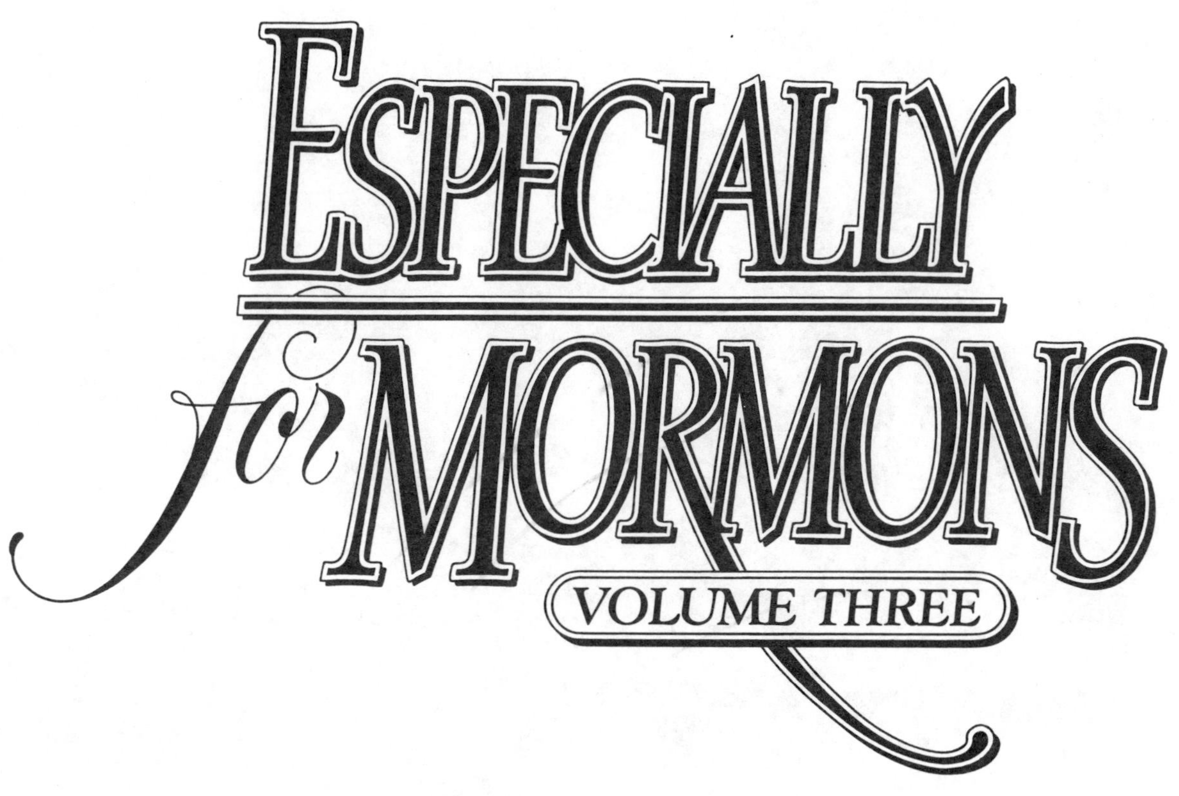


**Stan and Sharon Miller**

Kellirae Arts
Provo, Utah

16th Printing, 1996



KELLIRAE ARTS

P.O. BOX 300

PROVO, UTAH 84603

# FOREWORD

"The greatest battles of life are fought out daily in the silent chambers of the soul."

--David O. McKay

Some of the sweetest portions of the Scriptures are those which tell of love, faith in Christ, and an admonition to be obedient so as to avoid pitfalls of those who have travelled life's roads before. Contained herein are these same pleadings, but in words of many of our contemporaries who have experienced their own personal struggles and written their observations so all can learn.

Most people will never write a book, but oftimes a happy mother, a yearning student, or a busy father may take occasion to pen a pensive thought during a moment of reflection. These are the sorts of things that have made ESPECIALLY FOR MORMONS a favorite around the Church — because they are written by you!

Of course, words from the wise and learned are included as well. Hopefully, the combination will add a moment of inspiration to a discouraging day, or bring to mind just the illustration for that lesson or talk you have been asked to prepare.

For all of you, young and experienced alike, here is ESPECIALLY FOR MORMONS Volume Three, with love.

## ACKNOWLEDGEMENTS

Attempt has been made to acknowledge each contributor by name. However in many instances authorship is indeterminate. We express deepest appreciation to each person whose writings appear herein. We are sure each shares our desire to have his writings reach and inspire as many people as possible.

We especially express appreciation to so many who have sent us their own original stories or poems, hoping that someday there may be a third volume published in which their writings might be included. These submissions, along with encouragement from hundreds of interested readers have helped us to compile this collection of outstanding poetry, prose, and appropriate thought. Hopefully, you can feel the spirit of each writer as you enjoy their ponderings and expressions of faith.

Dedicated to Devon, Kelli, and all the rest . . . with love.

# INDEX OF SUBJECTS

# AGE

Maturity is the ability to think, speak, and act your feelings within the bounds of dignity. The measure of your maturity is how spiritual you become during the midst of your frustrations.

* * * * *

Middle age is when your clothes no longer fit, and it's <u>you</u> who needs the alterations.

-- Earl Wilson

* * * * *

<u>Beatitudes for Friends of the Aged</u>

Blessed are they who understand my faltering step
and palsied hand.

Blessed are they who know that my ears today must strain
to catch the things they say.

Blessed are they who seem to know that my eyes are dim
and my wits are slow.

Blessed are they who looked away when cocoa spilled at
the table today.

Blessed are they with a cherry smile who stop to chat
for a little while.

Blessed are they who never say, "You've told that
story twice today."

Blessed are they who know the ways to bring back
memories of yesterdays.

Blessed are they who make it known that I'm loved,
respected and not alone.

Blessed are they who know I'm at a loss to find the
strength to carry the Cross.

Blessed are they who ease the days on my journey
Home in loving ways.

* * * * *

# AMERICA

These are the times that try men's souls. The summer soldier and the sunshine patriot will, in this crisis, shrink from the service of their country; but he that stands it NOW, deserves the love and thanks of man and woman. Tyranny, like hell, is not easily conquered; yet we have this consolation with us, that the harder the conflict the more glorious the triumph. What we obtain too cheap, we esteem too lightly: it is dearness only that gives everything its value. Heaven knows how to put a proper price upon its goods; and it would be strange indeed if so celestial an article as FREEDOM should not be highly rated.

-- Thomas Paine

* * * * *

## Rights and Obligations

AMERICA is a unique land of many rights - and obligations.

* AMERICANS have the right to go to a church, synagogue or temple - or not go.
- and an obligation to respect this right in others.

* AMERICANS have the right to say what they think - individually, or collectively.
- and an obligation to hold their tongues when it will hurt their country.

* AMERICANS have the right to select those in public office.
- and those in public office have an obligation to serve with honesty, integrity, wisdom and selflessness.

* AMERICANS have the right of protection for their lives, homes and property.
- and an obligation to respect the laws of the nation.

* AMERICANS have the right to enjoy the greatest progress made by any nation on earth.
- and an obligation to do an honest day's work to contribute to that progress.

* AMERICANS have the right to enjoy the abundance of this nation.
- and an obligation to share this abundance with those less fortunate.

Americans have many rights - but also many obligations.

* * * * *

"I long for the day when the schools have unlimited funds to draw on and the Pentagon has to hold bake sales to buy tanks."

-- Terry Herndon

* * * * *

"It is in vain, sir, to extenuate the matter. Gentlemen may cry peace, peace, but there is no peace. The war is actually begun. The next gale that sweeps from the north will bring to our ears the clash of resounding arms. Our brethren are already in the field. Why stand we here idle? What is it that the gentlemen wish? What would they have? Is life so dear, or peace so sweet, as to be purchased at the price of chains and slavery? Forbid it, Almighty God! I know not what course others may take, but as for me, give me liberty, or give me death!"

-- Patrick Henry

* * * * *

## Our Flag

Standing here so close to you,
It seems that I am seeing you
For the first time.
Yet, I cannot remember
The first time I ever saw you,
Though I remember quite well
The first time I ever touched you.
It was the Fourth of July.
I paid a dime for you.
I did not know then
That you could not be bought
But that men would give for you
All that they had --
Even their lives.
I did not know
That what I held in my hand
Was not you;
No one told me.
But, of course,
Those things can't be told;
Each person must learn them
For himself.
I did not know that you had
A heart that could feel,
A mind that could think,
And a body that could work;

But I know you now
For what you are
I've learned my lesson.

You are a mother
Waiting for a word from her son,
And the word never comes.
You are a father
Working patiently,
Hoping for a better day,
A better world --
Tomorrow.
You are proud young men
With light and laughter
In their voices.
You are the hands of young women
Roughened and hardened by work.
You are a mother
Holding her first born
Tenderly close to her breast,
And wearing a Distinguished Service Cross
And a Purple Heart
Pinned on her dress.
You are the boys and girls
Offering their pledge to you
In the school houses of America.
You are men and women
Of every language, of every color,
Of every creed.
Going to the church of their choice
On Sunday morning.
You are the noise of the busy city;
The peace of the country side
At the twilight hour,
You are all of these
And something more:
You are Truth,
And Truth is Freedom;
"You shall know the Truth," he said,
"And the Truth shall make you free."

Yes, I know you now;
I can see you clearly;
You have changed.
You are not new and stiff and shiny
As you were on that summer day
So long ago.

You are stained with tears;
You are dirty with sweat;
You are torn and bleeding,
But you have wept before;
You have toiled before;
You have bled before,
And I know in my heart
That when this that is upon us
Shall have passed away
You will still in Freedom be flying
Over a people born to be free.

Historical Information

On a misty, foggy, Sunday afternoon, in the month of January, 1944, the late U.S. Senator, Robert S. Kerr, at that time Governor of Oklahoma, members of the American Legion, and I were seated on the Atoka, Oklahoma High School stage waiting to begin the memorial service honoring the young men of Atoka County who had given, in the Second World War, "...even their lives."

It was 2:30 o'clock p.m., time to start the service; still we waited. I was neither anxious nor impatient; I had been asked by the Commander of the American Legion to say something about the Flag, and I knew what I wanted to say, so I had not bothered to make a copy of it. A little later, the audience became quiet; when I looked toward the entrance of the auditorium, I understood why. Walking down the aisle toward the front were the families of the young men for whom the service had been planned. Suddenly, I felt that I could not stand, face those people, and say what I had decided to say. At that moment, with a shock, I realized that I did not remember a thing I had intended to say; I thought of leaving the building by the stage exit, but I could not do that when I remembered the young men and their families who had no avenue of escape.

When my name was called, I walked to the front of the stage, and for a long moment looked at the Flag standing close by ...Then I heard myself saying, for the first time, the lines of "Our Flag" that have been repeated countless times since that misty, foggy Sunday afternoon in the month of January 1944.

I wondered -- could Governor Kerr have been right when he said to the audience, "I came here from Oklahoma City to give the memorial services, but there is nothing left to say; the few lines you have just heard have said it all...for all time...for all people... ."

-- Grace R. Stewart

* * * * *

## The Price They Paid

Have you ever wondered what happened to those men who signed the Declaration of Independence?

Five signers were captured by the British as traitors, and tortured before they died. Twelve had their homes ransacked and burned. Two lost their sons in the Revolutionary Army, another had two sons captured. Nine of the fifty-six fought and died from wounds or the hardships of the Revolutionary War.

What kind of men were they? Twenty-four were lawyers and jurists. Eleven were merchants, nine were farmers and large plantation owners, men of means, well-educated. But they signed the Declaration of Independence knowing full well that the penalty would be death if they were captured.

They signed and they pledged their lives, their fortunes, and their sacred honor.

Carter Braxton of Virginia, a wealthy planter and trader, saw his ships swept from the seas by the British Navy. He sold his home and properties to pay his debts, and died in rags.

Thomas McKean was so hounded by the British that he was forced to move his family almost constantly. He served in the Congress without pay, and his family was kept in hiding. His possessions were taken from him, and poverty was his reward.

Vandals or soldiers or both, looted the properties of Ellery, Clymer, Hall, Walton, Gwinnett, Heyward, Ruttledge, and Middleton.

At the Battle of Yorktown, Thomas Nelson Jr., noted that the British General Cornwallis, had taken over the Nelson home for his headquarters. The owner quietly urged General George Washington to open fire, which was done. The home was destroyed, and Nelson died bankrupt.

Francis Lewis had his home and properties destroyed. The enemy jailed his wife, and she died within a few months.

John Hart was driven from his wife's bedside as she was dying. Their thirteen children fled for their lives. His fields and his grist mill were laid waste. For more than a year he lived in forests and caves, returning home after the war to find his wife dead, his children vanished. A few weeks later, he died from exhaustion and a broken heart.

Norris and Livingston suffered a similar fate.

Such were the stories and sacrifices of the American Revolution. These were not wild-eyed, rabble rousing ruffians. These were soft-spoken men of means and education. They had security, but they valued liberty more. Standing tall, straight, and unwavering, they pledged: "For the support of this declaration, with a firm reliance on the protection of the Divine Providence, we mutually pledge to each other our lives, our fortunes, and our sacred honor." They gave us an independent America. Can we keep it?

* * * * *

# CHARACTER

This above all; to thine ownself be true and it must follow, as night the day, Thou canst not then be false to any man.

-- Shakespeare

* * * * *

Talent is developed in tranquility - Character in the rushing stream of life.

* * * * *

Character is a victory - not a gift.

* * * * *

You will never have a greater or lesser dominion than that over yourself. The height of a man's success is gauged by his self-mastery: the depth of his failure by his self-abandonment. He who cannot establish dominion over himself will have no dominion over others.

-- Leonardo de Vinci

* * * * *

It is easy in the world to live after the world's opinions. It is easy in solitude to live after our own; but the great men is he who in the midst of the crowd keeps with perfect sweetness the independence of solitude.

-- Ralph Waldo Emerson

* * * * *

To say no at the right time, and then stand by it, is the first element of success. He is the wise man who, for all his life, can keep mind and soul and body clean.

-- David Starr Jordan

* * * * *

God hath entrusted me with myself.

-- Epictetus

* * * * *

Thought is action in rehearsal.

-- Freud

* * * * *

Self-discipline is doing what you know you should do when you don't want to do it.

-- N. Eldon Tanner

* * * * *

Character is the aim of true education; and science, history, and literature are but means used to accomplish this desired end.

-- David O. McKay

* * * * *

Whenever you violate a principle - you get a short-term gain, but a long-term loss.

-- Rodney Turner

* * * * *

Are you part of the inn crowd, or are you one of the stable few?

* * * * *

The greatest battles of life are fought out daily in the silent chambers of the soul.

-- David O. McKay

* * * * *

Sign over an arch leading to a university campus: "You are not what you think you are, but what you think, you are."

* * * * *

Character is not built in an emergency -- merely exhibited.

* * * * *

The people who object to rules are people who don't obey the rules.

-- N. Eldon Tanner

* * * * *

To profit from good advice requires more wisdom than to give it.

* * * * *

Try to become the kind of person that people are anxious to see you, and after you leave, they have a lot of thinking to do.

* * * * *

Be grateful for your problems, because if you didn't have them, you wouldn't be here, and if they were less difficult, we would get someone with less ability to take your place.

(Sign in executive lounge in a large company's office building.)

* * * * *

Most of the work in the world is not done by geniuses. It is done by ordinary people who have learned to apply their talents and abilities to accomplish those responsibilities which they have accepted.

* * * * *

## The Aging Process

If I should grow to a ripe old age,
May I possess some bit of individuality, charm and wit,
That I may not be discarded
When I am withered, worn and weak,
But sought after and cherished
Like a fine antique.

-- Unknown

* * * * *

A chain is no stronger than its weakest link;
A brain is no stronger than its weakest think;
A grain is no stronger than its weakest seed;
A man is no stronger than his weakest deed.

* * * * *

A little seed lay in the ground,
And soon began to sprout,
"Now which of the flowers all around,"
It mused, "shall I come out?
The lily's face is fair and proud,
But just a trifle cold;
The rose, I think, is rather loud,
And then it's fashion's old.
The violet is very well,
But not a flower I'd choose;
Nor yet the Canterbury bell,
I never cared for blues.
Petunias are by far too bright
And common flowers besides;
The primrose only blooms at night
And peonies spread too wide."
And so it criticized each flower,
This supercilious seed;
Until it woke one summer hour,
And found itself a weed.

-- Mildred Howell

* * * * *

These hands are shaped like my Heavenly Father's.
Divine hands, made
To work and build,
To serve and bless.
Clean hands, free
Of mark or stain
From wrong doing.

These hands are shaped like my Heavenly Father's.
Let them never do
The things a child of God
Should never do;
Or touch the things
A child of God
Should never touch.

These hands are shaped like my Heavenly Father's.
Thou in whose image I was made,
Help me to discern
That which is right
In thy sight.
Give me strength.
And the will.

Heavenly Father; help me to control these hands.

-- Ira J. Markham

* * * * *

## Your Mental Vitamins

| | |
|---|---|
| Vitamin A | Our friends; they will build the bony structure of our character and keep it firm. |
| Vitamin Bl | Our self respect; good grooming will give us just that increase in energy needed to land or hold that better job. |
| Vitamin C | Usefulness; when a person no longer feels useful to someone somewhere the tissue becomes dry, wrinkled and old age begins. |
| Vitamin E | Work with our hands; no matter how hard our mind works, we need to do some work with our hands to conserve our vitality. |
| Vitamin K | Fun; unless we derive fun from our work and our play, our life blood is soon lost as we become automatons instead of personalities. |
| Vitamin B6 | Personal freedom; we have learned that when we say to an individual "you must not change your job, your doctor, your house, your church, unless you have permission" we destroy that individual's morale and self-confidence. |
| Vitamin Bl2 | Faith in God; lacking faith in God, we have no faith in ourselves and no love for our fellowman. |

* * * * *

## Make Mistakes Pay

A man's not bad who makes mistakes, for he's a man who tries ... To make, then recognize, mistakes just shows that he is wise ... It's only in the grandstands where the perfect players stay ... They criticize and know it all ... yet they don't act or play ... They tell just how it should have been ... and really pour it on ... revealing in so many ways ... that brains oft go to brawn ... The fellows down there playing see the errors that they make ... and profit by them too, you'll note ... their future is at stake. The man who boasts of no mistakes ... makes one that's big and bad ... he daily fails to utilize the talents that he has ... He is the over-cautious type ... Is scared of every deal ... in other words he is the brake on his own Progress wheel ... The men who have attained success ... have conquered interventions ... For them there is no top-most rung ... they simply add extensions.

-- Ethel D. Posegate

* * * * *

## The North Side

"A ship-building company had this statement in its advertisement: 'All of our timber comes for the north side of the mountain.' Why the north side? What does that have to do with timber?

After investigation, I found out that the best timber grows on the north side of the mountain because of the rigors of Mother Nature. The snow is deeper and the cold is colder, the winds are stiffer, and the warmth is not so warm as on the south side of the mountain. The very harshness of the weather is a contributing factor to the toughness of the timber.

Human character is not much different from timber. How often the best in personality grows on the north side of the mountain. We grumble about our hardships and difficulties, yet those very difficulties help us to grow and become nature persons. Each can look at his own life and see that the times when he made the greatest personal progress was probably when life had him on 'the north side of the mountain.'"

-- Edmond H. Babbitt

* * * * *

## Just for Today

Just for Today I will try to strengthen my mind. I will study. I will learn something useful. I will not be a mental loafer. I will read something that requires effort, thought, and concentration.

Just for Today I will exercise my soul in three ways. I will do somebody a good turn, and not get found out; if anybody knows of it, it will not count. I will do at least two things I don't want to do - just for exercise. I will not show anyone that my feelings are hurt; they may be hurt, but today I will not show it.

Just for Today I will have a quiet half hour all by myself and relax. During this half hour, some time, I will try to get a better perspective of my life.

Just for Today I will have a program. I may not follow it exactly, but I will have it. I will save myself from two pests: hurry and indecision.

Just for Today I will be agreeable. I will look as well as I can, dress becomingly, talk low, act courteously, criticize not one bit, not find fault with anything, and not try to improve or regulate anybody except myself.

Just for Today I will try to live through this day only and not tackle my whole life problem at once.

Just for Today I will adjust myself to what is and not try to adjust everything to my own desires. I will take my "luck" as it comes and fit myself to it.

Just for Today I will be happy. This assumes to be true what Abraham Lincoln said, that, "Most folks are as happy as they make up their minds to be."

* * * * *

## Gratitude

A boat was sinking somewhere off the Pacific Northwest Coast during a violent storm. A crowd had gathered to watch the battered vessel being pounded to pieces on the rocks off shore. Some sturdy men launched a life boat and pulled frantically at the oars to reach the ship in time to rescue the seamen who clung to their fast-disintegrating vessel.

As the small life boat came struggling back to shore, someone cried out, "Did you save them?"

"All but one," came the answer through the storm. "There was one we couldn't reach."

Then a young man stepped forth from the group and called, "Who will come with me to get the other man?"

Then his grey-haired mother cried out, "Oh Jim, please don't go! Please don't risk your life - you are all that I have left."

Onlookers knew that this boy's father had been drowned at sea and years ago his brother, Bill, had sailed away and had never been heard from since.

But the boy replied, "Mother, someone has to go."

A few others joined him and together they launched their boat and pulled from the wreck, while those on shore anxiously waited.

Finally, the boat was seen to pull away from the wreck and headed again for the shore. The crowd watched as the small frail craft was beaten by the wave. At every plunge of the boat it looked as if it would be crushed like an egg shall. There was silence on the shore as the watchers prayed. For an hour the desperate struggle continued until the life boat was near enough to hail, when someone shouted, "Did you get the other man?"

Then in a high, clear, triumphant shout over the roar of the surf came the young man's voice saying, "Yes...and tell mother that the man we rescued is Bill!"

* * * * *

Keeping His Word

One day a Spaniard who was talking to a Moorish student, became very angry, because the student challenged his religion. Pulling out his sword, the Spaniard said, "My God would not have such as you live. Die you coward!" and he killed him, leaving his body by the roadside. As he was hurrying away, a band of students came down the road, seeing what had been done, and they started after the murderer. He knew the road, better than they, and so, taking a hidden turn, he dropped over a wall into the garden of a wealthy Moor. Seeing the man working among his beautiful flowers, he ran to him, fell on his knees before him, and cried, "In my haste I killed a man who loved not God. Save me from the mob at the gates. I have done what seemed right. Save me, I beg of you."

"If thou hast done wrong, thou should surely be punished," said the old man, "but it is better to avenge oneself slowly. I will share with thee this peach which I have picked from the tree. When we have eaten together, thou canst be assured of my protection. When night cometh, I will come unto thee." So saying he locked the man in the garden house and went to sit on his porch. Hardly had he seated himself when he heard the sound of many people who were wailing; they came nearer to his home; they knocked at his gate; and the servant admitted them. "What hast thou here?" asked the Moor as they entered the gate. "We have the body of thy son, thine only son," answered a student, for he hath been killed by a Spaniard not far away from thine own roadway. Let us leave him here and go quickly, that we may join in the search for the man who wronged thee." Without a word he let them depart; then he shut himself in his room and fell on his face. This son was his one great joy in life, for all honored and loved him. In his garden house sat the man who killed him. He had only to say the word, and the men would take him away and kill him.

Should he say the world? Ah, but to that man he had promised life and liberty. They had eaten together; to wreck vengeance upon him was unthinkable, for he was a Moor.

All day long he paced back and forth in the room that overlooked the sea, now black with wind and rain. In his soul was a great storm. As the mourners listened, they said one to another, "Behold, how he loved him. He grieved even as a mother." When night fell, he called all his servants to his room, and saying he wished to be left alone in his grief, he sent them each unto his own home. When the last had gone, he went to the garden house and slowly unlocked the door. As the man came forth, the Moor stood before him and said in a voice that made the prisoner tremble, "Thou art a Christian, yet thou hast killed my only son in thine anger; his body lieth in my house. Thou oughtest to be severely punished, but I have eaten with thee. I gave thee my word, and my word shall not be broken. I leave thee to thine own God, believing that thou must answer to him for the breaking of his own law. Come!" With trembling footsteps the old man led the young man to the street where one of his fleetish horses was ready for him to mount. "Go," said the father. "Go far, while the night may be a help unto thee. God is just, and God is good. I thank him that I have no load such as thine to carry. It were easier to carry sorrow than shame. My son's memory shall be to me as the sunlight and the moonlight, as the fragrance of the violet and the beauty of the rose, as the cooling breeze on a weary day. Thou hast taken his life, but couldst not take away what he has been to his father. That is mine. Go, and may thine anger never again cause thee to break the law of thy God. Go." As the sound of the swiftly moving horse's hoofs died away, the old man went again to stand by the bier of his son, his only son. "Better thou art here than there my son," he said. "And thy father hath still kept the faith that he taught unto thee."

-- Margaret White Eggleston

* * * * *

# CHASTITY

It is easier to suppress the first desire than to satisfy all that follow it.

-- Benjamin Franklin

* * * * *

Your virtue is worth more than life. Please, young folks, preserve your virtue even if you lose your lives. Do not tamper with sin. Do not permit yourselves to be led into temptation. Conduct yourselves seemly and with due regard, particularly you young boys, to the sanctity of womanhood. Do not pollute it.

-- David O. McKay

* * * * *

Speaking in the area conferences in France, Holland, Finland, Germany and Denmark in August, 1976, President Kimball gave this counsel on chastity:

"The Lord and His Church have no tolerance for these sins (of immorality). But the Lord greatly loves the repentant person and forgives most sins when totally repented of.

"There is no forgiveness without true repentance, and one has not repented until he has bared his soul and admitted his actions without excuses or rationalizations and really suffered intensely. He must admit to himself that he has sinned without the slightest minimizing of the offense and that it is as big as it really is.

"The Church is not softening its standards nor abandoning its God-given tenets. When the sun grows cold and the stars no longer shine, the law of chastity will still be basic in the Lord's Church."

* * * * *

When we learn that physical gratification is only incident to, and not the compelling force of love itself, we have made a supreme discovery.

Expressions of love are not ugly unless they are used in an ugly way. The prostitution or misuse of these powers becomes all the more lamentable because the power itself and the righteous expression of it are pure and beautiful and sanctified.

To seek some satisfaction by yourself is but to experience guilt, morbidity, and degradation. Such indulgence is neither necessary nor desirable.

-- Spencer W. Kimball

* * * * *

We have no right to go near temptation, or in fact to do or say a thing that we cannot honestly ask the blessings of the Lord upon, neither to visit any place where we would be ashamed to take our sister or sweetheart. The Good Spirit will not go with us on to the Devil's ground, and if we are standing alone upon the ground belonging to the adversary of men's souls, he may have the power to trip us up and destroy us. The only safe ground is so far from danger as it is possible to get. Virtue is more valuable than life. Never allow yourself to go out of curiosity to see any of the "undercrust" in this world. We can't handle dirty things and keep our hands clean.

-- Heber J. Grant

* * * * *

You may search all the ages for a person who has had no problems, you may look through the streets of heaven asking each one how he came there, and you will look in vain everywhere for a man morally and spiritually strong whose strength did not come to him in struggle. Do not suppose that there is a person who has never wrestled with his own success and happiness. There is no exception anywhere. Every true strength is gained in struggle.

-- Richard L. Evans

* * * * *

A Mother's Advice to Her Daughter

A kiss is a sacred way of expressing love, deep affection, admiration, and respect. It is not a way of saying "goodnight." It is not a way of saying, "thank you for a good time." And especially, it is NOT a way to get a thrill or entertain each other. Respect and admiration must be a part of the love you feel for a person before a kiss will mean anything. Naturally, you can't feel love, respect, and admiration for every person you date and so naturally you don't kiss every person you date. In fact, there are VERY FEW who will merit enough respect for you to kiss. We are taught to practice moderation in all things. If, after dating one person for awhile, your love and respect for him grows; then, a kiss is the best way to show him your love for him. But it will remain a sweet expression of love only if you remember that a kiss is sacred. To remain sacred it must be given in the right atmosphere, with the proper attitude, kept in small doses, and it must not be an every-date occurrence. A kiss brings a couple closer together; it helps their love and respect for each other to grow IF it is used the way it is meant to be used in the attitude of LOVE and PURITY.

* * * * *

I said I would have my fling.
    And do what a young man may;
And I didn't believe a thing
    That the parsons had to say.
I didn't believe in a God
    That gives us blood like fire.
Then flings us into hell because
    We answer the call of desire.

And I said "religion is rot,"
    And the laws of the world are nil;
For the bad man is he who is caught
    And cannot foot his bill.
And there is no place called hell:
    And heaven is only a truth,
When a man has his way with a maid,
    In the fresh keen hour of youth.

And the money can buy us grace,
    If it rings on the plate of the church;
And money can nearly erase,
    Each sign of a sinful smirch.
For I saw men everywhere,
    Hot-footing the road of vice!
And women and preachers smiled on them
    As long as they paid the price.

So I had my joy of life;
    I went the pace of the town:
And then I took me a wife,
    And started to settle down.
I had gold enough and to spare
    For all of the simple joys
That belong with a house and a home
    And a brood of girls and boys.

I married a girl with health
 And virtue and spotless fame
I gave in exchange my wealth
 And a proud old family name.
And I gave her the love of a heart
 Grown sated and sick of sin.
My deal with the devil was all cleaned up.
 And the last bill handed in.

She was going to bring me a child,
 And when in anguish she cried,
With love and fear I was wild --
 But now I wish she had died.
For the son she bore me was blind
 And crippled and weak and sore!
And mother was left a wreck.
 It was so she had settled my score.

I said I must have my fling,
 And they knew the path I would go;
But no one told me a thing
 Of what I needed to know.
Folks talk too much of a soul
 From heavenly joys debarred --
But not enough of the babes unborn,
 By the sins of their father scarred.

* * * * *

## Make Own Rules Supplement God's

Elder Hartman Rector Jr. of the First Council of the Seventy said man might supplement God's commandments with some of his own. Speaking at the Sunday afternoon General Conference session in the Tabernacle, Elder Hartman Rector said our man's commandments should help us more easily live God's laws.

Elder Rector illustrated what he meant by relating his experience in the military. "I spent twenty-six years flying the Navy's airplanes. It was very exciting to see how close I could fly to the trees. This is called 'flat hatting' in the Navy, and it is extremely dangerous.

"When you are flying just high enough to miss the trees and your engine coughs once, you are in the trees. Now let's pretend that the Navy had a commandment: 'Thou shalt not fly the airplane in the trees.' As a matter of fact, they did. In order to really be free of the commandment, it becomes necessary for me to add a commandment of my own to the Navy's commandment, such as, 'Thou shalt not fly closer than 5,000 feet to the trees.' When you do this, you make the Navy's commandment of not flying in the trees easy to live.

"Admittedly," said Elder Rector, "the latter commandment is your own addition, and care should be exercised that you do not get it mixed up with the law and expound it as the law."

Elder Rector applied the principle of making personal commandments to single adults. "It is so important that young people, who are unmarried, erect barriers against temptation to help them avoid the compromising situations. May I suggest:

1. Never go into a house alone with one of the opposite sex.
2. Never enter a bedroom alone with your companion.
3. Do not neck or pet.
4. Never park on a lonely road with just the two of you alone.
5. Do not read pornographic literature.
6. Do not attend R or X-rated movies.
7. Do not spend time in drinking or gambling establishments.

Elder Rector described Joseph's actions when Potiphar's wife attempted to seduce him. "The scripture records that Joseph stoutly resisted the advances to Potiphar's wife, but one day as he went into the house to 'do his business,' it so happened that 'there was none of the men of the house there within.'

"Now, this is always a dangerous situation and should be avoided if at all possible," Elder Rector said. Potiphar's wife became particularly insistent, even to taking hold of his coat and attempting to draw him near to her. But Joseph did the very best thing he could do under the circumstances. 'He left his garment in her hand, and fled, and got him out.' (Gen. 39:12) Or, in today's language, he ran," Elder Rector said. "Maybe that doesn't sound like a very sophisticated thing to do, but sometimes running is the only thing to do."

* * * * *

## The Heart of the Rose

She put her arm around him and kissed his forehead. "Let's don't be angry on our last night," she begged.

"Why did you do it?" he asked. "I know you heard what I said to Rose, but what is she to you?"

"A great deal," she responded, "but not so much as the boy I love so dearly -- the boy I have been a mother to, and yet I haven't been a true mother, for I never have talked to you of these things because they were hard. You see, I have failed in my duty."

Instantly he was all tenderness. He drew her down into his boyish long arms and laid his head against hers. "You have not failed in anything, you darling!" he cried. "But it wouldn't hurt me. I'm a man. All the fellows do that way."

"How do you know?"

"They tell about it. We don't all talk about it in a crowd, but just when we are together, like John and me."

"Does John treat Rose that way?"

The boy grew warm in a minute. "He'd better not; he went too far to suit me tonight."

"Why did he?" she asked quietly. "You were rather free towards Dorothy."

"Dorothy is different; she's a -- she's -- well, she's a jolly good fellow, but Rose -- well, I like Rose, and every fellow had better keep his hands off her. I don't want a girl all the fellows can love, but I'm different. Those things don't hurt a fellow; he's coarser and -- well, it's expected of him."

"But they do hurt you," she said. "The little book of memories that Rose gave you this afternoon told a story of its own. I am going to tell you this story."

He looked away into the distance, and she began.

"Once there was a man who went into a garden. All around him were beautiful roses of all colors. But he chose a little white bud for his. He chose it because it was pure and white, but most of all because it was closed. No other person could see into its heart. While he was waiting for it to unfold, he walked around to enjoy the other flowers. He studied their coloring and he breathed their perfume. For a long time he enjoyed this; then he wanted to get nearer to these roses, to handle them. Other travelers were handling them and they seemed to enjoy themselves more than he did. So he touched one rather timidly; others he was not so careful with. At last he grew tired and wandered back to his own rosebud and lo! it had opened. It stood the whitest and most fragrant rose in the garden, and its heart was the dewiest and most tender. But he remembered the crimson roses and it seemed too white. Then he could not detect its fragrance for he had killed his sense of smell by its abuse with the other roses, some of which stood as high and beautiful as before, but others were left bruised and broken by his ruthless desire to please, yes, to indulge himself. As he plucked his own rose, he was aware of no sense of joy over it, except from pride, for many travelers cast him envious glances. But he could not see its unusual beauty; he could not get the fragrance from its heart, because his sense of sight had been dulled by the brilliancy of the other flowers and his sense of smell by their odor.

"Nor did he think of the little buds in the garden that he had touched and then left. They would perhaps open, but the petals he had touched would always be brown and torn. The passersby might not see them when the flowers had opened and revealed their hearts, but the men who had plucked them would - not at once, but when they had become less entranced and were seeking for defects. Then perhaps they would throw the roses away. But the man who had the perfect rose -- the one which was perfect because it had been well protected -- did not know of the havoc he had wrought. He was too much interested in wondering why he did not enjoy his rose, why it seemed so commonplace and really tiresome. He did not know that it was he who had become unable to appreciate it, through his own indulgence begun in an idle moment, while he had waited for his flower to blossom."

She paused to look into his face. He was listening. Then she went on:

"You say you are a man; you have only thought of one side; you have only wanted the perfect rose. You may get one, but if you do, it will be one which has been carefully guarded. You are not intending to break or bruise the other roses; you are just going to handle them because the other boys do. You will enjoy their fragrance, but you will leave wounded petals. Then after a time, if you travel far enough into the garden, you will grow indifferent to the havoc you are doing and will carelessly crush the flowers. You may grow so cruel that you will enjoy it. There are men who do, and they started out as free from intention to harm as you are tonight. You caressed Dorothy: John caressed her. The next boy who comes along will find it easier to be free with her, and unless there is some one who cares enough to guard her she will be torn from the stem before she has blossomed. If you had kissed Rose tonight, it would have been easy for you to kiss her again. You haven't yet, have you?"

He shook his head.

"I am so glad," she continued. "It will be so much better for her. If she permits you these familiarities, she will permit others the same ones. She may soon become as wreckless as Dorothy, and then we dare not think of the future. You can see now what a wonderful flower she promises to make. She is a perfect little bud. Would you not hate to think that you were spoiling the promise of that bud?"

"Forgive me for being so cross," he begged.

"Yes, dear, but we are going to look at your side now. God made you so that you have certain desires, certain cravings, that you are to control. Many men will say that they are only to be satisfied, but we know better. The first kiss you give to a girl thrills you -- really it is one of the greatest minutes of your life. The next girl you kiss seems less of a pleasure. Then after a while it becomes a mere habit; it loses all sense of enjoyment. Stronger desires than kissing arise and soon you are not the man God intended you to be. You will have a low idea of women. Even your wife, if you get the sweetest and purest in the world, will not seem so to you. Marriage will not be a sacred fulfillment; it will be a commonplace event."

"And," she continued, "your future career as a man will be touched. You cannot think clearly or act quickly when any of the senses of your body have been impaired. Lust kills ambition, ability and power. I do not mean that every boy who starts in this way has the same fatal ending, but a great many do. There is the halfway place where many men stop; yet you will find they are not real men. It will be so much holier and better to stay at the beginning."

She sat silent, waiting for him to speak. At last he did. "Of course, Beth, I wouldn't want to go even half-way, now: I wouldn't even want to touch any roses but one. But I cannot see yet why I can't let her know that I care for her; I will be constant. I want her to like me."

She drew a sharp breath. "You mean you will crush the petals of your own rose, and then enjoy the heart when it is opened. When you come back, you may not even want that heart; you are just a boy. If you do, there will be times when you will see those crushed petals and be sorry. You might blame yourself, but you will probably blame Rose. You may grow so discontented that you will blame another man. If you know she allowed you these caresses, these little familiarities, you will think she would allow others."

He spoke with pride. "I know Rose."

"We will look at it from her side. After she realizes those petals have been crushed by you she may be afraid of the future. She may be afraid that you have wandered far into the garden and come back to her a worn-out traveler. She may be afraid that you will not appreciate her and that you will not deal rightly with her."

He laughed. "I am not afraid of that."

"Other girls just as constant in their friendship as Rose have felt that way," she said in a low voice.

"What do you mean?" he asked.

"My dear boy, I have a few wilted petals and I know how they feel. You see, I was like you are. There was no one to guard me and I did just what any girl will do who does not think. But I realized in time to save myself from only a few brown ones, and I want to save every girl I can. We were young and thought we knew our hearts. My, how they changed! But they couldn't change those bruised petals."

"Floyd, I want to give the world a noble man. That is the dearest wish of every woman. I want to give some woman a pure husband; and I want to give you life in its best and purest forms."

"I promise," he said in a low tone.

"It will not be easy, dear. You will have to refuse to listen to other boys, you will have to read only good books, and you will have to think pure thoughts. Rose's little book will help you. On the second petal -- and you must look at it every day -- is the little picture of Sir Galahad which your first teacher gave you. Do you remember it?"

He smiled as he quoted:

My strength is as the strength of ten,
Because my heart is pure.

--Mabel A. McKee

* * * * *

# CHRIST

Jesus said, in effect, "You take my name, and I'll take your sins."

* * * * *

## The Actor

One time there was a very prominent actor in New York City. He possessed a special oratorical gift which enabled him to completely captivate any audience. One night after his recitation, he was applauded tremendously, and as he came back on stage to take his bows, a lady in the crowd called for him to recite the 23rd Psalm. This request startled the actor, but being familiar with the scripture he consented to do so. As he delivered the recitation, he endeavored to mould and beautify it with all the color, emotion, and personality that the long hard years of work had taught him. His delivery was excellent. Nothing had been forgotten or omitted. The crowd burst into a thunderous applause and praised him for his noble talent. As the applause subsided, the actor called an old gentleman from the front row to the stage and asked him to also recite the psalm. The old man appeared nervous, but consented. As he turned to the crowd he closed his eyes and bowed his head. He spoke the words:

> The Lord is my shepherd, I shall not want.
> He maketh me to lie down in green pastures;
> He leadeth me beside the still waters.
> He restoreth my soul; He leadeth me in the paths
> of righteousness for his name's sake.
> Yea, though I walk through the valley of the shadow
> of death, I will fear no evil; for Thou art with me;
> thy rod and thy staff they comfort me.
> Thou preparest a table before me in the presence of
> mine enemies; Thou annointest my head with oil,
> my cup runneth over.
> Surely goodness and mercy shall follow me all the days
> of my life and I will dwell in the house of the Lord
> forever.

When the old gentleman finished, there was no thunderous applause; there were no cries of praise; but there was also not a dry eye in the crowd.

The young prominent actor faced the crowd and said, "Ladies and gentlemen, I know the words to the 23rd Psalm, but this man knows the shepherd."

* * * * *

## A Second Coming - Would We Believe and Follow

If there should be, on Christmas Eve, a second coming - would there not be soon a second crucifixion? And this time, not by the Romans or the Jews, but by those who proudly call themselves Christians?

I wonder. I wonder how we today would regard and treat this man with his strange and frightening and "impractical" doctrines of human behavior and relationships. Would we believe and follow, any more than the masses of people in his day believed and followed?

Would not the militarists among us assail him as a cowardly pacifist because he urges us not to resist evil?

Would not the nationalists among us attack him as a dangerous internationalist because he tells us we are all of one flesh?

Would not the wealthy among us castigate him as a trouble-making radical because he bars the rich from entering the kingdom of heaven?

Would not the liberals among us dismiss him as a dreaming vagabond because he advises us to take no thought for the morrow, to lay up no treasures on earth?

Would not the ecclesiastics among us denounce him as a ranting heratic because he cuts through the core of ritual and commands us only to love God and our neighbors?

Would not the sentimentalists among us deride him as a cynic because he warns us that the way to salvation is narrow and difficult?

Would not the Puritans among us despise and reject him because he eats and drinks with publicans and sinners, preferring the company of winebibbers and harlots to that of "respectable" church members?

Would not the sensual among us scorn him because he fasts for forty days in the desert, neglecting the needs of the body?

Would not the proud and important among us laugh at him when he instructs the twelve disciples that he who would be "first" should be the one to take the role of the least and serve all?

Would not the worldly-wise and educated among us be aghast to hear that we cannot be saved except we become as children, and that a little child shall lead us?

Would not each of us -- in his own way -- find some part of this man's saying and doing to be so threatening to our ways of life, so much at odds with our rooted beliefs, that we could not tolerate him for long?

I wonder. I wonder if we are any more prepared for the second coming than we would have been for the first.

-- Sydney J. Harris

* * * * *

## Brief Description of a Great Life
(A parallelism)

His father, Joseph, was a poor man who made his living through the honest toil of his calloused hands. His birth brought no special notice from the religious leaders of the day. Why should it? They had not anticipated such a prophet would be born at this time.

He grew up in obscurity, receiving only the common education given the back country people of that day. But he learned about life. He walked in the fields and saw the sparrow and the hawk, the wheat and the tares, the flowers blooming in the meadow and the barren earth. And he wondered about God and about man and his responsibility to both.

He learned line upon line and precept upon precept. In his early youth he confounded the ministers of his day, telling them things which they thought impossible for a mere child to know. Then he was left alone to ponder the wonders he had learned.

The heavens were opened unto him and he received a divine commission which prompted him to restore to the earth the gospel which was as old as the earth itself. He gathered about him a few disciples; not the learned and scholared men, but simple folk like himself. He commissioned his disciples with the same authority he had and told them to go forth and teach others. He ordained them with the same Priesthood he held that they might bind on earth and in heaven.

He devoted himself entirely to his ministry. The ordinary pursuits of men held no attraction to him for he had a mission to perform. He never acquired wealth, he scarcely had a place he could call home.

People loved him. All kinds of people loved him; the saint, the sinner, the strong and the weak.

He loved people. It was said of him that he could be no prophet for he was too much of a social being. He liked company and would invite the poor ones from the street to come and dine with him.

He was hated and persecuted. Some of his own disciples turned away and he was betrayed into the hands of enemies. When he was in his thirties he sealed his mission with his blood rather than deny that he was God's anointed.

Even before the mobs formed, he had said that he would be killed.

On a day in late December, those who believed his words remember the occasion of his birth and thank God for his life and mission.

He was Jesus Christ.

The same also might be said about his Prophet, Joseph Smith.

Here, however, the parallelism ends for Jesus was divine, the Son of God. Joseph was but a man, chosen of God.

-- Kenneth J. Brown

* * * * *

## Inviting the Savior Into our Lives

One day when I really understood what Jesus Christ had done for me, I invited him to come into the house of my heart. And, as soon as I invited him, he came, without any hesitation. And, when he was there, he filled the house with joy. And, I wanted to run and tell all the neighbors about my guest and how wonderful it was to have him there.

When everything was settled, I said, "I hope you will stay and feel perfectly at home here." And, he said, "I'm sure I will, and now since we are new friends, why don't you show me around. I would like very much to see the library in the House of your Heart." And so I did.

Now in my house, the LIBRARY is very small and has very thick walls and is filled with everything I have read. Books, magazines, news articles, everything I have seen, like television shows, movies, plays; all the Sunday School lessons I have listened to, the sermons, the lecturers, they're all there in the library. And his eyes gazed over all the things that were on the shelf. And, I was a little embarrassed that there was so much trivia there. I wished that more scriptures and church books were really mine and on the shelf. And, I suggested to him that maybe I could stand a little bit of renovation in this room, and he agreed, that maybe we -- together -- could add more worthwhile things to the library.

You see, the library is a very important room because it's the study so-to-speak of the mind -- a sort of control room for the whole house. It affects the lighting, the electricity, and everything else in the house.

And, then he said he would like to see the DINING ROOM; and I took him in. Now in my house, this is a very large room because this is the room of appetites and desires; and it was stacked with all kinds of boxes and things. And, I told him I was always hungry, but I never seemed to be satisfied. And He told me that it was because I was eating the wrong things. He said, "If you would diet as I do, you would never feel hunger; for I live on the word of the Lord, the Father." And, then He offered me a taste of it; and it was delicious -- and oh, the flavor of it. And, I agreed with Him that this alone satisfied, and I knew that I would spend less time in the dining room now that he was a guest in the house.

Next, he asked if he could see my WORKSHOP. Now I had a workshop; it was down in the basement. And, we went down and looked at the workbench and produced much. He looked everything over and said that I had a lot of good equipment, but that I really hadn't used it to produce much. Oh, there were a few gadgets and trinkets and half finished projects, but nothing really of great value. And I said, "Well, if I wasn't quite so busy maybe I could do better. I know all the tools are there, but I'm awkward and clumsy, and I really don't know how to use them." So, he said, "Would you like to be able to use the tools in your workshop?" And, I said, "Oh yes, would you help me?" And he said, "I was wondering if you would ask me." And, so he stood behind me and put his great powerful hands over mine and guided them, and He showed me how to use the tools in the workshop. And, with his hands directing mine, I marveled at the work of art that came out. And, I said, "Now that you have helped me, I am going to come into the workshop often, and this will be a fun room to come to. Will you always help me?" And He said, "Yes, if you invite me to, but I never come unless I am invited." And so we left the workshop and the next room we went into was the DRAWING ROOM.

Now this was a small, quiet, peaceful place in my heart for deep thoughts and meditation, and he seemed pleased with it and comfortable there. And, so He said, "Let's meet here often at least twice a day and we can have long talks together, and you can tell me about all your activities and all your ambitions and all your problems -- and we'll talk it over together every day. I thought that sounded wonderful. So, I made an appointment with him every day that I would do that; and I did at first, faithfully. But then I got too busy, and sometimes I would forget to come in the morning. And, sometimes I would forget to come at night. And, sometimes days would go by, and we never had a talk at all. Now it wasn't that I didn't want to talk to Him, it was just that I was so busy and had a lot to do. Then, one day as I went to leave, I noticed Him standing in the doorway of the drawing room. And, I said, "Have you been waiting there every morning for me?" And He said, "Yes, we had an appointment, and you haven't been here for a long time." And I said, "You're a guest in my house, and I have neglected you; and I'm sorry." I had called on Him when I was in need, to come and help me, and He always came, but that was about the way I used Him. When things went well, I didn't really think we needed our chat as well as we did when things were bad. And so I decided that it had been a very one-sided relationship, and I also realized that he missed me. So I said, "Maybe there's something I could do for you; you've done so much for me." And he said, "Yes, there's a great deal you could do for me. I was wondering when you would want to help me."

"I have so many projects and so many things that need to be done. I could use a good friend like you. For one thing, I have no money in the world at all. I only have yours to use. Would you let me use some of yours?" Yes, of course. "And there are people I just cannot see. I could send you and commission you to go and represent me. Would you do that?"

But then one day I got rebellious and I said, "You demand too much of me. Can't I have anything to myself. After all, I have things I want to spend my money for, and you're always there needing something." Now that wasn't a very nice way to treat a person, especially a guest. And then he said, "Look at the things of my projects, and who benefits from them." And, then I really was ashamed because everything I did benefitted me as well as others and not Him personally. So I continued His work.

And then one day He said, "There is a peculiar odor in this house, and it's coming from that locked closet. And, although you've let me go into every room in the house, that one door has always been locked, and you've never let me in." Now that made me mad! I had let him into every room in my house; I ran and did his errands for him; I let him use my money, and now he wanted to look in my secret closet. So, I said, "I hold the key, and I will not let you in that closet. It's very small, only about two feet by four feet. The rest of my house is large enough and is perfectly presentable; so it shouldn't make any difference." And he said, "I cannot stay in this house if you do not give me the key to the closet." And, so he left.

Oh, I was sad. And great despair and gloom and depression came over me. Because you see, once having had Him as a guest in my home, life was unbearable without Him. And so I went and tearfully pleaded with Him and begged Him, "Come back, and I will give you the key to the closet and I will withhold nothing from you -- I cannot stand to live without you."

And so I gave Him the key, and He opened it. And, then quickly and efficiently he cleansed out those things that were dead and rotten that I wanted to feel were not there and wanted to ignore. He cleaned the whole closet out, fumigated it, painted it, and He made it perfectly acceptable. Afterwards, I said, "I'm so ashamed that you know what was in my closet." And then He said, "Why I see only a house that is totally acceptable to me." And then I knew why I loved Him so. And why of all my biggest of brothers only this one could love me enough to clean out my closet. And then he said, "You know, I've cleaned out so many closets, but it's a strange thing. I can never remember afterwards what was in them."

After a few moments, I said, "I get so tired of cleaning all the time, I go from one room to the other trying to keep up in the drawing room, in the dining room, the workshop, and in the library, but I always seem to be behind. I was wondering if you could take over the whole house like you did the closet, and you could be the owner, and I would be the guest and sort of helper or servant. And we'll switch positions. Instead of me calling on you to help me, you can call on me to help you. Is it possible?" And he said, "Why yes, that's why I came the first time you invited me." So I ran and got the deed to my house and I signed it over to Him and I said, "It is yours, it belongs to you, and I withhold nothing from you."

After I gave him the deed, He immediately started remodeling the house because he was not content to own a cottage. He was the architect, the planner, the builder, and told me eventually we would end up with a magnificent castle. It would take a while to build, but we would build it together. So he started the remodeling. He was the master of the house, and I was the servant, and I did whatever he bid. And there were times when clouds came and gathered around the house, clouds of war, hate and sin. And they beat on the house and demanded entry. But because He was the Lord of the house, it has a firm foundation and none of it was allowed to enter. Inside the house there was warmth, peace, and tranquility regardless of what was outside.

He told me as time went on that he would move my house to another city. He would take care of all the arrangements, and I wouldn't even have to know the day it took place or when. He said that I would be in a city where he had the deed to all the houses and there would be no storms or darkness, and I would like the neighbors better. It sounded wonderful, and I looked forward to it with eagerness. And, I looked back so long ago when I first invited Christ to come into the house of my heart as a guest, and thought about the many years it took to have the courage to give him the deed to the house. And I wondered why I had been so stingy and had reluctantly wanted to turn it over because he showered me with gifts and took care of all the remodeling, and I was always the debtor.

-- Author Unknown

* * * * *

The girl wiped a tear from her eye and wondered for perhaps the hundredth time that day what his reaction would be. She had known and kept her secret for two weeks now and she could no longer keep it from him. He told her he would be coming to see her today, anytime now, she must compose herself. This weather was certainly no help. It had been hot, very hot, even for April. The spring rains were few and very far between; then, when it did rain or sprinkle it became humid, clothes stuck to your body and homes were stifling to be couped up in. Today was really no different except that she had to tell him. She told her mother and father three days before. Her remembrance of those first few anxious moments of the revelation caused her to tremble. They had been very understanding, but, then her parents were those that she could always rely upon and trust for support and backing. It had been hot that day, too, but last night it rained and now the atmosphere was a thick, heavy mantle. It certainly didn't help ease the apprehension that was gripping her. The sun was blasting in the cloudless sky with its flames seeming to scorch the plants and dry, brown earth as she watched out the door for her beloved. The girl's mind raced over what she had to say and how she should say it. She was in a quandry over whether to blurt it out or lead up to it gradually. Should she be hesitant and shy about it or bold and straight forward?

I'll wait and see him, then depending on his mood I'll tell him," she thought. "Or perhaps..." There he is, at the corner, she hurried back into the sparsely furnished room and sat down so she wouldn't appear to be too anxious to meet him today.

The young man that rounded the corner on his way to see his girl was lighthearted. The morning had been successful. He received two work orders for his particular skill of carpentry and had fillers out for three more. Now he was to see his girl. They would be married soon and now that he was starting to do well financially, he was looking forward with an eager heart to marriage to this young woman who had captured his heart. She is lovely, he thought, what more could a man want than a beautiful, considerate, understanding wife and financial security? His heart quickened as he neared her door, and he thought briefly of the greeting kiss he would receive. There she was ... seated, looking like a beautiful statue carved in pure white marble. She rose to greet him with arms open wide to embrace him. Their greetings tumbled forth words of affection and endearment between two young people whose love and forthcoming marriage seemed made in heaven. Suddenly, without realizing what she was doing, the girl found herself saying, "I have something to tell you, something vitally important to both of us." "What is it, my love?" he asked. "Sit down, here, beside me." They sat, the young woman and the young man, side by side quietly for a long minute in silence. Without raising her eyes from the floor, the girl, her heart pounding an irregular rhythm, slowly said, "I'm going to become a mother." "Of course you are, many times. We are going to have a large family." "No, no. You don't understand," she said. He won't understand what I must say, she thought - he will be angry.

After a pause to rephrase her statement she continued. "No, I'm going to have a child very soon. I'm pregnant now." The silence that settled over the room was alive with tension and, as yet, unanswered questions. The young man stared unflinching into the brilliance that poured through the opened door. He suddenly felt the oppressive heat that poured through surrounding him. Funny, how he hadn't noticed it before. The sweat was running down his forehead in a trickle that caused him to wrinkle the folds of flesh over his eyes and rub the irritating perspiration out of his eyes. His mind raced ahead to future actions to be taken. Fleetingly he asked himself if he should walk through the door never to return or perhaps he should tenderly put his arm around her and reassure her that everything was all right. The law said that he could publicly ridicule and shame her.

"What happened? How could you let this happen to you?"

She heard and felt the hurt in his voice. What could she say that would sooth this young, dynamic man she loved so much? Trying to put herself in his place, she could easily imagine the shock and indignation of learning of the pregnancy of his fiance. Especially knowing that the child was not his own. Blinking back the tears that threatened to burst forth, the girl answered, "It was special, a dear and holy experience. It didn't just happen. It was a planned wonderful happening. Can you believe that?" The young man's trust in this special young woman had never before been challenged; he had never had cause to distrust her or have angry words with her. Now this - probably the most shameful thing that could happen - had occurred. He experienced a sudden feeling to shame and ire. He involuntarily shuddered and rose to his feet. Her eyes didn't leave his figure as he strode about the room - first to the window - then the door. Her heart seemed to stop, then race ahead as she saw his tall, lean figure pause in the open doorway and look upwards into the cloudless, still sky. His mind was a jumble of ideas and thoughts, crowding each other, each calling to be examined in depth. He was aware that his body was tense. He realized how tired he had become - what a change from the happiness and lightheartedness he had experienced just a few moments before. A rueful smile crept across his face and he bowed his head, gazing at an insect making his painful way through the dust outside the door. What a simple life animals lead, he thought. They mate only to create and don't know the agony caused by love! This girl had seemingly betrayed him, she had lead him to believe one thing ... with a deep sigh he relaxed. The tension ebbed out of his body and he turned to gaze into the shadows of the room. He blinked his eyes to see in the relative darkness. He opened his mouth to speak, but nothing came out, it was difficult ... he somehow couldn't bring himself to say what had been on his lips. He felt he must chastize her. But, for some strange reason, he could not stir himself to anger against her. She must have some explanation, a plausible, explainable reason. His heart went out to her as a feeling of calm descended over him.

She was still sitting quietly composed, in the center of the room. As he looked at her figure, so diminutive, he knew for a certainty the course he must follow. Slowly he crossed the few feet separating them and took her hands in his. When she rose at his bidding, he gently put his arm around this strange, exciting young woman and said, "I think I can understand your feelings. It's strange to me and a little frightening, but, I can understand." The girl's eyes misted and smiled as she nodded to herself and said, "Yes, He said you would understand. I love you." Suddenly, his heart soaring, he took her in his arms and, smiling down at her upturned face, asked, "What shall we call him?"

"Jesus...Jesus...a name fit for the Gods."

* * * * *

## Jesus Christ, the Son of God
(As Told by James, of This Elder Brother)

> What I am about to say and the manner of its saying is in response to a request made by those who planned this program. Some of the things I shall mention are based on the accepted accounts; some are imaginary. You will recognize each of these without further comment from me. What liberties I have taken with established texts are also easily recognized and need no explanation. However, I should like to tell you that I shall take liberty with two proper names in the sense that I have chosen to use these names in English as derived from the Aramaic tongue, the language spoken by the Jews at the time of Christ, rather than from the Greek from which these names usually come down to you. I shall have to make myself somebody else. You will forgive me for that.

Let me introduce myself as being James. I have four brothers. Jeshua is the oldest - my elder brother. Joses, Simon, Judas are my younger brothers. I have three sisters.

We lived quite simply in a little town called Nazareth. We had to live simply. My father was a carpenter. The carpenter's trade was dull business in our town. We made furniture as needed by the townspeople; we repaired furniture; we built houses; and we built stables and other shelter.

As small boys we often sat upon the roof of our house in the cool of the evening, and we would ask mother and father for stories. One story we liked especially well was how the angel came to each house in Mizraim and spared the first-born of those whose houses were marked with the blood of the sacrificial lamb. Then we liked, too, how when our people were in the wilderness, they were fed manna.

I asked my mother, "What is manna?"

She said, "I do not know, only that they were told that they must gather only enough for the day, for if they took more, it would spoil."

And the story of how the quails miraculously became food for them when they were desperately hungry. Those stories brought the ancient customs of our people to my mind.

But our favorite story was the one about the time when Father and Mother and Jesua went to live in Mizraim shortly after Jeshua was born; how when they had no money, some men from the East had visited them and had given them gold and frankincense and myrrh as a birth gift to Jeshua. She told how they had said that they had followed a star to our door.

We would ask, "Was Jeshua born in a stable?"

Mother would say, "Yes, but when these men came, we had moved from the stable into a house. It had been several days before we could obtain the lodgings, but your father searched and finally found a place."

"Was there a star?"

Mother said, "I did not see it, but the men said that a star showed them which way to go and indicated where to find us."

"Why did you go to Mizraim?"

"An angel came and warned us," said my father, "to leave and not come back until we were told, so we felt we needed to obey. It was fortunate for us that the men gave us gifts, for with the gold, we purchased asses to go to Mizraim - four of them, and with the money from the sale of the frankincense and the myrrh, we lived in Mizraim until it was safe to come home."

And how excited I became when my mother told me about the great sandstorm which they met on the way, which so suddenly came up that they could not pitch their little tent. How they were enveloped in the terrible wind and darkness of blowing and drifting sand. They struggled on and fortunately fell into, literally, a caravan with tents pitched and safe. The caravan leaders took them in, preserved them; and, from then on, they accompanied the caravan to Mizraim. Those were our favorite stories as we would sit on the roof of our house looking up at the stars.

Daily we learned our trade. Father was a hard taskmaster in the sense that he insisted that we learn - that is, all but Jeshua. He had liberty. He used to take long walks alone. Sometimes, as we grew older, He would be gone two or three nights; and Mother would worry about Him. Father, upon His return, never rebuked Him.

I would hear him say, "Jeshua, was your trip fruitful?"

"Yes, Father."

"Did you find what you sought?"

"I found fourfold," He would reply.

It is easy now, looking back, to see what He meant. I think our friend, Matthew, who wrote so extensively of His life, truly said He "grew up with his brethren, and waxed strong, and waited upon the Lord for the time of his ministry to come. And he served under his father, and he spake not as other men, neither could he be taught; for he needed not that any man should teach him." (Inspired Version, Matthew 3:24,25.)

It was on THAT day - that day when Mother prepared a special feast for us. She had procured a lamb and cooked it with vegetables into a most tasty dish. When we were through eating Jesua arose, kissed his sisters, embraced Father and each of us, and gave honor especially to Mother and said goodbye.

"The time has come, Mother. I am thankful to you for being my mother - and to you, Father, for your care of me."

Later we asked Mother why He must leave, and she said: "He is going to His work. God, His Father, has called Him."

"What work?"

"I cannot tell you. I am not quite sure myself. I know only that He is to save the people. I have not told you before, but now you should know that when He was born, an angel commanded your father to name Him "Jeshua," "The Anointed One." The angel told your father that He was born to save the people from their sins. How He will do it, I do not know; but He is leaving us now to begin that work.

"Is He a prophet?"

She nodded and said, "He is a prophet."

I never forgot that.

Then Jeshua came home. We had news of His work in nearby towns - how He healed the sick, and was teaching a new kingdom, a different kingdom than one we knew. We hardly had expected Him back so soon, but we were glad to see Him. Many friends called, and a feast was had in His honor. The Rabbi invited Him to read on the Sabbath. So we went - Father, Jeshua, I, Joses, Simon, and Judas - sitting on the little cushions on the man's side of the synagogue. Then the Rabbi invited Jeshua up to read. He asked the Rabbi for the roll from Esaias, and when it was procured, opened it and then He read. I can still remember the words:

"The Spirit of the Lord God is upon Me, because the Lord hath anointed Me to preach good tidings unto the meek; he hath sent Me to bind up the brokenhearted, to proclaim liberty to the captives, and the opening of the prison to them that are bound; to proclaim the acceptable year of the Lord, . . ." (Isaiah 61:1,2). Here He stopped. There was something in His manner which held everybody in close attention. My father was leaning forward slightly, hardly breathing.

Then, "This day this scripture is fulfilled in your hearing." (See Luke 4:16-30.)

There was an indrawn gasp of the assembled people. I turned to Father.

"What is He saying?"

My father turned and whispered to me, "Don't forget this, for this is true. He is saying that He is the person of whom Esaias was speaking."

"Is He the Messiah?"

"He is the Messiah."

There were accusations; and someone shouted, "Blasphemy!"

Another yelled, "If you are that prophet, let us see you do the works they say you do in Capernaum. You look to me like Jeshua, the son of old Joseph there."

Jeshua replied, "No prophet is accepted in his own country."

The whole audience seemed to be pulled by an intense anger. They arose to take Him, shouting that they would throw Him over a cliff nearby; but He stepped down and walked to the door and out, they appearing not to see Him.

My father smiled, "He will come to no harm. He has His work to do."

There is no need of my telling you all that He taught or all that He did. These things have been written, and well written, by my friends and associates.

I regret only one thing. One of our later associates, Dr. Luke, wrote an account of His life to the Greek people. I wish that He had not translated the name of my brother into that language. Proper names need not be translated, but the Doctor did it. Sometimes when I hear people now speak of Jesus Christ, I have to stop and catch myself before I realize that they are talking about my elder brother, Jeshua, the Anointed One.

The writings tell well enough of the accusations, the death - and of His resurrection. It was not until after that - when the excited Mary had told Peter and John, and they had seen the empty tomb - that we began to have clear in our mind what He meant when He so often had said He would rise the third day.

Sometime after this we were sitting on the roof of our old house in Nazareth. Peter and the apostles had organized the Church. I was appointed to be president of the Nazareth Branch. As the stars shone that night on us with all the glory of their clear beauty, I felt impelled to ask,

"Mother, was Jeshua the Son of God?"

"Yes, my son."

"But Joseph was His father."

"No, Joseph was not His father. Joseph was your father, but not His father."

"Then who was His father?"

"I have told you. He was the Son of God."

She continued.

"Years ago I was visited by an angel who told me that I should bear a son who would be called Jeshua, the Anointed One, the Son of God. Your father had intended to break the engagement when he discovered that I was expecting a baby. The angel commanded him to marry me and raise the child. These things, my sons, we have carried in our hearts all through the years: the joy of rearing, the pride of His accomplishments, the puzzlement in our souls when He did what we least expected and when He taught new doctrine. Yet we waited, knowing God's will would be done: the agony of frustration at His death and the sight of His glorious resurrection have at least each one been put in its proper place. Remember always, my sons and daughters, He is the Son of God, literally and finally. Your mother gave Him His earthly tabernacle. Your father was privileged to act as His foster father."

I can see my mother now as she sat there in the dignity of her old age, silver-haired as she bore witness that their Jeshua, Jesus Christ to the Greeks, was the Son of God, the Redeemer. As Esaias said, ". . .Wonderful, Counsellor, the mighty God, the Everlasting Father, the Prince of Peace." (Isaiah 9:6)

She said to us, "Let us never forget it."

Well, let you and me never forget it either. He is the Son of God. He is the Prince of Peace. He is your Saviour; He is my Saviour. He was resurrected; He did establish this Church. Let us all be united in that testimony, in His holy name, Amen.

-- S. Dilworth Young

* * * * *

## CHRISTMAS

When the song of the angels is heard no more,
When the Bethlehem star has gone from the sky,
When the kings and the wise men have returned to their homes,
When the shepherds are back in the fields with their flocks,
Then the real work of Christmas should eagerly begin,
To spread the Christian message,
To lift up the unbelieving,
To make whole the broken hearted,
To break the bonds of sin,
To purify the national purpose,
To exalt the destiny of all mankind,
And to set our eyes on those eternal goals
That the Son of God established in His day.

* * * * *

### No More Darkness

The clouds moved lazily, the air was still,
As the old man wearily trudged the hill.
His eyes were dimmed, blind from birth
He had never beheld God's wondrous earth.

But his hopes were high for he had heard it told
That a Messiah had come, as prophesied of old.
He stumbled and fell mid the crowd and throng
Pitied by the weak, pushed aside by the strong.

When ready to despair from life's sorrow and scorn
A voice pierced the air, "Blessed are they that mourn!"
Humbly he listened, while the crowd made mirth
"Blessed are the meek, they shall inherit the earth!"

With tears overflowing, his knees fell to the sod,
"Blessed are the pure in heart, they shall see God!"
He lifted his head, by the illumination overcome
And beheld there fore him, the Master . . . the Son!"

Tears clouded his eyes, then in darkness they closed,
But for one precious moment, he had seen with his soul.
Then a light brighter than a galaxy before him spread
And he knew he never again in darkness would tread.

He recounted the scripture . . . "Unto you is born this day"
A Saviour . . . A Master . . . Christ . . .the Light and the Way!"
"Peace on earth" at last in his heart he could find.
The same blessings of Christmas is still given to mankind!

* * * * *

## Pattern of Love

I didn't question Timmy, age nine, or his seven-year-old brother, Billy, about the brown wrapping paper they passed back and forth between them as we visited each store.

Every year at Christmas time, our Service Club takes the children from poor families in our town on a personally conducted shopping tour. I was assigned Timmy and Billy, whose father was out of work. After giving them the allotted $4.00 each, we began our trip. At different stores I made suggestions, but always their answer was a solemn shake of the head, no. Finally, I asked, "Where would you suggest we look?"

"Could we go to a shoe store, Sir?" answered Timmy. "We'd like a pair of shoes for our Daddy so he can go to work."

In the shoe store the clerk asked what the boys wanted. Out came the brown paper. "We want a pair of work shoes to fit this foot," they said. Billy explained that it was a pattern of their Daddy's foot. They had drawn it while he was asleep in a chair.

The clerk held the paper against a measuring stick, then walked away. Soon, he came with an open box, "Will these do?" he asked. Timmy and Billy handled the shoes with great eagerness. "How much do they cost?" asked Billy. Then Timmy saw the price on the box. "They're $16.95," he said in dismay. "We only have $8.00."

I looked at the clerk and he cleared his throat. "That's the regular price," he said, "but they're on sale; $3.98, today only." Then, with shoes happily in hand the boys bought gifts for their mother and two little sisters. Not once did they think of themselves.

The day after Christmas the boy's father stopped me on the street. The new shoes were on his feet, gratitude was in his eyes. "I just thank Jesus for people who care," he said. "And I thank Jesus for your two sons," I replied. "They really taught me more about Christmas in one evening than I had learned in a lifetime."

-- Jack Smith

* * * * *

## The Spirit of Christmas

The Omnipotent Weaver straightened His loom and turned,
with a practiced look,
To the endless mountain of variant threads and the open
pattern book.
He weighed each strand with a thoughtful smile,
and sorted them carefully --
A myriad of colors and priceless threads in silent symphony.

First on the loom went a thread of pure gold,
pressed firm by the Master's hand,
Till it lay in its place like the soft caress of a
hovering angel band!
Next was a priceless silver thread placed close to the
golden one,
Encrusted with diamonds and precious stones
in the brilliance of noonday sun!
The Master wove in the magic folds a pattern of warmth
and cheer --
Good will and giving and selfless thoughts
and compassion throughout each year!

Slowly and surely the Weaver toiled;
soon He finished, and then
Came a dusting of frankincense and myrrh
for the hungry souls of men.
The shining Hosts of Heaven then all crowded into the room
To admire the Weaver's masterpiece as it came from off the loom!

"Magnificent work, oh Father," an angel whispered low.
"What will You call its name, then,
and to whom does this rare gift go?"

The Master smiled and breathed a prayer
as the velvet folds unfurled --
"I'll call it the Spirit of Christmas --
My gift to the mortal world."

-- Sue Allen

* * * * *

## The Magi

Sensitive men
Inflexible will.

The wise men scanned the distant night-blue sky.
They were men born to a life of quest,
And they watched for a promised sign while others scoffed:
"Nothing good will come out of Judea,
And no star shall arise."
"We shall see the brightness of a great new light.
The sign will come.
We shall follow where it leads
And find the Prince who is worthy to be served."
Friends looked on with strange and alien eyes
And said, "Vain dreams bring no money.
You are chasing shadows."
But the wise men heard only the call
Of age-old prophecy.
Saw only the diamond star.

Sensitive men
Inflexible will.

All night long the three men traveled.
They shared their food,
The stars at night.
How close men grow when caused to share a purpose!
They drank from the same springs,
Shared the ever-eager urge to attain their goal.
They traveled late into the night,
Rose much earlier than the sun.
They covered rocky slopes, level plains, and fertile fields;
They followed silver rivers.
They would not be deterred.

Sensitive men
Inflexible will.

They scanned the distant night-blue sky.
They rode through stubble fields and groves of trees.
They watched the sun go down each day -
Its crimson spires up and spreading color
Through the rays of gold.

At last the perfect star pulsed in the east.
Their jars of frankincense and myrrh and box of gold grew heavier
With each passing night and day.
Yet they followed
Till at last they found the Holy Child
In his mother's arms.

Sensitive men
Inflexible will.

No longer need they scan the distant night-blue sky.

-- Alta Craw Williams

* * * * *

It is almost time for Christmas
And everyone is gay
Wishing each other the joys
They feel in their hearts today.

I have much joy in my heart
And thanks and gratitude, too,
For my many, many friends
And the things you say and do.

The Lord gives all of us trials
Hoping to make us strong,
And without the help of each other
We would probably all go wrong.

This year is closing much brighter
Than at one time I thought it might.
It has been your thoughts and faith and prayers
That are helping to make things right.

The Lord has heard your petitions,
My life has been spared for a time.
I am grateful for all of your prayers,
And to Him who has listened to mine.

Adversity must come to all,
But it is easier to understand
When things have turned out right again,
That the Lord did have a plan.

We all need to be reminded
We agreed to the joy and the pain
That must be suffered in this life
So we could live with Him again.

So at this Christmas season,
Since we've received the plan from above,
Let's put second the things of the world
And start with the Savior's gift of love.

-- Joyce Wilde

* * * * *

## True Christmas Joy

'Twas the day before Christmas, a long time ago
And our beautiful earth was all covered with snow;
Down the street with their sleighs came two manly boys,
Who paused at the window to look at the toys.

Already two others were there looking in;
But their faces were sad, and their clothes old and thin.
And the little one said, "Is it because we're so poor
That Santa doesn't come to our house anymore?"
The older one patted his wee brother's head,
And hugged him up closely, as softly he said:
"Oh, maybe he will come tonight, little Tim,
If we ask in our prayers for the Lord to send him!"
The little face smiled, but the boys saw a tear
In the eye of the one who quelled little Tim's fear.
Then slowly and sadly the waifs went their way
To the place they called home, where that night they would pray.
The boys, with their sleighs, followed closely behind,
And neither one spoke, but in each childish mind
A beautiful thought said as plain as could be:
"I'll share with those poor boys what Santa brings me."

When the two reached their home, to their father they ran,
And eagerly told him their unselfish plan.
He was proud of his boys, who now felt that same love
That sent our dear Savior from His Home above.
Next morning, still thrilled with their beautiful thought,
They scampered downstairs to see what Santa brought,
And they, with the help of their father and mother,
Selected the presents for Tim and his brother.

And as the first light of dawn came into view
The two went their way with the toys bright and new,
And crept very quietly up to the door
Where they'd seen the boys enter the evening before.
As they hurried back home toward their own Christmas joys,
They could not even dream how the other two boys,
On finding that Santa had really been there,
Sent their joy to the One who had answered their prayer.
That night, when the "Santas" were ready for bed,
With a hand of their father on each curly head,
They knew, as they thought of two poor, happy boys,
What's the truest and choicest of all Christmas joys.

-- Jennett Morrell

* * * * *

## Christmas Eve on the Desert

Tonight, not one alone am I, but three --
The Lad I was, the Man I am, and he
Who looks adown the coming future years
And wonders at my sloth. His hopes and fears
Should goad me to the manly game
Of adding to the honor of my name.

I'm fate to him -- that chap that's I grown old,
No matter how much stocks and land and gold
I save for him, he can't buy back a single day
On which I built a pattern for his way.

I, in turn, am product of that boy
Who rarely thought after Selves. His joy
Was in the present. He might have saved me woe
Had he but thought. The ways that I must go
Are his. He marked them all for me
And I must follow - and so must he -
My future Self - Unless I save Him!

Save? - Somehow that word,
Deep down, a precious thought has stirred.
Savior? - Yes, I'm savior to that "Me."
That thoughtful After Person whom I see! -
The thought is staggering! I sit and gaze
At my two Other Selves, joint keepers of my days!

Master of Christmas, You dared to bleed and die
That others might find life. How much more I
Should willingly give up my present days
To lofty deeds; seek out the ways
To build a splendid life. I should not fail
To set my feet upon the star-bound trail
For him - that After Self . . . . . .

Tonight, not one alone am I but three -
The Lad I was, the Man I am, and he
Who is my future self - nay more
I am his savior - that thought makes me four!

Master of Christmas, that Star of Thine shines clear -
Bless thou the four of me - out here!

-- Harrison R. Merrill

* * * * *

## The Carol that Never was Sung

The first Christmas Eve, of course, was a very important event. The birthday of the Child called for the biggest celebration the heavenly hosts had ever had. Even the Carols, held in reserve for ages for some really special event, would be sung.

The choir was to be one of Heaven's very best, with some exceptionally rich angelic tenors and basses brought in from the glee club to help out. All the stars had been rubbed with a special polish, and one brand-new star added just for the occasion. The Carols were quite puffed up with pride and excitement, and they all promised solemnly to be on hand in plenty of time.

On the great night, everything went off fine. The stars shone as they had never shone before; the angel choir outdid itself in paeans of joy, and the Carols were a great success. There was only one little flaw, and hardly anyone even noticed it. One of the Carols didn't get there in time.

In fact, it didn't get there at all. It was quite a sweet Carol, the angels singers told each other a little sadly. It had been a pity not to have sung it.

The Carol was very penitent. It had stopped on the way, it explained vaguely. Something had got its attention, and it had stopped, and been late. Questioning by the choirmaster produced little more. The Carol got vaguer and vaguer as the questions became sharper and sharper. Only one thing it seemed sure of.

It would never happen again, the Carol promised. But it did, every year. And finally, when nearly twenty long centuries had gone by with the last Carol still not sung, they brought the situation to the Throne Room. There they explained more in sorrow than in anger, about the Carol that was always late. Then, at a sign, they left, and the last Carol was summoned. The Last Carol was ashamed and frightened and hung its head as it stood in the Throne Room and explained with no more vagueness, why it had been late.

Each year had been something different, it admitted. Sometimes it had been a man in a dungeon. Often it had been men and women whose spirits had fallen low in the face of great obstacles, whose faith in love was almost extinguished and who could not join in the rejoicing over the Child's birthday.

Always, explained the Carol simply, it had seemed important to stop with these for ahile, and somehow it had always meant being late. "But next year . . . . ," began the Carol, but the voice from the Throne interrupted.

"Next year," said the Voice, "you will do as you have done. Next year and for many years to come. For you are the Carol that must be voiceless until all men sing together in a mighty chorus that covers the earth. Only in the hearts of men who have seen the vision," said the voice, "can you honor the Child, until all men love each other as He loved them."

"Then," said the Carol wistfully, "must I be silent forever?" "Not so," said the Voice, and the full choir of angels had never sounded so richly majestic. "They flee from it in fear and greed, but with their fear there is a shame, and through their greed shines love. One day they will cast out their fear and let love lead them into the rich habitation I have prepared for them. Then," said the Voice, "all men will join in singing the sweetest carol of all . . . . THE SONG OF UNIVERSAL BROTHERHOOD."

-- Alfred Hassler

* * * * *

## Silent Night
(How it came to be written)

On Christmas Eve, 1818, in the little Alpine village of Oberndorf in northern Austria, it was snowing hard. The people of the little town had long before gone to bed and all was quiet and still. But there was one light still burning. It shone from the study window of the young priest, Joseph Mohr.

Joseph Mohr had not been able to go to sleep that night and he had been pacing up and down his study, pausing now and then to look out of the window at the silent, snow-covered scene before him. He was deeply worried. Christmas, a day of music and rejoicing, was almost there and as yet he had seen no way to overcome the disappointment he knew was in store for his congregation.

The truth of the matter was that the church organ was in need of repair and there was no repairman in the town of Oberndorf. And the heavy snows had made it impossible to get one from anywhere else.

He was thinking of this and at the same time was remembering a conversation he had had the preceding summer with his friend, Franz Gruber, a school teacher in the town of Arnsdorf, not far away. Gruber was also an accomplished musician and played the organ in the village church. One day, as was their custom, they had been sitting in the pastor's garden singing together to the accompaniment of Gruber's guitar. Suddenly Gruber had stopped in the middle of a hymn and turned to his friend.

"Father," he had said, "do you realize that of all these Christmas songs we've been singing none expresses the real Christmas spirit?"

"You are right, my friend," the priest answered. "Perhaps one day someone will write a song that will tell simply the meaning of the Holy Night."

"Why should not that someone be you?" asked the schoolmaster.

Joseph Mohr had laughed. "And will you write the music if I do?"

"Of course," Gruber replied. "And I'm quite serious about this. I'm sure you can do it."

In the weeks that followed this conversation, Joseph Mohr had tried to write that song. But somehow, try as he would, the words simply didn't come; and now on Christmas Eve he felt a little sad as he thought of the service the next evening with no organ and no new song to sing to his people as he had planned.

As he stood at his window now, lost in thought, he suddenly realized that someone was struggling through the deep snow toward his house. He rushed to the door and went out to help his exhausted visitor into the warmth of his fire. It was a woman, too breathless to speak for some moments, but at last she was able to tell her story.

She had come over the mountain from the cabin of a friend of hers who that night had given birth to her first child, a son.

"And Father," the woman concluded, "her husband, who is a young woodcutter, is very anxious that you come and bless the new mother and the babe this very night."

"Of course I'll go." the priest answered.

"But the snow is getting very deep now," the woman protested. "I came as I promised him I would, but I'm sure he'll understand if you wait until morning. 'Twas not snowing hard like this when I left their house."

"I don't mind the snow. And the walk will be good for me," Joseph Mohr answered. "I'm feeling too wakeful to go to bed anyway. You stay here until you're rested before you go home."

Bundling himself up in his warmest clothes and taking a stout cane to help him, the priest started out. It was several miles to the woodcutter's cabin and the heavy snow made it difficult to walk, but when he arrived and opened the door he caught his breath at the scene before him. It was one he would never forget.

There was the new mother in her bed smiling happily at her husband, who was kneeling in adoration before a crude wooden crib in which lay his newborn son. It seemed to Joseph Mohr that he was looking at a scene that had taken place in B thlehem of Judea many ages before.

The young woodcutter felt the sudden draft of cold air and rose quickly to his feet. "Welcome, Father, " he cried. "I didn't expect you to come when I realized how hard it was snowing; but I'm grateful you're here."

Proudly he led the priest over to the cradle where the child lay and Father Mohr admired the baby and then gave him and the mother his blessing.

Although the woodcutter wanted the priest to partake of some refreshment before he left, Father Mohr replied that he must be on his way. Bidding goodbye to the happy parents, he set out for home - but this time the way didn't seem quite so hard. The snow was no longer falling but the branches of the pine trees bent low under their heavy white mantle. The stillness in the forest was awe-inspiring. As he plowed through the drifts the pastor kept thinking of the little family he had just left. Truly this had been a holy night.

At home, he could hardly wait to take off his coat and warm his stiff fingers. Then he sat down at his desk and began to write. It was early morning before he finished and fell exhausted upon his bed for a little rest.

But he didn't stay there long. Soon he arose, ate his breakfast and hurried out again. This time he went in the direction of Arnsdorf where his friend Franz Gruber lived. When Gruber opened his door Joseph Mohr handed him the manuscript containing the words he had written in the early morning hours.

"My friend," the priest said, "here is a new Christmas Song. Will you set it to music as you once promised?"

Franz Gruber's eyes shone as he read the beautiful verses. Grasping the pastor's hand he said, "I shall do my best. And we'll sing it at the service tonight. My guitar will be our accompaniment."

That evening the congregation gathered in the little church at Oberndorf to hear their priest preach his Christmas sermon. After he had finished telling them the meaning of the Star of Bethlehem, Franz Gruber came and stood with him. The altar candles cast a soft glow around them as together they sang the hymn their combined talents had produced.

As the last words, "Christ the Savior is born" were heard, the people in the little church were filled with a reverence they had not known before. But they couldn't have realized that they were having the privilege of hearing for the first time a song that in years to come would be the best loved of Christmas carols.

Silent Night! Holy Night!
by Joseph Mohr and Franz Gruber

Silent night! Holy night!
All is calm, all is bright.
'Round yon Virgin Mother and Child!
Holy infant, so tender and mild,
Sleep in heavenly peace, Sleep in heavenly peace.

Silent night! Holy night!
Shepherds quake at the sight!
Glories stream from heaven afar,
Heav'nly hosts sing, "Alleluia!"
Christ, the Savior, is born! Christ, the Savior, is born!

Silent night! Holy night!
Son of God, love's pure light!
Radiant beams from Thy holy face
With the dawn of redeeming grace.
Jesus, Lord, at Thy birth,
Jesus, Lord, at Thy birth.

* * * * *

## Rudolf - That Amazing Reindeer

On a December night in Chicago several years ago, a little girl climbed onto her father's lap and asked a question. It was a simple question, asked in children's curiosity, yet it had a heart-rending effect on Robert May.

"Daddy," four-year old Barbara asked, "Why isn't my Mommy just like everybody else's mommy?"

Bob May stole a glance across his shabby two-room apartment. On a couch lay his young wife, Evelyn, racked with cancer. For two years she had been bedridden; for two years, all Bob's income and smaller savings had gone to pay for treatments and medicines.

The terrible ordeal already had shattered two adult lives. Now Bob suddenly realized the happiness of his growing daughter was also in jeopardy. As he ran his fingers through Barbara's hair, he prayed for some satisfactory answer to her question.

Bob May knew only too well what it meant to be "different." As a child he had been weak and delicate. With the innocent cruelty of children, his playmates had continually goaded the stunted, skinny lad to tears. Later at Dartmouth, from which he was graduated in 1926, Bob May was so small that he was always being mistaken for someone's little brother.

Nor was his adult life much happier. Unlike many of his classmates who floated from college into plush jobs, Bob became a lowly copy writer for Montgomery Ward, the big Chicago mail order house. Now at thirty-three, Bob was deep in debt, depressed and sad.

Although Bob didn't know it at the time, the answer he gave the tousled haired child on his lap was to bring him to fame and fortune. It was also to bring joy to countless thousands of children like his own Barbara. On that December night in the shabby Chicago apartment, Bob cradled his little girl's head against his shoulder and began to tell a story . . .

"Once upon a time there was a reindeer named Rudolph, the only reindeer in the world that had a big red nose. Naturally people called him Rudolph the Red Nosed Reindeer." As Bob went on to tell about Rudolph, he tried desperately to communicate to Barbara the knowledge that, even though some creatures of God are strange and different, they often enjoy the miraculous power to make others happy.

Rudolph, Bob explained, was terribly embarrassed by his unique nose. Other reindeer laughed at him; his mother and father and sister were mortified too. Even Rudolph wallowed in self pity.

"Why was I born with such a terrible nose?" he cried.

"Well," continued Bob, "one Christmas Eve, Santa Claus got his team of husky reindeer - Dasher, Dancer, Prancer, and Vixon ready for their yearly trip around the world. The entire reindeer community assembled to cheer these great heroes on their way. But a terrible fog engulfed the earth that evening, and Santa knew that the mist was so thick he wouldn't be able to find any chimney.

Suddenly Rudolph appeared, his red nose glowing brighter than ever. Santa sensed at once that here was the answer to his perplexing problem. He led Rudolph to the front of the sleigh, fastened the harness and climbed in. They were off! Rudolph guided Santa safely to every chimney that night. Rain and fog, snow and sleet; nothing bothered Rudolph, for his bright nose penetrated the mist like a beacon.

And so it was that Rudolph became the most famous and beloved of all the reindeer. The huge red nose he once hid in shame was now the envy of every buck and doe in the reindeer world. Santa Claus told everyone that Rudolph had saved the day and from that Christmas, Rudolph has been living serenely and happy."

Little Barbara laughed with glee when her father finished. Every night she begged him to repeat the tale until finally Bob could rattle it off in his sleep. Then, at Christmas time he decided to make the story into a poem like "The Night Before Christmas" and prepare it in bookish form illustrated with crude pictures, for Barbara's personal gift.

Night after night, Bob worked on the verses after Barbara had gone to bed for he was determined his daughter should have a worthwhile gift, even though he could not afford to buy one . . .

Then as Bob was about to put the finishing touches on Rudolph, tragedy struck. Evelyn May died. Bob, his hopes crushed, turned to Barbara as his chief comfort. Yet, despite his grief, he sat at his desk in the quiet now lonely apartment, and worked on "Rudolph" with tears in his eyes.

Shortly after Barbara had cried with joy over his handmade gift on Christmas morning, Bob was asked to an employee's holiday party at Montgomery Wards. He didn't want to go, but his office associates insisted. When Bob finally agreed, he took with him the poem and read it to the crowd. At first the noisy throng listened in laughter and gaiety. Then they became silent, and at the end, broke into spontaneous applause. That was in 1938.

By Christmas of 1947, some 6,000,000 copies of the booklet had been given away or sold making Rudolph one of the most widely distributed books in the world. The demand for Rudolph sponsored products, increased so much in variety and number that educators and historians predicted Rudolph would come to occupy a permanent niche in the Christmas legend.

Through the years of unhappiness, the tragedy of his wife's death and his ultimate success with Rudolph, Bob May has captured a sense of serenity. And as each Christmas rolls around he recalls with thankfulness the night when his daughter, Barbara's questions inspired him to write the story.

* * * * *

## The Most Beautiful Thing

The sides of the path were covered with rugs of white snow. But, in the center, its whiteness was crushed and churned into a foaming brown by the tramp, tramp of hundreds of hurrying feet. It was the day before Christmas.

People rushed up and down the path carrying armloads of bundles. They laughed and called to each other as they pushed their way through the crowds.

Above the path, the long arms of an ancient tree reached upward to the sky. It swayed and moaned as a strong wind grasped its branches, and bent them toward the earth. Down below a haughty laugh sounded, and a lovely fir tree stretched and preened its thick green branches, sending a fine spray of snow shimmering downward to the ground.

"I should think," said the fir, in a high smug voice, "that you'd try a little harder to stand still. Goodness knows you're ugly enough with the leaves you've already lost. If you move around any more, you'll soon be quite bare."

"I know," answered the old tree. "Everything has put on its most beautiful clothes for the celebration of the birth of Christ. Even from here I can see the decorations shining from each street corner. And yesterday some men came and put the brightest, loveliest lights on every tree along the path - except me, of course." He sighed softly, and a flake of snow melted in the form of a teardrop and ran down his gnarled trunk.

"Oh, indeed! And did you expect they'd put lights upon you so your ugliness would stand out even more?" smirked the fir.

"I guess you're right," replied the old tree in a sad voice. "If there were only somewhere I could hide until after the celebrations are over, but here I stand. . . the only ugly thing among all this beauty. If they would only come and chop me down," and he sighed sorrowfully.

"Well, I don't wish you any ill will," replied the fir, "but you are an eyesore. Perhaps it would be better for us all if they came and chopped you down." Once again he stretched his lovely thick branches. "You might try to hand onto those three small leaves you still have. At least you wouldn't be completely bare."

"Oh, I've tried so hard," cried the old tree. "Each fall I say to myself, 'this year I won't give up a single leaf, no matter what the cause', but someone always comes along who seems to need them more than I," and he sighed once again.

"I told you not to give away so many to that dirty little paper boy," said the fir. "Why you even lowered your branches a little, so that he could reach them. You can't say I didn't warn you then."

"Yes, you did at that," the old tree replied. "But they made him so happy. I heard him say he would pick some for his invalid mother."

"Oh they all had good causes," mocked the fir. "That young girl, for instance, colored leaves for her party, indeed! They were your leaves!"

"She took a lot, didn't she?" said the old tree, and he seemed to smile.

Just then a cold wind blew down the path and a tiny brown bird fell to the ground at the foot of the old tree and lay there shivering, too cold to lift its wings. The old tree looked down in pity, and then quickly he let go of his last three leaves. The golden leaves fluttered down and settled softly over the shivering little bird, and it lay there quietly under the warmth of them.

"Now you've done it!" shrieked the fir. "You've given away every single leaf! Christmas morning you'll make our path the ugliest sight in the whole city!"

The old tree said nothing. Instead, he stretched out his branches to gather what snowflakes he could that they might not fall on the tiny bird.

The young fir turned away in anger, and it was then he noticed a painter sitting quietly a few feet from the path, intent upon his long brushes and his canvas. His clothes were old and tattered, and his face wore a sad expression. He was thinking of his loved ones and the empty, cheerless Christmas morning they would face, for he had sold not a single painting in the last few months.

But the little tree didn't see this. Instead, he turned back to the old tree and said in a haughty voice, "At least keep those bare branches as far away from me as possible. I'm being painted and your hideousness will mar the background."

"I'll try," replied the old tree. And he raised his branches as high as possible.

It was almost dark when the painter picked up his easel and left. And the little fir was tired and cross from all his preening and posing.

Christmas morning he awoke late, and as he proudly shook away the snow from his lovely branches, he was amazed to see a huge crowd of people surrounding the old tree, ah-ing and oh-ing as they stood back and gazed upward. And even those hurrying along the path had to stop for a moment to sigh before they went on.

"Whatever could it be?" thought the haughty fir, and he too looked up to see if perhaps the top of the old tree had been broken off during the night.

Just then a paper blew away from the hands of an enraptured newsboy and sailed straight into the young fir. The fir gasped in amazement, for there on the front page was a picture of the painter holding his painting of a great white tree whose leafless branches, laden with snow, stretched upward into the sky. While below lay a tiny brown bird almost covered by three golden leaves. And beneath the picture were the words, "The Most Beautiful Thing Is That Which Hath Given All."

The young fir quietly bowed its head beneath the great beauty of the humble old tree.

-- Roma Story Whipple

* * * * *

## The White Kid Gloves

The dictionary defines happiness as good luck, prosperity, a state of well-being, and whenever I read the accepted description, it interests me to remember that the moment of happiness I cherish out of a lifetime was attended by no one of those things. On the contrary, luck had been so long absent as to become a stranger, prosperity was not even around a distant corner, and I was running a low fever.

The winter when I was sixteen, my father suffered a series of paralyzing business reverses. He was the owner of a small, independent company which he had founded and built into a comfortable position, and which he loved with the devotion of a man who understands responsibility and appreciates work. A series of misadventures, which began in the middle of the year, culminated in October with the default of a note he had signed for a friend in cheerful confidence, and he was forced to pay out of his working capital the sum of $25,000. He found that he was almost penniless and that recovery lay months, even years, in the future -- if at all.

The times were inflationary, and almost the bitterest pill to swallow was prosperity flourishing on all sides of him but eschewing his path. He had established a standard of living commensurate with his prospects, which included a pleasant house with a sizeable mortgage, a wife he loved to indulge, and two spoiled children, Stanley and me.

My father was not a man to burden his family with business worries, and during the early days of his troubles he maintained silence. As the number of his employees diminished and then vanished altogether and his working hours increased, he was forced to take my mother into confidence. I do not know to what extent she was frightened by the facts, for she never gave a sign, past dispersing with the maid-of-all-work and the yard man, and the assumption of the full role of cook and housekeeper, with my brother and me as her assistants, positions which did not fill me with enthusiasm.

While I fretted at the ironing board and my brother grumbled as he stoked the furnace or raked the leaves, my mother was able to sing at her work and my father summoned a kind of haunted cheer in our presence.

It was only after we had been driven abovestairs to attack our homework that the burden of unease seeped through the house. I would lean over the banister in the dark and observe my parents, clinging together on the sofa as if they occupied a bit of driftwood in a raging ocean, and pick up bits and pieces of their conversation:

"But, Whit, could you sell the business?"

"I don't know, I suppose so -- at a loss."

"It would relieve you of a burden. You could always get a job."

"That might solve things. Gabbardt would take me on. Or I think so."

"But you don't really want to sell it, do you?"

"No, I believe in it -- if we can weather this spell."

"I believe in it, too," my mother would declare loyally. "We'll find a way. Now, you're not to worry about it another minute!"

The dominion of money over human beings is a devastating thing. It is, as everybody knows, inedible and of no use in building a fire, and in any elemental situation it is worse than useless, but in the limits of our society too much can be a danger and too little a bludgeon. I do not suppose that my father and mother ever thought we should actually go hungry or cold, but they knew that the quarterly note on the house mortgage would roll around inevitably, along with the insurance premiums and the taxes and the fuel bills and the grocery accounts, and that credit and honor are inseparable.

I had not the experience at the time to know how their minds ran around in tortured circles, like frightened squirrels caught in a maze, but I have since had reason to discover.

"I don't know how to tell you this, Eloise," my father said one night as he stood before the fireplace, drumming his whitened knuckles on the mantel and looking away from her, "I've taken a job."

"You've decided to give up the business?" she asked, her voice gray.

"No," he said. "I'm on the night shift at the Eldorado Hotel - night clerk. Would you like a room, lady, double bed?"

"But, Whit," my mother cried, "you can't work day and night!"

"You underestimate me," he answered brightly.

"Oh, Whit," moaned my mother. "How can you joke about it?" And she began to cry.

My father enfolded her in his arms and nuzzled her hair. "Now, don't blubber," he ordered. "You know I can't stand a crying woman."

She moaned afresh.

"You'll wake the children, sweetheart," he chided. "And, anyway, it's only temporary. Just think, they're going to pay me regularly."

My mother took a dim view even of a regular stipend. But the matter was settled.

I scuttled up from the landing as they began to turn out the lights. My cheeks were hot with shame. My father - working in a cheap hotel. I didn't know anybody whose father was a night clerk. It was mean and horrid, something I could not admit to my friends. I felt very rebellious . . .

If life had been uneasy heretofore, after my father began his double duty it became more so. He used to stumble home at 6:00 a.m., sleep until noon, then eat lunch, and set out for his empty office. He did not come home at dinnertime, and my brother and I rarely saw him except on Saturday and Sunday mornings, when we were not in school.

We missed him, but my mother was as one bereft. Most of the time she was too busy to mope, but during the long evenings I can remember her attacking the darning as if each raveled sock were a bitter enemy, staring out of the window into the night, or looking around our living room with its pretty chintres and books, deep sofa and rosey fire, as if she might never see it again.

Christmas had always been a splendid time for us. My father loved it as he loved all bright and social things - the flowing eggnog bowl and the people who came to call, the red satin ribbons and the mystery of packages, the turkey to be carved with a flourish, surprises. They were part of his nature. He set store by tradition, and his Christmas trees were a marvel of taste and originality, though he was very bad in the electrical province, and the strings of lights were always going off and reducing him to profanity.

My mother had a warm heart for Christmas, too. In that season her bustling hostess-ship reached its finest flower. The house was always rife with delicious smells -- baking fowl and spice and the scent of drying spruce. The doorbell never stopped ringing.

But as Christmas came on, general nervousness around the house increased. Nobody mentioned it and Stanley and I waited in vain for some cheering word.

"I want a bike," Stan said.

"I don't think we can afford it," I said, from the store of intelligence I had harvested eavesdropping. "I think we're poor."

"Are we?" my brother asked anxiously. "Who told you?"

"Nobody. I just think so."

"We still go to the movies," he pointed out.

"But _they_ don't," I said meaningfully. "They don't want us to be deprived."

"What's that?"

"Well, not to have things."

"Then they must want me to have a bike," Stanley concluded. "If I had one I could get a paper route. Then I could make money." Stan was always ready with a rationalization.

"I want something pretty," I said. "Something not practical!"

"Like what?"

"Like a party dress with a long skirt, and a pair of white kid gloves."

"A-a-ah. You're not going to any party."

"I am too. I'm going to Ruthie's Christmas dance, but I won't go in an old short dress, without gloves."

"Who wants an old pair of gloves," said Stan. "I want a bike. But don't tell anybody."

Time flowed into December. Still nobody said anything. My mother had a pleading look, as if she were waiting for father to speak, but he seemed impervious to the brash advance guard of the Yule. We began to feel both betrayed and dogged. The bicycle and the white kid gloves ceased to be desires and became causes. We whined aloud, though it made my mother cringe. We complained at our housework.

"Maybe it isn't coming this year," I said at last, banging the pots and pans about after dinner.

"What isn't coming?" my mother asked.

"Christmas!"

"Christmas always comes for people who have the right spirit."

"Not to us!"

"Christmas comes in your heart."

"But not like last year," I wailed. "Nothing's the same any more. Nothing." I began to sniffle, and rushed up to my room.

She followed me.

"The real job of life is giving - not getting," my mother said. "You probably won't believe me now, but you'll find out."

"But that's just it," I complained. "I want to give, too, but I haven't anything to buy it with. I haven't any money!"

"Darling, I haven't either," my mother said sadly. "You're a grown girl. You'll have to find your own way. Please don't mention this to your father."

"I never see him, anyway."

"No more do I. And I'm afraid it's harder on me than on you. Now, wash your face."

I applied for a job in the school cafeteria, not as a waitress, but as a dishwasher, since I could not bear the thought of moving among my schoolmates collecting their soiled trays. After my last class I made my way to the steamy kitchen by subterfuges and lied out of after-school projects and sodas with uncompromising duplicity. I did not much mind the job, though it was tiresome work, but my snobbery despised the thought of stigma. I was paid $2 per week, and since Christmas was three weeks away, I could not hope for more than $6. Nobody knew about this venture. I could not bring myself to tell even Stan.

I didn't see much of Stan, anyway. I got home late, and Stan was usually gone. Sometimes my mother was gone. The whole close-knit structure of our household seemed to have fallen apart. We were all silent and secretive, and when we were together we did not find anything to talk about. My mother's eyes looked for mine, but I held myself aloof. My father made wistful little jokes at Sunday morning breakfast, but I would frown instead of laughing. It did not occur to me that night-clerking was as hard for him as dishwashing for me.

"I'm making _him_ a pipe rack," Stan said to me. "In manual training."

"But he doesn't smoke a pipe," I objected.

"I guess he would if he had one," said Stan. "I figure to get one to go with it."

"How?"

"I'm going to trade my knife," he said. "I know a guy who's got a pipe that's nearly new."

"What about _her_?"

"I'm making her a little box," Stan said, looking proud. "I'm carving her initials on it. She can put her beads and stuff in it. It's a real strong box."

I thought warmly of my $4 buried in the bureau drawer among my pictures of movie stars . . .

Christmas came on Wednesday this year. The Sunday before, my father came downstairs haggard but cheerful. I did not know until years later that he had finally scraped enough cash together to pay the interest and semi-annual installment on the house and we were sheltered for another six months.

"Well, I'm taking the day off," he announced, "to gather the Christmas greens. Who would like to accompany me on a search for a Christmas tree?"

"They're so expensive this year, Whit," my mother protested. "Don't you think we're all old enough to get along without?"

"Nonsense," said my father with his old authority. "Never too old for a Christmas tree. Besides, we have received a gift. Mr. Feeneman, an elderly guest at the hotel, has given me permission to raid his wood lot. In the spirit of our ancestors, we shall obtain a tree by dint of the ringing ax."

I loved to hear my father talk when he was in his oratorical mood, and the thought of a Christmas tree broke up the ido in my bosom. My heart lightened and Stan squirmed with excitement. As an added boon, my mother said she would remain behind and put the house to rights, so that we could get an early start. Dish-washing by now had become anathema and to be spared any session of it was more to be desired than rubies.

We set off through a light snow for Mr. Feeneman's wood lot, which turned out to be four miles in the country. My father made hearty comments upon the wholesome value of winter exercise, though I think this was to camouflage our lack of carfare. As we trudged, he pointed out the various trees to us and told us their Latin names. Awed by his unfailing crudition, I panted after his long steps, though I was tired enough to faint and the snow was running down my collar.

When we at last arrived at Feeneman's wood lot, it was the most unprepossessing acre of scraggy, leafless trees and brambles, without an evergreen shrub in sight. We went over it microscopically, and when we were just giving up Stan raised a shout from the farthest corner, and we rushed there, to find a lopsided little cedar, ravaged by wind and weather, old before its time. I thought it looked awful, but my father pronounced it prime. He unsheathed Stan's Boy Scout hatchet and began to chop.

The tree was very tough and my father was an inept woodsman. About halfway through the proceedings, a chip flew off the trunk and smacked Stanley in the eye. It was a small, jagged chip, and with the ardor of my father's chopping behind it, it landed with some force. One edge of it tore the tender skin under the eye, and a few drops of blood fell on Stan's round cheek. He yelped once, like a hurt puppy, and began to dig in his eye with his fist.

My father laid down the ax and went to examine it.

"It doesn't hurt," Stan said, backing off. "We got to finish chopping!" He seemed more worried about the Christmas tree than his personal wounds.

My father's face showed his concern, and there was another emotion on it -- the unsettling realization that he could not seem to do anything right.

"I'm sorry, Stan," he said. "I never had any idea. . ."

"Aw, Pop, it doesn't hurt," Stan insisted.

The eye was beginning to swell and discolor, and the painful look on my father's face increased. He went over the eye carefully to assure himself that it wasn't seriously injured.

"We could bandage it," I said, and brought out my handkerchief. My father tied it around Stan's head, and Stan, swaggering now, seized the hatchet and finished falling the cedar himself, to show that he was all right.

The bandage served a useful purpose, as a farmer, rattling by in an old truck, pulled up at the sight of our whoebegone trio and offered us a lift. As we three huddled in the rear holding onto our prize, I began to sneeze and was forced to attend to my nose with my mittens. The farmer put us out at our house, and Stan, acting wounded but valiant, dragged our solitary green to the door. My father looked shaken and I was having more trouble with my nose.

My mother came out on the steps. "What --?" she began.

"Madam," said my father, "I have given your son a black eye."

"My baby!" said my mother, enfolding her youngest, and Stan began to cry for the first time . . .

That evening we trimmed the Christmas tree. Nothing could disguise the fact that it was a dingy cedar, not shaped to bear the lovely loot of Christmas, but Stan was proud of it, and while he and my father affixed the stand, the light of happiness gleamed from his good eye. Through some inexplicable stroke on my father's part, the lights all burned brightly, and as I sat stringing the garlands of popcorn and cranberries, and my mother tied on the cherished old baubles of a dozen childhood Christmases, it seemed that our mutual estrangement vanished and we were a family again. This enabled me to partially ignore my throat, which was getting more sore by the minute.

By morning, my tonsils seemed to have closed off my windpipe, but I did not mention it. It was my last day in the cafeteria and I had to have the other two dollars. I took my accumulated wealth with me and after school I went shopping. The stores were crowded and I felt very warm and light-headed.

As I began to hunt for the things I had imagined buying, I soon discovered the inadequacy of $6. One by one I discarded my dreams, but I could not give up the thirst for luxury, and instead of the warm woolen socks my father needed, I came home with a pair of fine black silk ones, embroidered with a clock. Though my mother could have done with a pair of stout gloves, I chose a ruffly nightgown of some sleazy pink stuff, since it was what I would have wanted. For Stanley, I got a bicycle bell, knowing full well he hadn't got a bicycle, but it seemed to me that if you could not have what you heart desired, a bit of its music would be better than nothing. As I say, I was light-headed.

On Christmas Eve I felt awful. My throat ached, along with my head and all the other bones in my body, and my stomach kept turning over, so that I could not share in the frenzied celebration which marked the arrival of a twenty-pound turkey from Uncle Robert's farm. The presence of the traditional meat seemed to buoy my mother and to make her feel that the times were back in joint, while Stanley and my father responded to the thought of something besides chopped meat. But I was not hungry.

I wished for nothing so much as to lie still in the dark, but this was out of the question as the bubble and squeak of Christmas now rose to crescendo. I alternated between chills and burning, and resorted often to the bathroom to gargle or immerse my head with cold water from the tap. Between chores, I returned to my bedroom to admire my offerings. When I had time I thought about Ruth's party, which I still had hopes of attending, having assured myself if worse came to worst, I could wear my mother's old black dinner dress. In my fevered state this possibility seemed quite likely to me, though it never could have happened.

According to our customs, the Christmas tree was scheduled for the night of Christmas Eve. My father had got the night off from the hotel. When I came into the room in the late afternoon Stan was laying the fire on the hearth. Three forlorn little packages, wrapped up by Stanley in scraps of paper and string were disposed under the tree. I arranged my three around them.

"I guess that's all," I said hoarsely.

"I guess so," Stan said. "I hope you like what I got you."

"I will."

"You want me to tell you what it is?"

"No, no. I want to be surprised. I <u>have</u> to be surprised!" I cried out with passion.

"I wasn't going to tell you, anyway," he said.

At dinner I could not eat.

"She's too excited," my mother said. "She can't take anything calmly. She looks as if she had a fever."

I shrank from the hand she put out to explore my brow.

My father leaned over and, putting his forefinger under my chin, he tipped up my hot face. "My little girl," he said, "is turning into a beauty."

The effect of his almost forgotten tenderness sent a shiver down me and I had to swallow harder than usual to stop the blinding tears. My love for him ached like a tooth. The lump of anxiety and worry and fear of the months past got mixed up in my sore throat and everything hurt terribly, all at the same time. I could not keep from wishing I were dead, a natural emotion at sixteen when the possibility is remote.

By the time I had regained composure the inevitable dishes had to be washed, but I was almost grateful to have something to occupy me until eight o'clock. I offered to let Stan off from the drying to be alone, for I was afraid another word would send me flying into little pieces, but gallantly he insisted, not to be outdone in generosity.

Embarrassment fell on Stan and me in the kitchen. Our friendship was deep and lasting, but neither of us could talk about it, so we did not talk. We hung about in the kitchen after we had finished, not knowing what to do with ourselves. Then we heard my mother at the piano and my father's sweet, true voice singing Silent Night. The year before, we had raced like little children, but now we walked sedately, and Stan stood back and let me go in first.

The fire blazed and the room was soft with candlelight from the stubby storm candles set in the old brass candelabra. The little red and green bulbs glowed like jeweled fruit on the cedar tree. A snowfall of packages piled around the base, and to one side, refracting the firelight, stood the gleaming bicycle. Stan's mouth dropped, and I thought with almost my first pure unselfishness, that I had rather he had got it than to have had anything myself.

It is impossible to say more about the intimacy of the scene which ensued. It happens multiplied millions of times in the season, and you had best remember your own time. The happy cry which leaps from a young girl's lips when she draws from its tissue wrappings her first long party dress, even if it be fashioned from her mother's old taffeta negligee, is an old story. Surely you, too, have unwrapped your first pair of long white kid gloves with the dear little buttons at the wrist - the beautiful, delicate, white kid gloves which mean that you are a grown woman, forever above the soil of childhood. And if they were the product of sacrifice you cannot escape my intention.

It was late when we settled back from charged emotions of exchange to sip the cider. Stan was in a stupor of pleasure, swathed in his new sweater my mother had knitted up in the school colors and assaulting our ears with the brassy twang of the bicycle bell. My father was already wearing his new shoes (my mother's present), and his old ones, lined with the gray soles cut from old laundry boards to keep the damp from the holes, stood grotesquely under the Christmas tree. He was smoking the pipe that had been smoked only a time or two before and coughing, while he fondled his silk socks, his face alive with awareness that they were the best money could buy.

My mother had put on her pink night gown over her dress, and it became her. She sat tracing the initials of her name which Stan had carved into the box top, with gentle pride. I stroked my treasures alternately. I could not keep from touching what I loved. Stan had made me a fan, and it was the crowning touch of frivolity.

"Why, it's midnight," my mother said, aghast. "It's been a long day. Run along to bed."

A slight discussion followed which could be solved only by Stanley's being permitted to take his bicycle upstairs with him. He swore he could not be parted from it overnight. I then persisted that I must try on my dress and gloves and show them off. A strange lemancy had descended upon our parents. These things were permitted.

I stood before the mirror in my room. The dress had a low neck which showed all the smooth curve of my shoulder. I swished my skirt, caught up my long white gloves, and swept out of the room in imitation of my favorite movie heroine. I touched the hair at the back of the neck tentatively and smiled an enigmatic smile. I paused on the landing in my made-over finery, drawing on a glove. All my senses responded to the sibilance of silk and the softness of the glove against my bare arm. As I preened in the dark, enjoying the rash decciletage of the dress and the unaccustomed flow of skirt around my ankles, I leaned over the banister in a last excess of childish eavesdropping.

My father and mother were standing before the hearth. I saw how stooped his shoulders were and the new frost in his dark hair.

"Whitney," my mother said in a voice of happy puzzlement, "however did you do it - the bicycle, the gloves - ?"

"I don't blame you, Ellie, for thinking I've been at the hotel's till. It looks too foolish for our busted economy. But it was luck, honey, the Barton luck!" He summoned a grin. "So help me, I won the bike on a punchboard at the drugstore. I went in there the other night to get a cup of coffee and a doughnut, and there was one hole left in the board. What did I have to lose but a cup of coffee?"

"Oh, Whit!" she cried. "You went hungry."

"Just a tin-horn gambler," my father said. "But you've got to take a chance now and then!"

"But the gloves -"

"Well, I saved five dollars. I've been walking home from the hotel. Need a breath of air after an all-night stretch, you know."

My mother didn't speak.

"I had luck again," he said. "There was a bunch of measly-looking gloves on a table marked 'Clearance' and right down in one corner was this pair - just what the doctor ordered - and dirt cheap! Only $2.95."

"They're beautiful! You've made them both so happy."

"When you're sixteen," my father said, "Or just twelve, you deserve to be happy. And when you're an old man, you can't bear it if, now and then - at Christmas, say - you can't make wishes come true. You can't bear it, Ellie, being a failure to your children!"

"Don't say a thing like that. They've never wanted for anything in their lives!"

"But it's not enough - food and shelter and advice. You've got to give them something else, some kind of symbol of what the world can hold - something to reach for. Anyway," said my father, his voice trailing off into a whisper, "my luck didn't last."

"You can only have so much luck, Whit," my mother said.

He faced her, and his face was broken up and he swallowed painfully. "I haven't got anything for you, Ellie," he said. "I bought you a bottle of that stuff you like - that lilac stuff. But I got tangled up in the damn bicycle chain and fell down. I broke it!"

His despair was comic, and the picture of my debonair father entwined in the chain of Stan's new bike was funny enough to tickle anybody. I wanted to giggle, and I waited for my mother's laughter.

But she didn't laugh. She turned toward him, so that her full face was toward me, and such radiance burned on it, such an expression of pride and faith and hope and love, that I was forced to drop my eyes.

"I love you," she said. "I'd rather be married to you than to any man alive!"

They were motionless, two figures in a freeze, immobilized by the force of mutual feeling. They moved at the same time, without volition, melted together, entwined, touching - man and woman, but one entity.

It was then that my moment of happiness broke over me in brilliant, prismatic splendor. All finite things dissolved, the horizons of the earth rolled back, the firmament deepened, and I could hear that strange music which falls upon the inner ear only a few times in life. All the voices of all the angels sang in my head and every beat of every heart. I knew that the secret of life was almost in my grasp. I looked up the long arches of the years, and they beckoned. I leaned toward the future, abandoning fear.

I was dizzy with my untrammelled ability to see what cannot be seen with the physical eye, to see beyond the little limitations of the human orb into the extensions of the spirit. I turned upon my infinite pinnacle and saw them far below - the two loving figures who had given me the secret. How small they were and far away, and how my heart surged toward them.

My father had straightened up and was standing tall, and my mother's laughter spilled out. From my eminence I knew that they were invincible as long as they had breath, and even after.

In this eternity which occupied only a second in time, I had continued to tug at my other glove without knowing it. Now I drew it off and looked at it and pulled at the fingers to smooth them. Then I turned and went back upstairs. I could not intrude further on what I had witnessed and I did not want to see anybody . . .

On Christmas morning I had a high fever, and thickly over my swollen face the rash had materialized. The doctor, summoned from his own Christmas, sniffed at the door and almost before he had looked at me he made the diagnosis. "Measles," he said. "Fine thing for a great, strapping girl! And fine time to have the measles!"

But nothing could touch me. I could not even regret too deeply the loss of the Christmas party. I was quite happy to lie in the dark and ponder my thoughts.

There was compensation in the measles, for if I had had to go to the Christmas party, my father would have discovered what he never in all his life knew: both of the white kid gloves he had struggled to buy were for the right hand.

-- Margaret Cousins

* * * * *

# DETERMINATION

Keep your face to the sunshine and all shadows fall behind.

-- Helen Keller

* * * * *

Don't be afraid to take a big step if one is indicated. You can't cross a chasm in two small jumps.

* * * * *

Perhaps the most valuable result of all education is the ability to make yourself do the thing you have to do, when it ought to be done, whether you like it or not; it is the first lesson that ought to be learned, and however early a man's training begins, it is probably the last lesson that he learns thoroughly.

-- Thomas Henry Huxley

* * * * *

## Goals

Life's goal: To achieve a synthesis between creed and conduct.

If you chase two rabbits, both will escape.

The trouble with not having a goal is that you can spend your life running up and down the field and never scoring.

-- Bill Copeland

* * * * *

Nowadays the four-minute mile is commonplace for champion runners, but at one time it was scarcely thought possible. Tha man who proved it could be done was the British medical student, Roger Bannister - the man with the will to win.

He had been disappointed at his performance in the 1952 Olympic Games and had just about decided to give up running and concentrate on his medical training. He told his coach this.

"Roger," said his coach, "I think you are the man who can break the four-minute mile. I wish you would give it one last chance before you quit."

Roger went home and thought about this. Before the night was over, he had crystallized in his mind in the form of an iron will the determination that he was going to break the four-minute barrier before he quit running.

He knew what he must do. He would have to study between eight and ten hours a day in order to get through medical school. He would have to train for four hours a day, run to build up his body to a peak of perfection, go to bed early, sleep nine to ten hours a night so that his body could recuperate - all this to build up for that great day. He was willing to pay this price in addition to his previous training. For several months he went through a routine just like that.

Finally came that day for the four-minute mile. It was a bad day for the competition. It had rained for five hours and there was a sharp wind blowing, which made it a slow track. But Roger was not deterred. He told his running mates what he was going to try for. They encouraged him, shook his hand, and said they would do what they could to help by pacing him.

The first lap was right on time - 57.5 seconds. Because of the slow track, all the runners had to push in order to maintain that pace for the second lap, but when they finished it they were still on time - 1 minute 58.2 seconds. Then they went into the third lap, the hardest of all. This is when fatigue starts setting in. Roger and his running mates were tired, but at the end of the third lap, they were still on time - 3 minutes and 0.5 seconds in all. They were on their way to the first four-minute mile in history.

Roger said afterwards that he had never been so tired in his life as when he started that fourth lap. As he went around that first turn, his steps began to falter and he felt dead. His head was throbbing, his lungs were bursting, and his mind began to say to him, "Slacken up, and just try for a win." But as if in reply, something welled up inside of him and said, "Roger, if you run until you collapse on this track, you are going to make this four-minute mile. If your knees hit this track, you are going to do it. For all these months you have trained, and you've got to." So instead of slacking the pace, he fought off the pain, picked up his knees and began sprinting. Numb and tired as his legs were, he forced them to go.

As he hit the last curve, again his stride began to break. Describing it later, he said that there seemed to be an eternity in those fifty yards to the tape. But he closed his eyes, gritted his teeth, and forced himself to hold stride as he pounded down the stretch. Finally, he took that one last step which broke the tape, and he collapsed into the arms of his manager-coach. His time was 3 minutes 59.4 seconds. Roger Bannister had broken through the four-minute mile barrier.

* * * * *

# ENDURANCE

Private victories preceed public victories.

* * * * *

The reason people fall away from the church is the same reason people fall out of bed - because they aren't in it far enough.

-- Jay Osmond

* * * * *

Nothing in the world can take the place of persistency and concentration on one thing at a time. Talent will not; nothing is more common than unsuccessful men with talent. Genius will not; unrewarded genius is a proverb. Education will not; the world is full of educated derelicts. Persistence and determination alone are omnipotent. The watchword "hang on" has solved and always will solve problems of the human race.

-- Calvin Coolidge

* * * * *

## Vigilance of Life

In this world I've gained my knowledge,
And for it I've had to pay,
Though I've never been to college,
Yet I've heard the poet say
Life is like a mighty river
Rolling on from day to day
Men are vessels launched upon it,
Ofttimes wrecked and cast away.

Do your best for one another
Making life a pleasant dream,
Help a wan and weary brother,
Pulling hard against the stream
Some succeed at every turning
Fortune favor every scheme
Others, too, though more discerning
Have to pull against the stream.

If the wind is in your favor
And you've weathered every squall
Think of those who luckless labor
Never get fair winds at all
Don't give way to foolish sorrow
Let this keep you in good cheer
Brighter days will come tomorrow
If you try and persevere
Darkest night will have a morning
Though the sky be overcast
Longest lane will have a turning
And the tide will turn at last.

-- W. A. Perkins
(Written about 1876 - taken from his Great Grandson's journal, Samual Job)

* * * * *

One day recently, when we were having lunch with some friends, one of the guests had to leave early. Had to drive her thirteen-year-old to a friend's house, she explained.

"Couldn't he ride his bicycle?" someone ventured. "Or even walk?"

"Heavens no," she said. "It's at least a mile from our place."

A minor and commonplace episode, surely. And yet it left us thinking. A mile, she said. At least a mile.

In the summer of 1844, in an ox-drawn covered wagon creeping along the rugged Oregon Trail, a pioneer named Sager and his wife became ill and died. With them in the wagon were their seven children: two boys, the oldest thirteen; five girls, the youngest a tiny baby.

The Sager orphans stayed with the wagon train until it reached Fort Hall, a British trading post. But there the courage of its leaders faltered. The trail to Oregon seemed too desolate and dangerous. They decided to head southwest to California instead.

But John Sager, age thirteen, remembered what his father had said about the importance of settling Oregon, of holding that territory for the United States. The night the wagon train changed its plans, he wrote a note saying that he and his brother and sisters were going back east with the scout Kit Carson, who happened to be passing through Fort Hall. In the morning the Sager orphans were gone.

But John Sager was not with Kit Carson, and he was not heading east. Abandoning the heavy wagon, he turned the slow-moving oxen into a pack-train. Driving a cow to furnish milk for the baby, they headed west across the burning plains, seven children, all alone. Day after day they crept on under the burning sun. At night they shivered around a tiny camp fire. The baby became feverish and could not eat. The smaller children wanted to turn back. John made them go on.

Three hundred miles from Fort Hall, sunburned, half-starving, in rags, they came to what is now Boise, Idaho. A kindly trader fed them, tried to persuade them to stay, but John had heard of a missionary-doctor two hundred miles farther on, across the rugged Blue Mountains. He thought the doctor might save his baby sister. So he went on.

Now the brief summer was ending. As they came to the mountains, it grew very cold. The oxen were dying and had to be abandoned. The eight-year-old girl fell and broke her leg. John packed it in snow and reduced the swelling and put her on the back of the emaciated cow. He made a sling and carried the three-year-old on his back. The baby in his arms weighed almost nothing.

Over the mountains they went, on frostbitten, bloody feet. By now they were scarecrows, all of them. The cow's hooves were split and broken; she moaned constantly. But they went on, and on, and on, until one day they staggered up to the house where the missionary-doctor lived with his wife.

That kindhearted woman thought that the baby was dead. But after she warmed it and forced a few drops of milk between its blue lips, it uttered a whimpering cry. And John Sager, watching, gave a kind of croak that might have been a laugh.

The doctor and his wife had recently lost a child of their own. They persuaded the Sagers to stay and adopted them. So that was how John, his brother and sisters came to Oregon. Five hundred trackless miles, alone. And yet, not really alone. The greatness that made America walked with them, every step of the way.

-- from On To Oregon by Honore' Morrow. Movie, "Seven Alone"

* * * * *

## Trials

You perhaps recall the story of the blacksmith who gave his heart to God. Though conscientious in his living, still he was not prospering materially. In fact, it seems that from the time of his conversion more trouble, affliction and loss were sustained than ever before. Everything seemed to be going wrong.

One day a friend who was not a Christian, stopped at the little gorge to talk to him. Sympathizing with him in some of his trials, the friend said, "It seems strange to me that so much affliction should pass over you, just at the time when you have become an earnest Christian. Of course I don't want to weaken your faith in God, or anything like that. But here you are, God's help and guidance, and yet things seem to be getting steadily worse. I can't help wondering why it is."

The blacksmith did not answer immediately, and it was evident that he had thought of the same question before. But finally he said, "You see the raw iron which I have here to make into horses shoes. You know what I do with it? I take a piece and heat it in the fire until it is red, almost white with the heat. Then I hammer it unmercifully to shape it as I know it should be shaped. Then I plunge it into a pail of cold water to temper it. Then I heat it again and hammer it some more. And this I do until it is finished."

"But sometimes I find a piece of iron that won't stand up under this treatment. The heat and the hammering and the cold water are too much for it. I don't know why it fails in the process, but I know it will never make a good horse shoe."

He pointed to a heap of scrap iron that was near the door of his shop. "When I get a piece that cannot take the shape and temper, I throw it out on the scrap heap. It will never be good for anything."

He went on, "I know that God has been holding me in the fires of affliction and I have felt his hammer upon me. But I don't mind, if only he can bring me to what I should be. And so in all these hard things, my prayer is simply this: Try me in any way you wish, Lord, only don't throw me on the scrap heap."

-- Lynell Waterman

* * * * *

## ESPECIALLY FOR MORMONS

Dare to be a Mormon,
Dare to stand alone.
Dare to have a purpose --
Dare to make it known.

* * * * *

You can be active in the church without being active in the gospel.

* * * * *

In our search for truth we must purge outselves of prejudice, for that closes the mind. Truth is often found in the most unexpected places - - A knowledge of truth will help men to be free, whether it comes by direct revelation as in the case of the prophets, from the written word as recorded in the scriptures, revealed as a result of research in the laboratory, in the flight of the astronaut as he circles the globe, or as revealed to a prayerful youth upon his knees in the sanctuary of a grove.

* * * * *

### I Am A Child of Royal Birth

I am a child of royal birth
My father is king of heaven and earth
My spirit was born in the courts on high;
A child beloved, a princess (or prince) am I.

I was nurtured there; I lived by His side,
In a home where patience and love abide.
My Mother was there in that glorious place,
Blessing her children with queenly grace.

I grew to the stature that spirits grow,
I gained the knowledge I needed to know.
I was taught the truth and I know the plan,
That God and the Christ laid out for man.
I was there when the stars of morning sang.
I mingled my voice when the heavens rang.
I was there to rejoice, to praise and applaud.
The shouts of joy from the Sons of God.

I waited my turn and I came to earth
Through the wonderful channel of human birth,
Then the curtains were closed and the past was gone;
On the future too, the curtains were drawn.
I live on the earth, and God willed it so,
With freedom to choose the way I should go.
I must search for the truth, I must serve and obey.
I must walk by my faith many miles of the way.

Someday I'll go back; I will answer the call,
I'll return with my records to the Father of All.
The books will be opened and so will my heart,
There will be rejoicing if I've done my part.
My Father, the King, with His infinite love
Will welcome me back to the mansions above.
The curtains will part and eternity
In its light and glory will open to me.

-- Anna Johnson

* * * * *

## Courting Temptation

The story is told of a man who once caught a poisonous snake by the nape of the neck and held it up to show his companions how clever he was. Much to his surprise it began to coil around his arm and to tighten until in agony the man released the serpent's neck long enough for the snake to strike, killing him.

So it is with many men. Some feel they can go where temptation and possible danger lurk without getting hurt. They think they can play with temptation and not reap the consequences. Such people are commonly surprised.

For example, some years ago a teacher was talking to a girl who had come to him in tears after being involved in morality problems. "I just don't understand," she said. "I prayed with all my heart that God would keep me from giving in to this temptation, and he let me down."

Then it was the teacher's opportunity to question her. "Did you know that this type of trouble might come if you continued keeping company with this crowd?"

"Yes," came her reply.

"Did you make an effort to find new friends and to leave this group?"

"No," she responded. "I felt God would cause everything to turn out all right."

Far too many of us expect God to direct our destiny with no effort on our own part. James E. Talmage has written:

"The plan of mortality involved the certainty of temptation. The intent of the supplication (from the Lord's prayer) appears to be that we be preserved from temptation beyond our weak powers to withstand; that we be not abandoned to temptation without the divine support that shall be as full a measure of protection as our exercise of choice will allow.

"How inconsistent then to go, as many do, into the places where the temptations to which we are most susceptible are strongest; for the man beset with a passion for strong drink to so pray and then resort to the dramshop; for the man whose desires are lustful to voice such a prayer and then go where lust is kindled; for the dishonest man, though he say the prayer, to them place himself where he knows the opportunity to steal will be found! Can such souls as these be other than hypocrites in asking God to deliver them from the evils they have sought? Temptation will fall in our way without our seeking; and evil will present itself even when we desire most to do right; for deliverance from such we may pray with righteous expectation and assurance."

* * * * *

## This Once Won't Matter

Society was surprised in 1964 by the sudden withdrawal of John Glenn, one of America's first astronauts, from the Ohio senatorial race. The news article which reported this withdrawal (Deseret News Editorial, 1 April 1964) stated:

> It's a sad and ironic thing that a man who has served through two shooting wars, orbited the earth three times and survived a risky capsule landing finds his career ended, or at least seriously threatened, by a fall in his own bathroom.

So it is with many men. They steel themselves against the big temptations only to find that by slipping and giving in to smaller, seemingly unimportant temptations, they have just as surely "ended or at least seriously threatened" their own future.

* * * * *

## The Call

Please follow me as I paint a picture of what might be. Suppose you have been called by the Bishop to be in his office at a certain time. Well, you tell yourself that you are tired of church jobs and you hope he hasn't called you in to give you another position. You decide that you'll keep the appointment, but you have all the answers ready.

The door is ajar, and so you walk in. At first you feel faint with fear, and you'd run away if you dared, for standing there where you expected the Bishop . . . was Christ. But the sweet smile on the Savior's face has overcome your fear and as He reaches out to take your hands in His, all that was in your mind when you came through the door has faded away.

Then Christ, not the Bishop, asks if you won't help Him. He tells you of the great need for service in His kingdom. Now you can feel the nail prints in His hands. Then He reminds you of His promises to those who serve Him. And through your tears you answer, "If you feel I am worthy I'll give my time and energy for you."

Well, Christ can't be in every Bishop's office, so the Bishop of your Ward is there with the same call . . . for the same purpose . . . with the same promise.

A call to serve in the Church of Jesus Christ of Latter-day Saints . . . in any office . . . is an opportunity for growth and service and happiness. It could be an invitation to greatness.

* * * * *

## Uphold the Hands of the President of the Church

We have some tight places to go before the Lord is through with this Church and the world in this dispensation . . . The power of Satan will increase; we see it in evidence on every hand . . .

Now the only safety we have as members of this Church is to do exactly what the Lord said to the Church in that day when the Church was organized (D&C 2:4-6). We must learn to give heed to the words and commandments that the Lord shall give through his prophet . . . There will be some things that will take patience and faith. You may not like what comes from the authority of the Church. It may contradict your <u>political views</u>. It may contradict your <u>social views</u>. It may interfere with some of your <u>social life</u>. But if you listen to these things, the promise is "that the gates of Hell shall not prevail against you. . ."(D&C 21:6).

As I thought of the role of President Tanner and myself as his counselors, I thought of a circumstance in the life of Moses, when the enemies of the Church in that day were just as they are in this day (Exodus 17:8-12). . . The hands of President Smith may grow weary. They may tend to droop at times because of his heavy responsibilities; but as we uphold his hands, and as we lead under his direction, by his side, the gates of Hell will not prevail against you and against Israel. Your safety and ours depends upon whether or not we follow the ones whom the Lord has placed to preside over his Church.

Let's keep our eye on the President of the Church and uphold his hands. . .

-- Harold B. Lee

* * * * *

## How To Discern When You Do and Do Not Have the Spirit

| When you have the Spirit -- | When you do not have the Spirit, or when Satan is prompting you -- |
| --- | --- |
| You feel happy and calm. | You feel unhappy, depressed, confused, frustrated. |
| You feel full of light. Your mind is clear. | You feel heavy, full of darkness. Your mind is muddled. |
| Your bosom burns. | You feel empty, hollow, cold inside. |
| You feel generous. | You feel selfish, possessive, self-centered. |
| Nobody could offend you. | Everything anyone does bothers you. You are always on the defensive. |
| You feel confident in everything you do. | You easily become discouraged. |
| You wouldn't mind everybody seeing what you are doing. | You become secretive, sneaky, evasive. |
| You feel outgoing, anxious to be with people. | You want to be alone. You avoid other people, especially members of your family. |
| You are glad when others succeed. | You are envious of what others do and of what they have. |

You want to make others happy. You bring out the best and say the best of others.

You are critical of others, especially of family members, and of authority.

You gladly and willingly perform church ordinances. You'd like to be in the temple for a while everyday.

You feel hesitant, unworthy to perform church ordinances; you don't want to go to the temple.

You feel you can magnify your church calling.

You wish you had another church job, or no job at all.

You feel like praying.

You don't want to pray.

You wish you could keep all the Lord's commandments.

You find the commandments bothersome, restricting, or senseless.

You feel you have control of your appetites and emotions: food and sleep in moderation, sexual restraint, diversion that is wholesome and moderate, calm and controlled speech, no anger, etc.

You become a slave to your appetites; your emotions become passionate; over-indulgence in food, sleep, sex, stimulating entertainment, strong anger, out-spokeness, etc.

You're generally just glad to be alive.

You wonder if life is really worth it.

* * * * *

# EXAMPLE

Example is not the main thing in life -- it is the only thing.

-- Albert Schweitzer

* * * * *

Show courtesy to others,
Not because they are gentlemen
But because you are.

* * * * *

The first great gift we can bestow on others is a good example.

-- Morell

* * * * *

If all Mormons would live their religion, our church would have no need of missionaries.

* * * * *

There are three ways to effectively teach a child: First is example, and second is by example, and third is through example.

-- Albert Schweitzer

* * * * *

I can easier teach twenty what were good to be done than to be one of the twenty to follow mine own teaching.

-- Shakespeare

* * * * *

A few words upon the subject of example: and these I speak particularly to my brethren, the Elders of Israel, yet they will apply to all classes of mankind. It is a rule with me, and always has been, to request nothing of the people that I am not willing to do myself, to require no obedience of them that I am unwilling to yield. Experience has taught me, that example is the best method of preaching to any people.

-- Brigham Young

* * * * *

"A little child on a summer morning stood in a great Cathedral Church. The sunlight streamed through the beautiful stained glass windows and the figures in them of the servants of God were bright with brilliant color. A little later the question was asked, 'What is a saint?' and the child replied, 'A saint is a person who lets the light shine through.'"

-- Anonymous

* * * * *

## What Will They Remember?

What will they remember when they think of me?
My virtues or vices -- which shall it be?
Will they think of a woman who tried very hard
To live the commandments of our dear, loving Lord?
Or a woman who could preach, it is true,
Then forget the things she told others to do.

Will they remember my dress so short and tight
That when I sat down -- well, it just wasn't right?
Or will they think of me as tastefully dressed
With clothes fresh and clean and neatly pressed?
And what of my actions -- did they depend on the crowd
For the course I would follow -- refined? or loud?

Did I repeat gossip and add a bit more?
Or remember that I was not so pure?
When asked to help someone, did I respond with a smile?
Or was I cranky and ornery, and gripped all the while?
Someone else's children -- did I treat as my own?
Or did I treat them so they left me alone?

Would they think me a lady by the things that I said?
Or grieved by the words that came from my head?

Will they remember me as a kind wife and mother,
And of being thoughtful of each sister and brother?
Let us pause a moment in this world full of strife;
How will they remember me, as I go through this life?

-- Grace Maxwell

* * * * *

## Thus A Child Learns

Thus a child learns; by wiggling skills through his fingers and toes into himself; by soaking up habits and attitudes of those around him, by pushing and pulling his own world.

Thus a child learns; more through trial than error, more through pleasure than pain, more through experience than suggestion, more through suggestion than direction.

Thus a child learns; through affection, through love, through patience, through understanding, through belonging, through doing, through being.

Day by day the child comes to know a little bit of what you know; to think a little bit of what you think; to understand your understanding. That which you dream and believe and are, in truth, becomes the child.

As you perceive dully or clearly; as you think fuzzily or sharply; as you believe foolishly or wisely; as you dream drably or goldenly; as you bear false witness or tell the truth -- THUS A CHILD LEARNS.

-- Frederick J. Moffit

* * * * *

## Numbed Condition

Some years ago one of my friends sent me a copy of a letter he had written to a man who needed a bridge to cross a difficult passage. It was addressed to "Dear Edgar."

Dear Edgar:

You told me of an experience you once had with a deer-hunting companion in the Uinta mountains late one fall in bitter cold and stormy weather. Your companion had become lost, panicky and exhausted from running over the mountainside. He had finally lain down under a pine tree, and by sheer luck you had come upon him before he froze to death. He was still conscious and could talk to you, but in his numbed condition, claimed he was not cold at all. No amount of coaxing on your part could persuade him to get up and move around. He begged to be left alone, insisting he was perfectly comfortable and got sore when you dragged him to his feet and made him move. He really cussed you plenty, you said, when you at last in desperation picked up a stick and laid one or two across his back until he moved to get out of the reach of it. You had to drive him more than a mile like that, for every time you got sympathetic and eased up with the stick, he'd lie down again. Finally, however, you got him moving faster and faster to get out of the way of the stick and his blood warmed up and began circulating so when he could think clearly again he thanked you with tears in his eyes time and time again for using the stick and saving his life.

I have the feeling since our conversation the other day that you, and hundreds of other good men like you, are in about the same condition spiritually as your hunting companion was physically. You came home from your mission all enthusiastic and for some reason you have grown cold. (I'll bet it's because of inactivity in the Church.) So cold you are numb, and can't think clearly in spiritual matters.

More than likely you have gotten sore at your home teachers because they would not leave you alone and probably cursed (to their backs) your quorum president and your bishop because they would not go away and quit bothering you. Am I guessing correctly?

- -

And so here again we need the Bridge Builders.

Here is our great opportunity to become the lighthouse for those who are in the fog for lack of understanding; here is our chance to build a harbor for the lost; a hitching post for the straying. Here is our chance to raise the spiritual, moral sights of the mediocre and to provide to even the brave a fire upon a mountain. Edwin Markham said:

We are blind until we see
That in the universal plan
Nothing is worth the making
If it does not make the man.

Why build these cities glorious
If man unbuilded goes?
In vain we build the world
Unless the builder also grows.

-- Spencer W. Kimball

* * * * *

Example

The Changing of the Guard

The bishop asked me later if I knew what time I had visited the old man that Sunday afternoon. I guess I did.

"Jamie, come in," said the old man. "And you've got Mark with you, too. Come on in, boys."

We stood in front of him as he lay in the hospital bed. "Mark, crank me up so I can get a good look at you." Mark looked at him with a puzzled expression. "Down at the foot of the bed, you see a big handle there? Looks like they took it from a Model T, don't it?"

Mark finally found it.

"You turn that a few times and I'll be able to see something besides the ceiling." Mark turned the handle and the upper end of the bed began to rise. "Not too much. I don't want to be bent double. There, that's fine."

"Jamie, it's good to see you." He put out his hand for me to shake. I knew he was pretty sick, because his grip was weak.

"I got permission from the bishop for Mark and me to come and give you the sacrament."

"I'd be pleased to take it, boys."

We closed the door to the hall, and I took a small slice of my mom's homemade bread from a bag and put it on a paper plate. Mark filled a plastic cup with water. I took the bread and carefully broke it and then knelt down and read the prayer. Then I held the plate while he reached down and guided a piece to his mouth. Then Mark knelt and blessed the water and handed him the cup. When he finished, he had tears in his eyes. "Thank you, boys."

Mark stayed for a few more minutes and then said he had to go home. He didn't know the old man like I did.

The old man and I sat and talked a little and watched the afternoon shadows move across the floor. He was very old. His face was tough, as if the wind and sun had carved out the soft flesh and left only the leathery surface. For sixty years he had farmed in the valley until his children had grown up and left, his wife had died, and he was alone with his garden, a plug horse named Blaze, and the Church.

I guess he'd always been in our ward, but kind of in the background. I remember he used to bear his testimony nearly every month, and whenever Dad took me to the welfare farm for a work project, he was always there. Today I thought of how we met . . .

When I turned fourteen and had to go home teaching, I was assigned to be his companion. He didn't have a car and I didn't drive then except during harvest time, so I rode my bike over to his place, now just a little out of town since things had grown so much since he first moved there.

In his living room was a round kitchen table with four chairs, a shag throw rug on the floor, and a reading lamp hung from the high ceiling. Lying on the table was a large copy of the Book of Mormon and a Bible.

That day he shuffled over to the reading lamp and switched it on. (Later he told me a horse had kicked him and left him with a limp.) He stood there looking at me, then reached in his back pocket and pulled out a large handkerchief and wiped his nose.

"Jamie, let's have a word of prayer." He grabbed the edge of the table for support and lowered himself to a kneeling position and folded his hands on the seat of the chair.

Then he looked up at me and said, "You kneel, don't you?"

I knelt down.

"Father in heaven," he began, "Jamie and me come to ask thee to help us as we go home teaching into the homes of the Saints."

It was a long prayer, and my knees were soon aching. I tried to shift my weight around to get a better position, but by the time I found it, he had finished.

"Jamie, help me up."

I reached down and put my arm under his elbow and pulled. He was a big man, and it was a struggle to get him on his feet.

He walked over to the window and looked out. "Come over here. Do you see the place over there by the big tree, and the place next to it down the road? On your way here, do you remember the place with the 'Rhubarb for Sale' sign nailed on the fence?" I nodded. "The Lord's given us stewardship over those families. Do you know what that means?"

"Yes, sir."

"What does it mean?"

"Well we've got to visit them once a month."

He rubbed one hand over his stubble beard. "Is that what you think it means?"

"I think so."

"You've got a long way to go, son . . ."

The nurse came in and gave him some pills. He didn't look very good. But when he talked, and you forgot about the chalky grayness of his face and his short, quick breaths, he was the same.

"Did you go fishing yesterday?"

"No, I'm waiting for you to get out so we can go together."

He looked out the window for a long time, and I thought he hadn't heard me. But after a few minutes he turned to me. "Jamie, you better learn to tie your own flies. I can't furnish you with free equipment your whole life."

"I will."

"I would have taught you before, but you were such a slow learner at fishing I thought I'd better wait."

The first time he offered to take me fishing behind his place, I brought the stuff my friends and I used when we fished from the old country bridge.

"What kind of a rig d'you call that? He looked at my large lead sinker and a treble hood with a wad of dried-up cheese stuck to it. "Here, let me see that. You're not supposed to club the fish to death," he said, as he took the sinker from the line. "And what's this?"

"Cheese."

"You bring your lunch?"

"I usually use worms or cheese for bait."

He shook his head. "I'll teach you how to fly fish. Then you'll know something about fishing."

He stepped into the river so he could get a free swing with his fly rod. "Look over there, just in front of the boulder." He whipped the fly line back and forth a couple of times to let the line, and then cast. The fly landed gently on the water above the boulder and then glided into the swirling water downstream from it.

Suddenly the water boiled as a German Brown rose up and took the fly. He carefully fought it to his side and then reached down and swished it up in his net. "You think you can learn to do that?" he asked, as he reached down into the net and pulled out the fish and gently dropped it back into the water.

Nearly every weekday afternoon that summer I'd go over to his place with my gear and we'd walk across his field to the river. He taught me how to cast a fly rod, where to cast, and what kind of flies to use for each part of the summer. "You got to find out what they're feeding on, Jamie. That's the secret . . ."

He slept a while because of the pills. The bishop stopped by to see him, but saw he was asleep and said he'd come back later.

The third month we went home teaching, Brother Johnson had just got a new horse. And so we walked out to the corral and took a look.

"Mort, how much you pay for that mare?"

"About a thousand dollars. Why?"

"She's a fine one. How come you spent so much money for her?"

"She's registered stock; she's got a good line."

Then Brother Johnson stopped and looked at the old man. "Why are you asking me a question like that? You been around horses your whole life."

"I never had a horse worth a thousand bucks. What will you do with her, sell her to the glue factory?"

"You know I'm not going to do that."

"Yep, I know that." He looked at the mare for awhile and then turned to Brother Johnson and said, "Mort, how long did your dad serve as a bishop?"

"About ten years, I guess. Why?"

"You come from a good line, Mort. As far as the Lord is concerned, you're registered stock. But you're no goot to the Lord the way you are now. It'd be less of a waste to sell that horse to the rendering plant than for you to keep away from the Church any longer. The Lord wants you back in harness, Mort."

Brother Johnson took the toothpick out of his mouth and flipped it on the ground. "You may be right," he said soberly . . .

Example

When the old man woke up, he was embarrassed that he'd fallen asleep. But I said it was okay. I didn't mind, and it was good for him to rest.

"Jamie, you been here too long. Your folks'll be worrying about you."

"They know I'm here."

He turned his head so he could get a look outside. "What day is it?"

"August sixth."

"August sixth. Now starting in a few days try an Adam with a number 14 hook. You got enough flies? If you need any, you know where they are."

He seemed to get some strength and he leaned forward.

"Now Jamie, you keep visiting them families, you hear? The Johnsons are coming along fine, but you ask the bishop to get the Scoutmaster over there to get their boy in Scouting." He grabbed my hand and squeezed it hard, and there was an urgency in his voice. "You keep yourself pure so's you can marry a beautiful L.D.S. girl in the temple when the times here. And get ready for your mission. You need to read the scriptures more than you do."

"I will."

He was still holding onto my hand. "Once on my mission I went and saw the changing of the guard. They marched into the courtyard wearing red uniforms and their buttons shone in the sun. The guards who'd been at their posts marched forward and --"

Before he could finish, the nurse stuck her head into the room. "I'm sorry but visiting hours are over."

He released his grip. "You'd better go, Jamie. Come back tomorrow if you can."

The next day when I got home from my softball game, my mom told me that the old man had died that afternoon.

I walked over to his place and down the path to the fishing spot on the river where we used to go and sat down on a rock. The river takes a bend just upstream from that point, and there's a hole where the eddy currents curl around in slow, lazy loops; and there he had told me the fish stay when they are feeding on a hatch of flies coming down the river. The spot is hard to find because of the growth of trees, and most people who fish it probably get their lines tangled in the fallen branches that lay hidden in the water; but he had told me where to stand and how to cast to avoid the hidden traps.

My thoughts were interrupted by a trout jumping clear out of the water for a fly. And then, for a moment, I could hear in my mind the words of the old man: "Don't whip the water, just let it glide down nice and easy. You're supposed to make the fish think that a fly is landing on the water and not that a tree has fallen into the river. How come you've never read the Book of Mormon? I want you to read it and tell the Johnsons about it. That'll be good practice for your mission."

And I remembered the last thing he had ever said about the changing of the guard.

I sat there for a couple of hours thinking about him, until it was dark, and I got up and walked back down the path and on to my home.

On my way, I stopped by the home of the Johnsons to see how they were.

-- Jack Weyland
Reprinted with permission,
"Improvement Era"

* * * * *

# FAITH

I believe in Christ as I believe in the rising sun -- not that I can see it, but that by it I can see everything.

* * * * *

On a new gravestone in England right after World War Two: "There is not enough darkness in all of the world to put out the light of one small candle."

* * * * *

Faith is what makes you feel the comfort of the hearth while you're chopping the wood.

-- Frank Clark

* * * * *

Do you sometimes think, "If I could just see Christ. If I could meet him. If I could talk to him personally, then this life would be easier." But you have seen him. You have met him. You have talked to him personally. This knowledge, believed in faith, can make life easier.

* * * * *

I would rather walk with God in the dark than go alone in the light.

-- Mary Gardiner Brajharel

* * * * *

"All the strength and force of man comes from his faith in things unseen. He who believes is strong; he who doubts is weak. Strong convictions precede great actions."

-- James F. Clarke

* * * * *

Why me Lord? Here I am
"In the thick of things" - Once I wasn't,
Someday I won't be. But here, right now,
I am.

Right in the middle of a strange,
mixed up, demanding world, and
with this nagging awareness within
me that you want me to DO something,
or say something, or BE something
that shall make a difference - - - -
It may not change the course of
history, but it may change the
course of some life. Mine? Here?
His? Theirs? Why me? I don't know.
I only know the unrest, the eagerness
on the one hand to charge off in
knightly splendor, the agony on the
other hand of not knowing the direction.
What would you have me do?

* * * * *

## Think of These Things

If you are ever plagued with doubt,
And question whether God's about,
Try thinking on some simple things;
You'll be surprised the peace it brings --
A sleeping child: A summer's day;
A puppy, awkward in its play;
The clean, washed air that follows rain;
A diamond-frosted window pane;
An apple tree all pink and white;
The stillness of a starlit night;
A fire crackling on the hearth;
The smell of freshly spaded earth;
A trail you knew once long ago;
A picket fence high-capped with snow;
A song your mother used to sing --
Why you can pick most anything
And you will find your answer there --
It's still God's World -- He's everywhere!

* * * * *

## A Condition of Effective Faith

A condition essential to the exercise of a living, growing, sustaining faith in Deity is the consciousness on man's part that he is at least endeavoring to live in accordance with the laws of God as he has learned them. A knowledge that he is wilfully and wantonly sinning against the truth will deprive him of sincerity in prayer and faith and estrange him from his Father. He must feel that the trend of his life's course is acceptable, that with due allowance for mortal weakness and human frailty he is in some measure approved of the Lord; otherwise he is restrained from supplicating the throne of grace with confidence.

-- James E. Talmage

* * * * *

## Persecution, Tribulation and Affliction

President Brigham Young pointed out that the intensity of Christ's suffering was induced by the withdrawal from him of the Father's Spirit. And I quote from Brother Young:

"...at the very moment...when the crisis came...the Father withdrew.... His spirit, and cast a veil over him. That is what made him sweat blood. He then plead with the Father not to forsake him. 'No,' says the father, 'you must have your trials, as well as others.'" (Journal of Discourses, Volume 3, page 206)

However, just as Jesus had to endure affliction to prove himself, so must all men endure affliction to prove themselves.

President Brigham Young is quoted as observing that the prophet was more perfect in thirty-eight years, with the severe tribulation through which he passed, than he would have been in a thousand years without it. (Speaking of Joseph Smith)

"For after much tribulation come the blessings. . ." (D&C 58:2-4)

-- Marion G. Romney

* * * * *

I had a companion, a fellow officer, who was a very rich man, highly educated. He was a lawyer, had great power, was self-sufficient and he said to me as we often talked of religion (because he knew who I was), "There is nothing in life that I would not like to have that I cannot buy with my money."

Shortly thereafter, he and I with two other officers were assigned to go to the city of Arras, France, which was under siege. It had been evacuated, and upon arrival there we thought there was no one in the city. We noted that the fire of the enemy was concentrated on the cathedral. We made our way to that cathedral and went in. There we found a little woman kneeling at an altar. We paused, respecting her devotion. Then shortly she rose, wrapped her little shawl around her frail shoulders, and came tottering down the aisle. The man among us who could speak better French said, "Are you in trouble."

She straightened her shoulders, pulled in her chin, and said, "No, I'm not in trouble. I was in trouble when I came in here, but I've left it at the altar."

"And what was your trouble?"

She said, "I received word this morning that my fifth son has given his life for France. Their father went first, and then one by one all of them have gone. But," straightening again, "I have no trouble; I've left it there because I believe in the immortality of the soul. I believe that men will live after death. I know that I shall meet my loved ones again."

When the little soul went out, there were tears in the eyes of the men who were there, and the one who had said to me that he could purchase anything with money turned to me and said, "You and I have seen men in battle display courage and valor that is admirable, but in all my life I have never seen anything to compare with the faith, the fortitude, and the courage of that little woman."

Then he said, "I would give all the money I have if I could have something of what she has."

-- Hugh B. Brown

* * * * *

## Farewell Skippy

Dear God:

I would like to tell you about my dog, Skippy. Skippy is very old now. He is so old he can barely walk around and when we go out riding in the car and take him with us we have to lift him in and out of the car. He can hardly see and is always bumping into the furniture and he can only eat things cooked into small pieces and milk and he don't eat much of that.

My pop is going to take Skippy into the woods and shoot him. My pop isn't a bad man at all, but he says he's got to because Skippy must be suffering. He says it's best for Skippy that he get shot. My pop told me about it this morning when he was loading the rifle. He said it had been on his mind for some time now, but he kept putting it off but he said he felt he had to do it now. I didn't want to cry and I didn't actually, but I guess some tears came to my eyes and my pop reached out and tousled my hair. I said, "Pop, do you have to shoot Skippy today?" And pop said, "Well, I think it best all the way around if we get this over with." And I said, "Would you please shoot Skippy tomorrow instead?" And my pop looked at me real close and kind of shrugged his shoulders a little and I said, "I would like to spend this last day with Skippy." And my pop said, "Well, all right." And he tousled my hair again.

So all day today I've been with Skippy trying to feed him at lunch time, although he won't eat much, and petting him. I put him in my red wagon and pulled him around over the neighborhood to all the places Skippy and I used to go.

Skippy lay in the wagon very still as if he knew he were taking all this in for the last time, and I felt very bad because I remembered how Skippy used to romp after me at these places and bark and prance around and chase leaves in the wind and scamper after squirrels. And then I felt worse than ever because I thought about pop taking Skippy out in the woods tomorrow and putting a rifle close to his head and Skippy letting him, because Skippy always let us do what we wanted with him, and then a big explosion coming and Skippy laying on the ground twitching a little and blood coming from him.

Then suddenly I thought of you, God, and that's why I came home and kneeled down here by my bed to pray to you about it. Nobody down here ever wants to die -- people, dogs or cats, no matter how old they get. But I'd appreciate it very much if you would let Skippy die before tomorrow. Because he's going to have to get shot anyway and it'd be nicer for him to just die than have to lay on the ground and twitch and have blood come from him.

I don't think Skippy is really any kind of special dog, God. I guess he's mostly just a little bit of everything; but, except for taking a nip at the milkman two times, he's been a very good dog. He minds well, and before he got very old, he would do a lot of tricks, such as bringing back sticks and balls that you threw and laying on his back and kicking his feet in the air and jumping through barrel hoops.

I'm not trying to tell you how to run your business, God, but sometimes I wish everybody didn't have to get old. Old people are the best people there are. They're always nice and kind and helpful but the trouble of it is they can't get around so well and they don't hear very good or see very good and pretty soon they just mostly sit in rocking chairs and then after awhile they die. Dogs are just about the same way. Skippy used to be so full of fun, always after something or other, but when he began to get old he moved around slower and less and less until now he can hardly get around or do anything at all.

Even the milkman that Skippy took a nip out of two times will tell you he's a nice dog. I guess he chased cars a little and also cats and squirrels, but it wasn't so much that he wanted to do any harm as it was that he liked to go after things. He just naturally had a lot of scampering in him. I know you like him, God, and I wouldn't be surprised if you made him your personal dog. He'd follow you wherever you went and if you didn't want him to he wouldn't bark too much. Anyway, if you let him die in a nice easy way, you know, not jerky and puttering, but soft and smooth and silky-like, like he was going on a swift non-stop electric train going to a place where he was going to be very welcome.

Pardon me for just a minute . . . There's somebody at the door. I'll be right back.

It was pop. He said to me, "I just wanted to tell you we won't have to shoot Skippy after all." Although I had the strangest feeling, I knew what he was going to say, word for word.

I said, "Why?"

And he said, "Skippy has just died."

I didn't say anything for a little while and then I said, "Do you know whether he wagged his tail just before he died?" Then my pop looked at me for about a half a second and then he said, "Yes, as a matter of fact, I think so."

God, I am back at my bedside and I want to thank you for being so nice about this. You'll get a swell dog up there in Skippy and I know you'll get along swell with him, and he won't cause you any trouble. Although if you have any milkman up there I'd be a little careful with him. Most of all, though, I want to thank you for making him welcome, and I know Skippy felt that way or he wouldn't have wagged his tail. Everybody down here, even people, would way tails if they had them when they're made to feel welcome. It is the most wonderful feeling you gave us.

Thank you so much dear God.

Arthur.

-- Harold Relfer

* * * * *

With Trust In God

"...in God I have put my trust: I will not fear what flesh can do unto me."
- Psalms 56:4

What were you doing on the afternoon of 10 June 1963? Probably you don't remember. But Ron Clark does. In fact, he will never forget. He was lying pinned beneath a two-ton cattle truck at the bottom of the desert wash. Beside him were several of his best friends -- dead. Around him was a bloody disaster that resulted when the big truck crashed backwards off a cliff, bearing the precious burden of forty-five people. Now thirteen of those forty-five were dead. Twenty more were injured. Ron himself was trapped near the front of the heavy vehicle where the greatest weight was. His jaw had been severely knocked out of joint when the truck went over, and his left leg was crushed under the truck.

As soon as he could pull his arms and right leg free, Ron set his jaw himself as best he could amid all the crying and screaming of the hurt passengers. The unhurt MIA Superintendent who had been accompanying the group of scouts, for whom this trip was to have been a super activity, was making the rounds, checking the extent of the damage. When he reached Ron he asked him how badly he was hurt. The young man tipped his head back.

"Charles," his voice trembled, "I've lost my leg." He couldn't feel a bit of life in his left leg, and terrible visions of the future raced through his mind. Despite the pain and worry, it was Ron who kept telling the others, "It's all right. They're going to get us out of here."

Ron was the last one pulled from the wreckage. Soon after he was taken to the Panguitch Hospital, his family arrived from Provo.

"I'm all right, Mother," he said.

This sixteen-year-old Explorer showed remarkable courage. And a few days later he was called upon to show perhaps even greater valor. He was sent home, where he had to be fed through a straw because he could not move his badly swollen jaw. He could hardly speak. He couldn't sing. For Ron that was very serious. All during his life he had brought a great deal of beauty and pleasure to the lives of those who heard his incomparable voice. When he was only twelve years old, he sang his way into the hearts of those at General Conference who heard his lovely renditions of "Listen, Dear Teacher," and "When He Comes Again." Only a year ago he had sung in a chorus at stake conference. His friends had sung with him then -- the same ones who helped plan the trip to Southern Utah.

He remembered how happy they all had been. Randy Miller, Lynn Merrell, Gary Christensen, Gary Rasmussen, Joe Erickson, and Gordon Grow -- all good friends.

Those were happy days. Ahead of him now was Gordon's funeral and the next day, the joint funeral for five of his closest pals. Ron could only get around a little with the aid of crutches when the stake president, Ben E. Lewis, called on him.

"Ronnie," he said, "the families want you to sing at the funeral service."

How could he? His jaw was too badly swollen for movement. Besides . . . these were five very special guys.

"You can do it," President Lewis promised, "if you will pray and if you really want to."

He really wanted to. The next few days were filled with prayer. He knew only the Lord could help him accomplish this incredible task.

The morning of the funeral, he couldn't eat; the jaw was rigid, and he spoke through closed teeth. Practicing beforehand was a fiasco . . . with those clenched teeth he could get no resonance or carrying power. But he had given his word.

His earnest prayers continued right up to the time he sat with his brother, Bob, in the choir loft of the old Provo Tabernacle. Then suddenly, minutes before he was to sing, an overwhelmingly peaceful feeling settled on him, and Ron turned to his brother. "I can move my jaw!" he whispered. "It feels all right!"

He picked up his crutches, limped on the platform by the organ, and with a faint smile, nodded to organist Byron Jensen. The young Explorer stood up tall and looked below at the flower-covered caskets bearing the bodies of the five friends he had buddied with practically all his life. How could he sing?

His voice rose, beautiful and pure. "May the Good Lord Bless and Keep You. . ." The unwavering notes filled the tabernacle and soared to heaven on the summer breeze. "Fill your dreams with sweet tomorrows. Never mind what might have been. . ." The melody was strong until the last, but then, he couldn't go on. He faltered, then whispered, "...till we meet again."

Tears coursed down the faces of the fifteen hundred sobbing people gathered in the Tabernacle -- tears shed not only for the five boys who had been taken, but tears also for the courage of a young Explorer with a puffy jaw.

As for that jaw -- immediately after the song, it locked again, and weeks passed before Ron could open it.

Nobody can tell Ron that miracles don't happen. He's had a few close calls since then, too, but he's now living the dreams of his life. He filled a mission in the Eastern Atlantic States, married his sweetheart, and has served in a Bishopric in Orem, Utah. But miracles don't happen all by themselves. It takes real faith, sincere prayers, and a lot of personal effort. In this case, all were supplied in abundance by a very strong man.

--Reprinted with Permission,
"Improvement Era"

* * * * *

# FAMILY

Oh, there's one who smiles on high, when there's love at home

* * * * *

"A happy family is but an earlier heaven."

-- Bowring

* * * * *

The trouble with being a parent is that by the time you are experienced, you're unemployed.

* * * * *

"The most important work you will do for the Church will be within the walls of your own home."

-- Harold B. Lee

* * * * *

"The only time we fail in the home is when we give up on each other."

-- Marvin J. Ashton

* * * * *

Babies are the nicest way to start people.

* * * * *

"I can think of nothing sweeter in all the world than a home where the father is holding and magnifying his priesthood and doing his duty, living the teachings of the gospel, realizing that his greatest responsibility is in his family; and with a wife who loves and sustains him in all his righteous endeavors; where the children honor and obey their parents."

-- N. Eldon Tanner

* * * * *

It is something to be able to paint a particular picture, or to carve a statue and so to make a few objects beautiful; but it is far more glorious to carve and paint the very atmosphere through which we look - to affect the quality of the day - that is the highest of arts.

-- Henry David Thoreau

* * * * *

Hold him a little longer,
Rock him a little more,
Tell him another story
(You've only told him four).
Let him sleep on your shoulder,
Rejoice in his happy smile,
He is only two-and-a-half
For such a little while!

-- Author Unknown

* * * * *

One morning my small son said to me at breakfast, "Daddy, may I read to you? I got nine out of ten for reading at school yesterday."

"Very good," said I, hardly glancing from my morning paper.

"May I?"

"Eh? May you want?" I demanded - being in haste and wishful to glance over the news and finish breakfast in next to no time.

"May I read to you?"

"Well, not now son! There's no time."

So off I went to catch a bus.

Home that evening, I told my little son that I would listen to his reading as soon as I had my supper. But somebody called, and I had to see him. And finally I went into my son's bedroom, and found him fast asleep, his cheeks wet with tears, a school reader open on his bed. Thus through this experience, I learned my lesson: to show my love for him a little more and for myself a little less.

-- Author Unknown

* * * * *

## Strengthening the Family

It has been stated that "salvation is a family affair...and that the family unit is the most important organization in time or in eternity."

The Church was created in large measure to help the family, and long after the Church has performed its mission, the celestial patriarchal order will still be functioning. This is why President Joseph F. Smith said: "To be a successful father or a successful mother is greater than to be a successful general or a successful statesman..." And President McKay added: "When one puts business or pleasure above his home, he, at that moment, starts on the downgrade to soul weakness."

The adversary knows "that the home is the first and most effective place for children to learn the lessons of life: truth, honor, virtue, self-control; the value of education, honest work, and the purpose and privilege of life. Nothing can take the place of home in rearing and teaching children, and no other success can compensate for failure in the home." (President David O. McKay)

Parents are directly responsible for the righteous rearing of their children, and this responsibility cannot be safely delegated to relatives, friends, neighbors, the school, the church, or the state.

-- Ezra Taft Benson

* * * * *

## A Family Is . . .

| | |
|---|---|
| A Family Is . . . | a deeply rooted tree with branches of different strengths all receiving nourishment from an infinite source. |
| A Family Is . . . | where character is formed, values are learned, ethics are created, and society is preserved. |
| A Family Is . . . | where all members contribute and share, cooperate and work, and accept their responsibilities toward the good of the group. |
| A Family Is . . . | where holidays are celebrated with feasting, birthdays acknowledged with gifts, and thoughts of days gone by kept alive with fond remembrances. |
| A Family Is . . . | where each can find solace and comfort in grief, pleasure and laughter in joy, and kindness and encouragement in daily living. |

A Family Is . . . a haven of rest, a sanctuary of peace, and most of all, a harbor of love.

-- Manny Feldman

* * * * *

Boy, We Really Have a Swell Bathroom, Haven't We?

He who believes knows that he belongs. But he also needs to feel himself an important and accepted part of a group. Young people want and deserve parents and a family they can be proud of. Their capacity to become worthwhile persons is strongly affected by the absence or presence of such a family, and by their own acceptance of the challenge to be a contributing responsible member of it. The influence of a good family is well-captured by this account from an unknown source:

"It was a gorgeous October day. My husband, Art, and I were down at the boat landing helping our friend, Don, drag his skiff up on the beach. Art remarked wistfully that it would be a long time before next summer, when we could all start sailing again. 'You folks ought to take up skiing like our family and have fun the year round,' Don said.

'Doesn't that get pretty expensive?' I asked.

Don straightened up and smiled. 'It's funny,' he said. 'We live in an old-fashioned house - legs on the tub, that sort of thing. For years we've been saving up to have the bathroom done over. But every winter we take the money out of the bank and go on a couple of family skiing trips. Our oldest boy is in the army now, and he often mentions in his letters what a great time we had on those trips. You know, I can't imagine his writing home, 'Boy, we really have a swell bathroom, haven't we?''"

* * * * *

To My Parents

Only a year ago I was six
sitting between you two on Sundays
wearing ruffled pinafores and golden finger curls
starting school by myself
I was grown up.

Not more than a few months ago I was nine
being in Campfire Girls with you, Mommy
hunting with you, Daddy
going to summer camp by myself.
I was grown up.

Barely a few weeks ago, I was thirteen
starting junior high school in orthodontic braces
being in plays, recitals, and programs
struggling to succeed by myself-I was a teenager.
I was grown up.

Yet but a few days ago I was sixteen
driving the car to high school
staying out late with friends and dates
experiencing the pains and pleasures of adolescence.
I was grown up.

Now I am eighteen
preparing to leave home and security
starting life on my own
wondering what lies ahead

Now as always you two are there - ready to help

I want to say thank you
And I will always come back
Because I love you, and
I am not grown up.

-- Kristin Koon

* * * * *

## Grandma

I know what makes a grandma grand --
She always has a treat,
A cookie or a piece of cake
An apple pie to eat.
And when we go to visit her
She gets the good things out,
And we don't have to ask for more
As long as she's about.

Then Mom will say,
"That's all today,
Don't give them any more,
You'll make them ill,
I know you will,
Tonight we'll walk the floor."

A Grandma never punishes
Or says that we are bad,
She always takes us on her knee
And tells us she is glad
To have us racing 'round the house.
And when we get too smart,
And Pop and Mom are awful cross,
She always takes our part.

Pa says it's funny grandma acts
The way she does today.
When he was grandma's little boy
He couldn't disobey,
Or only eat the things he liked
And get the stomach ache,
Or pick the chocolate frosting off
And never touch the cake.

When he was bad, he always had
The punishment to bear,
But we can be much worse than he
And Grandma doesn't care.

* * * * *

## What Shall We Give the Children?

In the long twilight of the year, the faces of the children grow luminous. Rosy with cold, arabesqued with snowflakes, leaning into the wind, or drowsing before the fire, their eyes large, they look and listen, as if they glimpsed the peripheries of miracle or heard a soundless music in the air. From the innocent kingdom of implicit belief to that uncomfortable arena where the implacable mind battles the intractable heart, the faces of children at Christmas are lighted with visions of things to come.

What shall we give the children?

It seems certain that they will travel roads we never thought of, navigate strange seas, cross unimagined boundaries, and glimpse horizons beyond our power to visualize. What can we give them to take along? For the whild shores of Beyond, no toy or bauble will do. It must be something more constructed of stouter fabric discovered among the cluttered aisles and tinseled bargain counters of experience, winnowed from what little we have learned. It must be devised out of responsibility and profound caring -- a homemade present of selfless love. Everything changes but the landscape of the heart.

What shall we give the children?

Attention, for one day it will be too late. A sense of value, the inalienable place of the individual in the scheme of things, with all that accrues to the individual -- self-reliance, courage, conviction, self-respect, and respect for others.

A sense of humor. Laughter leavens life.

The meaning of discipline. If we falter at discipline, life will do it for us.

The will to work. Satisfying work is the lasting joy.

The talent for sharing, for it is not so much what we give as what we share.

The love for justice. Justice is the bulwark against violence and oppression and the repository of human dignity.

The passion for truth, founded on precept and example. Truth is the beginning of every good thing.

The power of faith, engendered in mutual trust. Life without faith is a dismal dead-end street.

The beacon of hope, which lights all darkness.

The knowledge of being loved beyond demand or reciprocity, praise or blame, for those so loved are never lost.

What shall we give the children?

The open sky, the brown earth, the leafy tree, the golden sand, the blue water, the stars in their courses, and the awareness of these. Birdsong, butterflies, clouds, and rainbows. Sunlight, moonlight, firelight. A large hand reaching down for a small hand, impromptu praise, an unexpected kiss, a straight answer. The glisten of enthusiasm and a sense of wonder. Long days to be merry in and nights without fear. The memory of a good home.

* * * * *

## Twenty-one Memos From Your Child

1. Don't spoil me. I know quite well that I ought not to have all I ask for. I'm only testing you.

2. Don't be afraid to be firm with me. I prefer it; it makes me feel more secure.

3. Don't let me form bad habits. I have to rely on you to detect them in the early stages.

4. Don't make me feel smaller than I am. It only makes me behave stupidly "big."

5. Don't correct me in front of others if you can help it. I'll take much more notice if you talk quietly with me in private.

6. Don't make me feel that my mistakes are sins. It upsets my sense of values.

7. Don't protect me from consequences. I need to learn the painful way sometimes.

8. Don't be too upset when I say, "I hate you." It isn't you I hate but your power to thwart me.

9. Don't take too much notice of my small ailments. Sometimes they get me the attention I need.

10. Don't nag. If you do, I shall have to protect myself by appearing deaf.

11. Don't make rash promises. Remember that I feel badly let down when promises are broken.

12. Don't forget that I cannot explain myself as well as I should like. That is why I'm not always very accurate.

13. Don't tax my honesty too much. I am easily frightened into telling lies.

14. Don't be inconsistent. That completely confuses me and makes me lose faith in you.

15. Don't put me off when I ask questions. If you do, you will find that I stop asking and seek my information elsewhere.

16. Don't tell me my fears are silly. They are terribly real and you can do much to reassure me if you try to understand.

17. Don't ever think that you are perfect or infallible. It gives me too great a shock when I discover that you are neither.

18. Don't ever think that it is beneath your dignity to apologize to me. An honest apology makes me feel surprisingly warm toward you.

19. Don't forget how quickly I am growing up. It must be very difficult for you to keep pace with me, but please try.

20. Don't forget I love experimenting. I couldn't get on without it, so please put up with it.

21. Don't forget that I can't thrive without lots of understanding love, but I don't need to tell you, do I?

* * * * *

Dear Daughter:

I tiptoed in your room tonight and I looked down at you smilling in your sleep. You were so lovely my heart nearly broke; and I thought how very much like Sleeping Beauty a little girl is.

When I tuck you in at night, I never know how old you'll be when you wake. One evening you crawl on your dad's lap and throw your arms around his neck; the next morning you might be much too grown up for that sort of thing. You're so quickly approaching the awkward age: too young to drive the car and yet too old to be carried into the house half asleep on daddy's shoulder.

I have a secret I have never told you, Sleeping Beauty. You're going on a very exciting trip. You'll travel from yesterday all the way to tomorrow. It's a rapid journey and you'll travel light, leaving behind your measles, mumps, freckles, bumps, bubble gum, and me. I promise not to feel too hurt when you discover that the world is more important than your daddy's lap.

Yesterday you were blue-jeaned and pigtailed, the neighborhood's best tree climber. Tomorrow you'll be blue organdy and pony-tailed, and you'll view the world from a loftier perch -- a pair of high-heeled shoes. Yesterday you could mend a doll's broken leg with a hug; tomorrow you'll be able to break a young man's heart with a kiss. Yesterday you could get lost one aisle away from me in a supermarket; now I have to worry about losing you down another aisle to some strange young man.

You see, just at the point where your growing pains stop, mine begin. Yesterday you were kind of a pain in the neck when you were around; tomorrow you'll be an ache in my heart when you're not. Tomorrow you'll lay aside your jump rope and tie up the telephone lines. And that little boy that used to push you in the mud...well, he'll fight to sit out a dance with you.

The clock upstairs is counting the minutes for you, and the sky upstairs is saving its brightest stars, and the sun is waiting with its shiniest day. Oh, I, I can't expect you to live in a doll house forever. Sooner or later the butterfly sheds it cocoon and the smallest bird must try its wings. But when you grow up and out of my arms, when you finally get too big for my shirts, I'll still recall how you used to scatter dust and dolls impartially through every room in the house. But you spread sunshine too. The dust is settled, your mom picked up the dolls. But the sunshine will always fill the corners of our hearts.

So, here I am talking in your sleep. Because, well, if you saw this look on my face, you'd laugh; and if I spoke with this lump in my throat, I'd cry.

Yeah, honey, when I looked at you tonight you were a Sleeping Beauty. So I tiptoed over and I kissed you. You didn't wake up...I knew you wouldn't. According to the legend, only the handsome young prince can open your eyes, and I'm just the father of the future bride. So you sleep on, pretty thing. Tomorrow you'll wake and you'll be a young lady, and you won't even realize that you changed courses in the middle of a dream. But you might notice a little change in me. I'll look a little different somehow...a little sadder, a little wiser, but a whole lot richer.

Tonight I kissed a princess. And I feel like a king.

* * * * *

## A Moment Can Last Forever

Loading the car with the paraphernalia of our youngsters, ages three to nine, was hardly my idea of fun. But, precisely on schedule -- and at a very early hour -- I had performed that miracle. With our vacation stay on Lake Michigan now over, I hurried back into the cottage to find my wife, Evie, sweeping the last of the sand from the floor.

"It's six-thirty -- time to leave." I said. "Where are the kids?"

Evie put away the broom. "I let them run down to the beach for one last look."

I shook my head, annoyed by this encroachment on my carefully planned schedule. Why had we bothered to rise at dawn if we weren't to get rolling before the worst of the traffic hit? After all, the children had already spent two carefree weeks building sand castles and rambling for miles along the lakeside in search of magic rocks. And today they had only to relax in the car - sleep if they liked - while I alone fought the long road home.

I strode across the porch and out the screen door. There, down past the rolling dunes, I spotted my four youngsters on the beach. They had discarded their shoes and were tiptoeing into the water, laughing and leaping each time a wave broke over their legs, the point obviously being to see how far into the lake they could wade without drenching their clothes. It only riled me more to realize that all their dry garments were locked, heaven knew where, in the overstuffed car trunk.

With the firmness of a master sergeant, I cupped my hands to my mouth to order my children up to the car at once. But somehow the scolding words stopped short of my lips. The sun, still low in the morning sky, etched a gold silhouette around each of the four young figures at play. For them there was left only this tiny fragment of time for draining the last drop of joy from the sun and the water and the sky.

The longer I watched the more the scene before me assumed a magic aura, for it would never be duplicated again. What changes might we expect in our lives after the passing of another year, another ten years? The only reality was this moment, this glistening beach and these children -- my children -- with the sunlight trapped in their hair and the sound of their laughter mixing with the wind and the waves.

Why, I asked myself, had I been so intent on leaving at six-thirty that I had rushed from the cottage to scold them? Did I have constructive discipline in mind, or was I simply in the mood to nag because a long day's drive lay ahead? After all, there were no prizes to be won by leaving precisely on the dot. If we arrived at our motel an hour later than planned, no forty-piece band was going to be kept waiting. And how could I hope to maintain communication with my children, now and in later years, if I failed to keep my own youthful memory alive?

At the water's edge far below, my oldest daughter was motioning for me to join them. Then the others began waving, too, calling for Evie and me to share their fun. I hesitated for only a moment, then ran to the cottage to grab my wife's hand. Half running, half sliding down the dunes, we were soon at the beach kicking off our shoes. With gleeful bravado we waded far out past our youngsters, Evie holding up her skirt and I my trouser cuffs, until Evie's foot slipped and she plunged squealing into the water, purposely dragging me with her.

Today, years later, my heart still warms to recall our young children's laughter that day -- how full-bellied and gloriously companionable it was. And not infrequently, when they air their fondest memories those few long-ago moments -- all but denied them -- are among their most precious.

-- Graham Porter

* * * * *

<u>Promises to Peter</u>

This is for Peter Jay. He was born early this morning. (Preachers' sons should be born on Sunday morning.) Although he is less than twelve hours old, he is an unusual child. Dr. Arrandell said so. He has delivered some 3,000 babies and everyone of them was favored indeed to have him there. Such a wise doctor should know a bright child when he sees one. And, therefore, I would have a word with my new son.

This is a great life, Peter, and I'm glad you were born into it. We wanted you very much. For the past nine months we have been talking about you. Actually, we have been thinking of you for many years.

Your mother and I fell in love when we were very young. I remember the picnic when we sat in the park, talked about our babies, and named you. So you have been in our dreams for a long time. For five years after we were married there were no babies, and then Philip came. He did us so much good that the Lord looked down one day and said, "There is a couple in need of another baby." And here we are now, with three more because the first one did us so much good.

Philip, Karen, and Paul have taught me much. We've learned a lot together. Therefore, there are some thing I want to promise you.

<u>(1) First, I pledge that I will remember always that it takes a lot of love to make good children.</u>

You have the nicest grandpa. One day Dad Peterson and I were sitting in the living room and I asked him, "Dad, how did you ever produce a wonderful daughter like Martha?" He smiled and said, "Charlie, you can do anything you want with a child if you love him enough." He was right. As we work with people, we discover that security and stability come most to those people who have been most loved in their homes.

Of course, there will be some punishment. But what is punishment? It can be either for correction or revenge. I believe it is the nature of God -- both here and hereafter -- to punish only to make better. I promise you, Peter, that before I punish you, I will ask myself this question: "Am I punishing him for him -- or am I punishing him for me?"

The Chinese have a proverb which says, "He who strikes the first blow has run out of ideas." I feel like that, Peter. For me it is an admission of failure to administer physical punishment. It reveals that I don't think hard enough for better ideas. I don't mean that you will be over-indulged. It will be hard to draw the line, but whenever I don't know, I hope that I will always err on the side of love.

(2) Next, I promise you that I will never say "no" if I can possibly say "yes."

We see it often. Babies raised in a positive atmosphere develop much better personalities than those who perpetually hear the words, "no," "stop," and "don't."

Let me show you what I mean. This has to do with a dirty old bale of binder twine. When we moved from Nebraska to Oklahoma we brought it along. I had used it there to tie up sacks of feed and miscellaneous items. It cost something like $1.15. So I said, "Now Philip, you see this binder twine? I want you to leave it alone." But it held a strange fascination for him and he began to use it anyway when he wanted. I would say, "Don't," "no," and "You can't," but all in no avail.

That went on for six or eight months, and then one day I came home tired. There was the garage looking like a no-man's land with binder twine across and back and forth, and up and down. I had to cut my way through to get the car in. And was I provoked? I ground my teeth as I slashed at that binder twine. Suddenly, when I was halfway through the maze, a light dawned; I asked myself, "Why do you want this binder twine? What if Philip does use it?"

So when I went into supper that night, Philip was there and I began, "Philip, about that binder twine!" He hung his head and said, "Yes, Daddy?" Then I said, "Philip, I've changed my mind. You can use that old binder twine anytime you want. What's more, all those tools out in the garage that I have labeled "No", you go ahead and use them. I can buy new tools but I can't buy new boys." There never was a sunrise like that smile. "Thanks, Daddy," he cried. And there, guess what, Peter, Philip hasn't touched that binder twine since?

So there it is. I will say "Yes" everytime I can. A positive background for a little boy -- I hope I can give that to you.

(3) Here is my third promise: I pledge that I will really be with you when I am with you.

That may sound odd, but a little black-eyed lady in our church taught me a lesson. I was sympathizing with her one night because her husband was gone often. I said, "It must be hard to have him away from home." She smiled at me and said, "Oh, yes, but some men don't have to be home much." What she meant was that when he was home, he was <u>home.</u>

I sat with a young doctor recently. We were talking about this, and we decided that with people on schedules such as ours, it is important to be present when we are present. For instance, a little boy said to me not long ago, "The thing I don't like about our home is the newspaper." As we discussed it, he said that every night his daddy comes home, props the newspaper in front of him and says, "Now go away until I finish the news." Peter, there never has been anything in the news, there never will be anything in the news, but that you are more important than the news.

Time is a problem with daddys but you will be glad to know that we have one day a week at our house when to the church committees and to the people who call from distant places with, "Won't you give a speech at our banquet?" we say, "This is our night to lie on the floor and romp, to pop popcorn and play games." You know, I have never had anyone argue. They seem to understand.

Sometimes when I go away, you will go with me and we will stop at every other dime store and buy balloons, and eat hamburgers. We will talk about things you want to talk about like, "Why isn't a cow green when it eats so much grass?" "What's inside a nail?" or, "Is there really a man in the moon?" And sometimes if I come home and I am tired (too bad we leave our worst behavior for those we love the best), I hope you will remind me that I promised you -- one Sunday before you were twelve hours old -- that when I am home, I will really be home.

<u>(4) I pledge you now that I will try to see things from a child's point of view.</u>

I learned something the other day, Peter. I was fixing the high chair for you. I was down on the floor, and supper was on the table. You know something? The mashed potatoes on Paul's plate looked like a whole mountain of snow. Mother seemed to be a huge giant sitting there, and Karen was certainly large for seven years. For just a moment, I caught a glimpse of how things look to little eyes.

Yes, when you come in shouting, "There's a cowboy pistol down at Danner's that makes smoke and I've got to have it right now," I promise that I will try to see it from your angle and arrive at a sensible answer.

The other day I was in a restaurant and a little girl said, "Mommy can I have another helping?" Her mother said, "No." Then the little girl asked, "Why not, mommy?" And her mother answered, "Because I said so." Well, now, I hope we will be able to talk and find some reasonable answers. So, I will try to see your point of view and not make the mistake of expecting you to be an adult too quickly. And, just as important, I hope I will try not to keep you a baby when you want to be an adult.

(5) Comes now a small item, but very hard sometimes. I promise to be a good waiter.

We had a wonderful Negro lady who took care of Philip, Karen and Paul until she moved away recently. When she left it was like a familiar tree going down outside the window. It left a big hole. Sometimes when we would scold your big brothers or sister, she would say: "Ah, now, he's only a little boy. Just let him grow. All he needs is a great big dose of waitin' on de Lawd."

When your Cub Scout mother calls and says that Peter has been naughty the last two meetings, when your teacher phones to inform us that Peter is having trouble with his arithmetic, I hope I will be able to produce a "great big dose of waitin' on de Lawd." So many things work out in time.

(6) And here is the top promise. I will do everything I can to put your hand in God's hand that you may walk forever with Him.

I see many people with their problems -- and numberless folks are lost in the high weeds. Yet I have never seen one of them but that their problem centers in this: They have lost their hold on the Hand of God.

You see, Peter, you don't really belong to me. God put you here. What is a baby? Science says that a baby is 14% coal tar, 19% calcium, 8% phosphorus, 11% magnesium, and so on. That is a baby, but some day, son, you will be married and have a baby of your own. And when the woman you love holds that baby in her arms, you will know that anything as wonderful as a baby had to come from God.

I hope that I will be able to make religion natural to you. It is natural. In fact, this relationship with God is the only thing that is 100% natural. We will pray together until it is easy for you to put your arms on the window sill of heaven and look into the face of God.

Before I put you back in your crib, I want to tell you something Philip once said. We had been out in the country for a ride. It was evening and we ran out of gas. We were talking along after we had been to the farm house, and I was carrying a can of gas. Philip was only picking up flowers, and then all of a sudden it got dark. Sometimes night comes quickly in the country. Philip came over and put his little hand in mine and said, "Take my hand, Daddy; I might get lost."

Peter, there is a hand reaching to you from the heart of the Universe. If you will lay your hand in the hand of God and walk with Him, you will never, never get lost.

-- Charles Shedd

* * * * *

## FATHER

A father is a guy who has snapshots in his wallet where his money used to be.

* * * * *

"Fathers are people by whose name the family is known..."

-- Richard L. Evans

* * * * *

Unlike the bishop, who will someday be released from his responsibility, the husband, and later the father, is never released. His position is an eternal one, and it cannot and should not be delegated to another. I say "should not," because in some cases this great assignment is lost by default. This is contrary to the Lord's will, President Joseph F. Smith said on one occasion: "This patriarchal order has it's divine spirit and purpose, and those who disregard it under one pretext or another are out of harmony with the Spirit of God's laws as they are ordained for recognition in the home." It is not merely a question of who is perhaps the best qualified. Neither is it wholly a question of who is living the most worthy life. It is a question largely of law and order.

-- Reprinted by permission,
Improvement Era
June 1967

* * * * *

### Ten Commandments for Husbands

1. Remember that thy wife is thy partner, not thy property.

2. Do not expect thy wife to be wife and wage earner at the same time.

3. Think not that thy business is none of thy wife's business.

4. Thou shalt hold thy wife's love by the same means that thou won it.

5. Thou shalt make the building of thy home thy first business.

6. Thou shalt cooperate with thy wife in establishing family discipline.

7. Thou shalt enter into thy home with cheerfulness.

8. Thou shalt not let anyone criticize thy wife to thy face and get away with it, neither thy father, nor thy mother, nor thy brethren, nor thy sisters, nor any of thy relatives.

9. Thou shalt not take thy wife for granted.

10. Remember thy home and keep it holy.

-- Roy L. Smith

* * * * *

## A Dad's Greatest Job

I may never be as clever
as my neighbor down the street.
I may never be as wealthy
as some other men I meet.
I may never have the glory
that some other men have had.
But I've got to be successful
as a little fellow's Dad.
There are certain dreams I cherish
That I'd like to see come true.
There are things I would accomplish
ere my working time is through.
But the task my heart is set on
is to guide a little lad.
And make myself successful
as that little fellow's Dad.
It's the one job that I dream of
It's the task I think of most.
If I fail that growing youngster,
I'd have nothing else to boast.
I may never come to glory.
I may never gather gold;
Men may count me as a failure
When my business life is told.
But if he who follows after
shall be manly, I'll be glad--
For I'll know I've been successful
as a little fellow's Dad.
For though wealth and fame I'd gather,
all my future would be sad,
If I failed to be successful
as that little fellow's Dad.

* * * * *

## Blessings of Being a Father to a Boy

We have never seen the Father here,
But we have known the Son,
The finest type of manhood
Since the world began.

And summing up the works of God
I write with reverent pen,
The greatest is the Son he sent
To prove the lives of men.

The Lord did not come down himself
To prove a man His worth,
He sought our worship through the Child
He placed here on earth.

How can I best express my life
Wherein does greatness lie?
How can I long remembrance win,
Since I am born to die?

Both fame and gold are selfish things
Their worth may quickly flee,
But I am father of a boy
Who came to speak for me.

In him lies all I hope to be
His splendor shall be mine;
I shall have don man's greatest work
If only he is fine.

For some day he shall help the world
Long after I am dead.
In all that men may say of him
My praises shall be said.

It matters not what I should gain
Of fleeting gold and fame.
My hope of joy depends alone
On what my boy shall claim.

My story must be told through him,
For him I work and plan --
Man's greatest duty is to be
The father of a man.

* * * * *

## A Father's Gift To His Son

Traveling on a railroad train recently, a prosperous business man said to E. Mitchell Hodges, the well-known writer: "Would you like to know what I'm going to give my boy for Christmas?"

Hodges said, "Yes," and thought what a costly present that father could easily afford to give his boy. The gentleman pulled out his purse and took from it a piece of paper which had written:

> "To my dear son: I give you one hour of each weekday and two hours of my Sundays, to be yours, to be used as you want them, without interference of any kind whatsoever."

Hodges silently reflected; I wonder how that boy will feel and what he will think when on Christmas morning he reads that slip of paper. If he is just an average boy, he will be very much dissatisfied. If he is an unusual boy, he will realize that his father has given him a gift of the greatest magnitude, something he can never repay.

"Tell me," said Hodges, "how did you happen to hit upon the idea of giving such an extraordinary present?"

The gentleman said: "The other day a young fellow, whom I had not seen since he was a kid about my boy's age, came into my office to 'make a touch.' His face and bearing carried the tell-tale marks of idleness and dissipation. He was simply a human derelict. "Robert," I exclaimed in amazement, "to see you like this...and you, with such a fine father."

"Well, I've often heard that Dad was a fine man," the boy answered. "All his friends have told me so. I never knew him. He was so much occupied with his business and his clubs that I only saw him occasionally at meals. I never really knew him."

Said the man, "That made me, 'he think furiously,' as the French say, and believe me, from now on I'm going to see to it that my son has a chance to know me."

* * * * *

## Five Memories I Would Like To Have

In 1926, the _Era_ carried a memorable confession of a college senior concerning his desires for fatherly companionship. The desires of young men seem as timely today as they did then.)

I wish I could remember one Fourth of July, or one circus day, or one canyon trip, in which my father had joined the boys, instead of giving us the money and equipment to go, while he and mother stayed home, and made us feel guilty by working while we played.

I wish I could remember one evening when he had joined us in singing, or reading, or tussling, instead of always sitting so quietly with his newspaper by the reading lamp.

I wish I could remember one month, or week, or day even, when he had made purposeful work out of drudgery by planning the farm work with us, instead of merely announcing each morning what that day's work would be.

I wish I could remember one Sunday when he had bundled us all into the buggy and taken all to church together, instead of staying home while we went in the morning, and leaving us home while he and mother went in the afternoon.

I wish that I could remember just one talk in which we had discussed together the problems and facts that trouble every growing boy, on which his clear and vigorous viewpoint might have shed such light and comfort, instead of leaving me to pick up the facts haphazardly as I might, and to solve the problems as best I could.

And yet, my conscience would cry shame were I to blame him, for no man could ever be more devoted to his family, more anxious for their welfare, more proud of their successes. His example has been a beacon to us. He just didn't know - and there is the pity of it to me - he just didn't know that we needed him.

He didn't know that we would rather have his companionship than the land he could leave us - that someday, maybe, we might make money for ourselves, but that never can we make for ourselves the memories that might have enriched and mellowed and molded our lives. I can't see a fathers' and sons' outing without a lump in my throat. . .

-- Reprinted by permission
Improvement Era, March 1969

* * * * *

## This Was My Father

Dad was strong in his religion as he was in all his beliefs. He sang in the choir with a true but penetrating tenor voice, and someone once described the hymns as "solos by Mr. Stewart, with accompanying voices."

Strangely, Dad never sang very loudly at home. We lived in a rambling house with a large front porch loaded with wicker furniture. The living room, high ceilinged and trimmed with dark woodwork, held a grand piano, around which we gathered for family singing. My sister, Virginia, played the piano, my other sister, May, played the violin and I played the accordian - after a fashion.

During these occasions, Dad sang very softly, so as not to cover up Mother's clear, sweet voice. Her name was Elizabeth, and he called her Bessie and adored her. Though small and gentle and not given to contention, she frequently had her way over him because she possessed patience and endurance.

Doing things with my father was always fun, for his imagination added a dimension to events. When at ten, I announced that I was going to Africa to bring back wild animals, my mother and sisters pointed out my age, the problems of transportation and all such mundane and inconsequential facts.

But not Dad. He brought home books about Africa, train and boat schedules for us to study, and even some iron bars which we used to build cages for the animals I was going to bring back. When the departure day approached and I was becoming apprehensive, my father brought home a newspaper that told of a wreck on the railroad that was to take me to Baltimore. This postponed my trip and, by the time the train tracks were repaired, he and I were off on a new and more exciting project.

When President Harding died, the funeral train was scheduled to pass through a town about twenty miles from ours. I wanted desperately to go and see this train, but Mother pointed out that there would be school the next day and that it would be a long trip. That ended the discussion.

But Dad did not forget. When the day arrived, he came to me and, in a voice as near a whisper as his nature would allow, said, "Jim, boy, it's time to see the funeral train."

We drove along without talking much, bound together by the comradeship of our adventure. When we came to the railroad station, a half dozen people were talking in hushed tones and looking down the tracks. Suddenly the tracks gave a low hum - the funeral train was coming!

Dad shoved two pennies into my hand and said, "Run, put them on the rails. Quick!"

I did as directed and jumped back to hold his hand as the engine thundered past, pulling a glass-windowed observation car in which we saw the flag-draped casket, guarded by the two Marines, their glistening bayonets at attention. I could hardly breathe, so overwhelming were the sight and sound.

After the train had roared off, I retrieved the two flattened pennies from the track. Dad put one in his pocket and I kept the other.

As we drove home, I examined mine and found that the two feathers of the Indian headdress had become a great plume. On the other side two slender stalks of wheat had grown and burst, as if the seed had ripened and scattered.

For years, Dad and I carried those coins flattened by the weight of history. And the knowledge of what we shared made me feel very close to him.

With his temperament, it was amazing how patient Dad could be, how subtle his discipline. I don't recall a time when he stood across my path; he always walked beside, guiding me with his own steps. When a neighbor's dog killed my dog, Bounce, I vowed to kill that dog in revenge, I vowed it day after day in the most blood thirsty terms, almost making myself ill with my own hate.

"You are determined to kill the dog," my father stated abruptly one evening after dinner. "All right, let's get it done. Come on."

I followed him to the store, to discover that he had tied the dog in the alley. He got a deer rifle out of stock, loaded it, handed it to me, then stepped back for me to do my bloody work. The dog and I looked at each other. He wagged his tail in a tentative offer of friendship and his large brown eyes were innocent and trusting. Suddenly the gun was too heavy for me to hold and it dropped to the ground. The dog came up and licked my hand.

The three of us walked home together, the dog gamboling in front. No word was ever said about what had happened. None was needed.

During World War II, I enlisted in the Air Corps and became part of a bomber squadron. When we were ready to fly overseas, Dad came to the farewell ceremonies in Sioux City, Iowa. We were very self-conscious with each other, talking in generalities, trying to conceal our awareness that, starting tomorrow, he could no longer walk with me. At the time of the greatest crisis in my life, he would have to stand aside.

At the moment of parting, he studied his shoes a moment, then looked at the sky. I knew he was searching for a final word to sustain me, but he couldn't find it. He opened his mouth, then shut it hard, almost in anger. We embraced, then he turned and walked quickly away. Only after he had gone did I realize that he had put a small envelope in my pocket.

That night alone in my bunk, I opened it and read, "My dear Jim, soon after you read this letter, you will be on your way to the worst sort of danger. I have had this in mind for a long time and I am very concerned...But Jim, I am banking on the enclosed copy of the 91st Psalm. The thing that takes the place of fear and worry is the promise in these words. I am staking my faith in these words. I feel sure that God will lead you through this experience...I can say no more. I only continue to pray. God bless you and keep you. I love you more than I can tell you. Dad."

Never before had he said he loved me. I always knew he did, but he had never said it until now. I wept. In the envelope there was also a small booklet bearing the title THE SECRET PLACE - A Key to the 91st Psalm. I began to read it. From that day, the little booklet was always with me. Before every bombing raid over Europe, I read some of it, and with each reading the meaning deepened for me.

"I will say of the Lord, He is my refuge and my fortress...His truth shall be thy shield and buckler. Thou shalt not be afraid for the terror by night, nor for the arrow that flieth by day...For He shall give His angels charge over thee, to keep thee in all thy ways. They shall bear thee up in their hands, least thou dash thy foot against a stone."

And I was borne up.

Dad had committed me to God, but I felt the presence of both throughout the war.

When Mother died in 1956, we buried her in the family plot in Indiana, Pennsylvania. With his wife gone, Dad could work up no new enthusiasms. Her quiet strength had sustained him, and with her gone he quickly withered away. It was a bleak January day when I saw him placed beside his ancestors, men who had lived longer than he had but who were perhaps less demanding of life. Most of the town came to the funeral with respect and grief.

After it was all over, I went to the hardware store and let myself in with a key I hadn't touched for thirty years. The interior smelled of metal, leather, oil and fertilizer, the odors of my childhood.

I sat at his scarred oak desk and idly pulled open the middle drawer. I held a clutter of pencils and paper clips and bolts and pain samples. Something glinted dully among them. I picked up the funeral-train penny with the flattened Indian face and the burst grain.

For a long time I sat there at his desk, fingering the Indian head penny and thinking. Then I put it in my pocket, took a last look at familiar and loved objects, and walked out of the store, locking the door behind me.

-- Jim Stewart

* * * * *

# FREE AGENCY

Free agency - right to work toward the goals of our choice, necessitates acceptance of the consequences of choice.

The Lord doesn't want any person in His kingdom who hasn't known bad and chosen good.

* * * * *

The mind is its own place to make a hell of heaven or a heaven of hell.

* * * * *

It is my right to be uncommon.
For I do not choose
to be a common man. If I can,
I seek opportunity.
I do not wish to be a
kept citizen, humbled and
dulled by having the government
look after me.
I choose to take the
calculated risk, to dream,
to build, to fail or succeed.
I choose not to barter
incentive for a dole.
I prefer the challenges of life
to a guaranteed existence,
the thrill of fulfillment
to the state calm of Utopia.
I will not trade my freedom
for beneficence
nor my dignity for a handout.

* * * * *

Obesity is a condition which proves that the Lord does not help those who help themselves and help themselves and help themselves.

* * * * *

"God gave to man part of his dignity. He gave to man the power of choice, and no other creature in the world has it. So he placed upon the individual the obligation of conducting himself as an eternal being. You cannot have any greater gift that could come to man or woman than the freedom of choice. You alone are responsible, and by wielding and exercising that freedom of choice, you grow in character, you grow in intelligence, you approach divinity, and eventually you may achieve that high exaltation. This is a great obligation. Very few people appreciate it. The roads are clearly marked -- one offering animal existence, the other life abundant. Yet, God's greatest creation -- man -- often is content to grovel on the animal plane."

-- David O. McKay

* * * * *

## On This Day

Mend a quarrel.
Search out a forgotten friend.
Dismiss suspicion, and replace it with trust.
Write a love letter.
Share some treasure.
Give a soft answer.
Encourage youth.
Manifest your loyalty in a word or deed.
Keep a promise.
Find the time.
Forego a grudge.
Forgive an enemy.
Listen.
Apologize if you were wrong.
Try to understand.
Flout envy.
Examine your demands on others.
Think first of someone else.
Appreciate, be kind, be gentle.
Laugh a little more.
Deserve confidence.
Take up arms against malice.
Decry complacency.
Express your gratitude.
Worship your God.
Gladden the heart of a child.
Take pleasure in the beauty and wonder of the earth.

Speak your love.
Speak it again.
Speak it still again.

-- Author Unknown

* * * * *

# FRIENDSHIP

A true friend walks in when the rest of the world walks out.

* * * * *

What wealth it is to have such friends that we cannot think of them without elevation.

-- Henry David Thoreau

* * * * *

Every man should have a fair-sized cemetery in which to bury the faults of his friends.

-- Henry Ward Beecher

* * * * *

Oh, the comfort, the inexpressible comfort of feeling safe with a person -- of never having to weigh thoughts nor measure words, but pouring them all right out, chaff and grain together, certain that a faithful hand will take and sift them, keep what is worth keeping, and with a breath of kindness, blow the rest away.

* * * * *

True friendship comes when silence between two people is comfortable.

-- Dave Tyson Gentry

* * * * *

Of all the gifts that a wise providence grants us to make life full and happy, friendship is the most beautiful.

* * * * *

Better are the blows of a friend than the false kisses of an enemy.

-- Thomas Becket

* * * * *

Since it has been my lot to find,
At every parting of the road
The helping hand of comrade kind
To help me with my heavy load,
And since I have no gold to give
And love alone must make amends,
My humble prayer is, while I live -
God, make me worthy of my friends.

* * * * *

By friendship you mean the greatest love, the greatest usefulness, the most open communication, the noblest sufferings, the severest truth, the heartiest counsel, and the greatest union of minds of which brave men and women are capable.

-- Jeremy Taylor

* * * * *

Friendship improves happiness, and abates misery, by doubling our joy, and dividing our grief.

* * * * *

There are two ways to make friends: One is to do something for people; the other is to let people do something for you.

* * * * *

## My Unknown Friends

It was the last morning of the four-day conference. Someone among us had asked for our prayers. We sat around the room, heads bowed, and prayed for an "unknown friend."

Through the corner of my eye, I watched my neighbor, sitting with closed eyes and rapt face. Four days before, on first seeing her modest dress, her quiet face, I had winced, thinking, this one's a wet blanket.

Now I watched her with affection, for I had come to know her as a warm, delightful person. All around the room I could see others whom I had thought dull or antagonistic or shallow, until I came to know them. How well the phrase "unknown friend" described these people! I had thought I was meeting strangers, but I was really meeting friends, waiting to be known.

Twelve hours later, I stood in line to board a plane home. The young man in front of me stepped back and stumbled against my bag, knocking it over. He muttered something under his breath. A sharp retort sprang to my mind, for I didn't like his long-haired looks anyway. Then the thought came: maybe this is another "unknown friend."

-- Ruth Bruns

* * * * *

## A Friend

Of all the treasures one can find
Until his life has reached its end,
There really isn't anything
Of greater value than a friend.
A friend is all you'll ever need
When times of crisis are at hand
And you are looking all about
For someone who will understand.
And when a sadness fills your heart
And only darkness you can see,
It helps a lot to have a friend
Who at your side right then can be.
Or if you feel a loneliness
That simply will not go away,
It's wonderful to have a friend
To bring you smiles across the day.
I know it would be hard for me
Without a loyal friend or two;
Especially the kind of friend
That I have always found in you.

* * * * *

## The Hands of a Friend

In a small chapel at Northwestern University, there is a statue of two hands raised in prayer. A simple statue - yet it has a strange story.

It goes back to the year 1490. Two young apprentices in France had often confided to each other their desire to study painting. But each of the friends, Hans and Albrecht, were too poor, and such study would take money.

Finally, though, they had a solution. Let one work and earn money while the other studied. Then when the lucky one became rich and famous, let him in turn aid the other. They tossed a coin and Albrecht won.

So while Albrecht went to Venice, Hans worked as a blacksmith. As quickly as he received his wages, Hans would forward them to his friend.

The months stretched into years, and at last Albrecht returned to his native land, an independent master. Now it was his turn to help Hans.

The two met in joyous reunion, but when Albrecht looked at his friend, tears welled from his eyes. Only then did he discover the extent of Hans' sacrifice. Hans' fingers could never handle a painter's brush.

And so it was in humble gratitude that the great artist, Albrecht Burer, painted a portrait of the work-ridden hands that had labored so that he might develop his talent. He presented his painting to his devoted friend.

That is why, as a symbol of friendship and sacrifice, the masterpiece was reproduced in the chapel at Northwestern.

-- Author Unknown

* * * * *

## Love Fails Not

Darkness filled the corners of the dungeon under the castle. All about on the hard floor lay men who had been arrested by the ruler's soldiers. Most of them had been condemned to death. A hopeless silence filled the room so that the low words of the young man outside the barred door sounded loud and angry.

"What did you do, my good friend, Pythias?" the young man demanded. "What did you do that so displeased the king?"

The prisoner at the door sighed. His hand reached through the narrow bars and touched his friend's arm. Since early childhood these two had always been together. Now Pythias knew that he was going to leave his friend forever and his heart ached at the thought of this separation.

"I did nothing, Damon," he insisted, "but the King has claimed that I am a rebel. There is nothing that can be done about it."

"Then what can I do for you?" Damon asked. "Shall I go to your home and comfort your parents?"

Neither of the young men had heard the great outer door open. They did not see the ruler as he came near to them.

"I would like to see them myself once more," Pythias' voice was hopeless. "I would come back here and pay with my life if I could only say farewell to them."

A loud laugh startled the two young men. Damon whirled and found himself face to face with his king. Quickly he bowed and waited for the ruler to speak. Again, the king laughed as he looked at the prisoner.

"So you would come back to die if I would let you go to your distant home?" he mocked Pythias and all the prisoners.

"I would come back," Pythias stated simply. "I promise."

"How do I know that you would keep your promise?" the king's eyes narrowed as he watched the man. "You are trying to cheat me. You cannot go."

"Then let me stay in prison in his place," Damon looked straight at the king as he made his request. "He has never broken a promise, but if he does not return, I will die for him on the day that is set for his execution."

The king was amused. This strange request would make a delightful story to tell to his friends. A young man who offered to die for his friend! This was the best jest of the year and he and his courtiers would watch it with interest.

Soon the prison door closed behind Damon, then Pythias was on his way home. The days passed and the day of execution came nearer and nearer. Day by day the king came to the prison to taunt the foolish young man. Again and again his cruel laughter rang out.

"If Pythias does not come back, it will not be his fault," Damon stated calmly. "Something will have happened to him."

At last the day for the execution arrived and Pythias had not returned. The king and his courtiers jeered at Damon as he was led from the cell.

"The man who dies for his friend, a false friend," they called out. "We told you that he would not return."

"He will come if he can," Damon said to himself as he walked straight and tall in the line of condemned men. "He will come if -- "

"Here he comes! Here he comes!" a soldier ran shouting to the king.

Damon smiled as he saw his friend. Pythias was hardly able to breathe. Storms and misfortunes had beset him all of the way back. He had feared that Damon would die before he could arrive. His face beamed with happiness when he found his friend alive. Quickly he fell into the line of prisoners and pushed Damon aside.

"I came," he panted.

"I knew that you would!"

The king could hardly believe his eyes and ears. Never had he known that there could be such friendship. His heart softened before such a great love.

"Go!" he said to the two young men. "Go back to your homes."

Then he turned to his stunned courtiers and added, "I would give all my wealth to have one such friend!"

-- A Greek myth adapted by Jewel Varnado

* * * * *

# GOSSIP

George Washington said, when asked by an officer what his battle plans were for that day, (in a whisper) "Can you keep a secret?" The officer said that he could. Then replied Washington, "So can I."

* * * * *

The best rule of thumb for character is to remember that if you can't be big, don't belittle.

-- Dana Robbins

* * * * *

## To The Critical

It seems common practice for people to talk about their friends and neighbors to criticize their seeming peculiarities and weaknesses. In fact, it is general that one would think that gossiping about and judging others were the thing to do.

The reason we cannot judge is obvious. We cannot see what is in the heart. We do not know motives, although we impute motives to every action we see. They may be pure while we think they are improper.

How can we, with all our weaknesses and frailities, dare to arrogate ourselves to the position of a judge? At best man can judge only what he sees; he cannot judge the heart of the intention, or begin to judge the potential of his neighbor.

Let us remember that the further out of line we are, the more inclined we are to look for error or weaknesses in others and try to rationalize and justify our own faults rather than trying to improve ourselves.

Gossip is the worst form of judging. The tongue is the most dangerous, destructive and deadly weapon available to man.

Let us determine now that in the heart of the campaign we will not indulge in vituperative talk of personalities which we so often hear. We must not rail against our brother and accuse him of lying and cheating, or being dishonest or immoral. Let us stand on principle, high principle.

Only by suspending judgement and guarding our tongues do we exhibit real charity.

-- N. Eldon Tanner

* * * * *

## A Good Day

I am proud of myself today. I could have heard some gossip about a neighbor, but I didn't. I am proud of my friend, too. She was in possession of this spicy bit, but didn't tell me about it. It was hard on both of us, her knowing and my wanting to know.

We were talking, this friend and I, and our neighbor's name was mentioned. My friend looked at me a bit quizzically and asked me if I liked her. I said that I did, very much.

"Oh," she said, "I used to, but I don't know, now. I saw something the other day. . ."

I waited for her to go on, but she didn't. She was waiting for me to ask, but I didn't. So we both just stood there, and didn't say anything at all.

I was curious about what she had seen, and could scarcely keep from asking. I weighed in my mind whether anything she could tell me would discolor my feelings for this neighbor. I decided that I would like her just as much no matter what my friend said. But I knew that what I heard now would come into my mind when I saw her again.

I don't know what went on in my friend's mind, but she must have struggled hard, for she loved to talk.

And so we took our leave of each other.

Later that day I met my good neighbor, for whom I still felt the same affection because I hadn't listened to some gossip about her. I was happy that there was nothing unfavorable to her to pop into my mind.

Yes, I am proud of myself, and of my friend, too.

-- Margaret Hardy

* * * * *

Charles W. Penrose spent years of service in the British Mission. In one of the districts where he established a branch of the Church, he did a very charitable act. Because there was no furniture in the place where the meetings were being held, he brought a small table and some chairs of his own for the use of the people. Later, when the branch was a little more self-sustaining, he took the furniture home which he had loaned.

A gossip, seeing a wagon taking some of the furniture from the meeting house, started a whispering campaign -- "sh--Brother Penrose is taking church property to his own house, etc., etc." When Brother Penrose heard "what he had done" he was very angry at first. He soon cooled off and wrote the inspiring words, "School thy feelings, oh, my brother--train thy warm impulsive soul."

* * * * *

Then speak no ill, but lenient be
To other's failings as your own.
If your the first a fault to see,
Be not the first to make it known,
For life is but a passing day;
No lip may tell how brief its span;
Then, O the little time we stay,
Let's speak of all the best we can.

* * * * *

# GRATITUDE

## Beauty

Sometimes I cry.
No, not for sadness,
But because happiness fills my soul,
And through my tears,
I realize that
My cup runneth o'er.

* * * * *

Man owes his very existence to a six-inch layer of topsoil, and the fact that it rains.

-- Richard L. Evans

* * * * *

## Sometimes

Sometimes, not often enough,
We reflect upon the good things
And those thoughts always center
Around those we love.
And I think about those people--
Who mean so much to me--
and for so many years
Have made me so very happy.
And I count the times I have forgotten
To say
"thank-you"
And just how much I love them.

* * * * *

## Let Us Give Thanks

Let us give thanks for this
wonderful day,
For the gift of life and the hope
to pray;
The heavens fair and the earth
so sweet,
The friends so dear that we chance
to meet.

Let us give thanks for the sunshine
bright,
The light of dawn and the stars
at night;
The springtime rain and the summer
breeze,
The mountains, the streams, and the
spreading trees.

Let us give thanks for these
blessings rare,
For a family dear and the love
we share;
The little ones and the smiles
they bring,
Such a goodly portion of everything.

Let us give thanks in a humble way
With a peace in our hearts as we
kneel to pray;
Our eyes and our souls ever looking
above. . .
Let us give thanks to our God of love.

-- Garnett Ann Schultz

* * * * *

## Everyday Thanksgiving

Even though I clutch my blanket and growl when the
alarm rings each morning,
Thank you, Lord, that I can hear.
There are those who are deaf.

Even though I keep my eyes closed tightly against the
morning lights, as long as possible,
Thank you, Lord, that I can see.
There are many who are blind.

Even though I huddle in my bed and put off the physical
effort of rising,
Thank you, Lord, that I have the strength to rise.
There are many who are bedfast.

Even though the first hour of my day is hectic; when
socks are lost, toast is burned, and tempers are short,
Thank you, Lord, for my family.
There are many who are lonely.

Even though our breakfast table never looks like the pictures
in the magazines, and the menu is sometimes unbalanced,
Thank you, Lord, for the food we have.
There are many who are hungry.

Even though the routine of my job is often monotonous,
Thank you, Lord, for the opportunity to work.
There are many who have no work.

Even though I grumble and bemoan my fate from day to day,
and wish my modest circumstances were not quite so modest,
Thank you, Lord, for the gift of life.

-- Author Unknown

* * * * *

## Gratitude

A young woman approached her minister. "My mother-in-law is breaking up my marriage," she sobbed.

"Is that so?" the minister asked. "How?"

"She interferes in our affairs continually. In everything we do she must give us advice, or offer suggestions. She went with us when we picked out our first home and made suggestions on how to decorate it, what kind of furniture to buy, etc. Now that we have children, she is always telling us how to manage them, or what to do for them when they are ill, or how to feed them and take care of them. I've had about all I can stand."

"I see," replied the minister. Then added gently, "She has gone through too many of the trials and vicissitudes of life not to offer advice to others who are meeting the same problems." Then he asked, "Isn't there something you can admire about her?"

"Oh, yes," the young woman hastily assured him. "She is generous to a fault. She offered to let us come and live with her when we were first married, and she is always giving us gifts, some of which I am sure she cannot afford. She is always happy to stay with the children, too, whenever I ask her, and sometimes when they have been ill she has stayed by their bedside night and day."

"Well," replied the minister after a moment's thought, "I know you are a praying person, as I have heard you say so. Now I suggest that tonight as you kneel before God you thank him that he has given you a mother-in-law who is so generous with herself, her talents, and her time. Then tomorrow night perhaps you can find some other fine trait of character in her for which you can be thankful. Will you do that?"

Hesitantly, the young woman promised that she would.

Some months later the minister took occasion to talk to her again, and asked her if her problem had been solved.

"Yes, it has," the young woman admitted. "As soon as I began cultivating gratitude in my heart for my mother-in-law's good qualities, I found I could no longer dislike her. It became sort of a challenge to me to find all the good I could in her. I discovered she was really a fine person, interested mainly in our welfare. My husband is her only son, and she is probably lonely, and finds fulfillment in taking unique interest in our lives. I can forgive that now that I realize that that quality is overbalanced by so many fine traits of character."

-- Author Unknown

* * * * *

## The Nine

My name is Ruben Ben Zoro. From my dress you may suppose that I am one of the ancient Jewish people, but I am not. I am a man of old Samaria. I come from a wealthy Samaritan family. And as I grew to man's estate, the blessings were multiplied upon me a thousand fold when Ruth, the lovely daughter of the priest, became my wife. Two sons were granted us--two beautiful boys.

And then one day, it all came to an end. It was no great calamity, it was simply a small reddish spot upon the flesh of my hand. . .a spot that would not heal. I hid the spot and spoke of it to no one. But my fear I could not hide. At last because I could not sleep at night, I went to the temple on Mt. Gerizim and showed it there to my father-in-law, the priest.

He greeted me kindly, and with rejoicing, as an old man does to the father of his grandchildren. Then I showed him my hand and the small reddish spot, and a great and overwhelming sorrow came upon him. He hid his face from me.

"I shall go to Ruth," he said, "I shall tell her that unexpected business has detained you and will keep you away from home a fortnight. By then. . .my son, . . .by then we shall know."

Fourteen days I spent there, in a lonely little room. . .fourteen days of mourning, of wild weeping and of desperate praying that God would spare me this dread thing. . .But he did not, and before the fortnight had passed I knew, and so, too, did my father-in-law.

"Will you see Ruth again?" asked my father-in-law, his voice shaking.

"No," I said, "I shall take the path here through the vineyard, and down to the olive orchard, and none shall know of my passing."

I did not notice the flutter of a blue scarf from behind the thick trunk of one of our oldest olive trees, until it was too late, for Ruth, weary of my long absence, had come with the children into the sunshine of the orchard. We shrank back, my father-in-law and I, but my son was too quick. His bright eyes caught the movement and he turned and saw us there. With a joyous shout, "Father, Father" he came running straight for my arms. My father-in-law. . .oh, may he be blessed, . . .stepped between us, caught the lad up in his arms and carried him away, bewildered now, and struggling. And Ruth, her face lovely with joy and surprise of my coming, gathered the little one in her arms and rose to come to me. Then, seeing my face, she hesitated, and my heart died within me as I drew the corner of my robe across my face and cried, in a voice harsh and rough with pain, "Unclean! Unclean!" And the love in her eyes changed to a dawning horror and a great fear as she stood clutching the child tightly to her breast. Then she turned and ran, stumbling along the path among the olive trees. The sound of her great sobbing came to me upon the breeze, . . .and I was left alone--Unclean!

I will not weary you with the telling of my suffering of the next few months. You all know the laws of our time concerning the leper. . .how we were forbidden to enter any town or approach any person save those afflicted as we ourselves were. There were none to care for our needs; our clothing became ragged and dirty; and we ate what was thrown to us in the streets.

I wandered alone those first months, I could not endure the sight of my fellow sufferers. Then the knowledge that in a short time, a few years, I too would be as they. . .blind perhaps, bony, crippled, wretched. . .misery without hope. No, it was unbelievable. Surely God would lift His curse and restore me to health and my loved ones as the Prophet Elisha of long ago had healed the leprous Syrian. But I knew there was no Elisha in Samaria nor in Israel either, and had not been for hundreds of years.

Then, one day, I joined a small group. There were nine of them, and when they first passed me in the field, I watched them in astonishment. They were hurrying! A leper has no need for haste.

I would have let them pass me by. . .I still had no desire for their wretched company. . .had it not been for the last among them. He was old and crippled and leaned upon a staff, and as he tried to run with the others, his staff broke beneath his weight and he fell almost at my feet crying to the others that they should wait. But they did not. In compassion for his trouble, I sprang forward and lifted the old man to his feet.

"May you be rewarded," he sobbed. "Help me. . .quickly. . .we must reach the highway! He is there, and we must see Him before He passes!"

So we hurried over the hill to the highway. There was a great crowd upon the highway, and here, standing apart from the rest were the eight who had hurried so and their voices were lifted in an agonized cry, "Jesus, Master, have mercy on us! Jesus, Master, have mercy on us!"

Just as we reached them the Man on the highway lifted His hand and as the voices about Him quieted, He called to us, "Go show yourselves unto the priests." Then He turned from us and the multitude closed about Him once again.

We stood and looked upon one another. "To the priests?" said one. "What have I to show the priest save my blinded eye and my leprous skin?"

But the old man who had leaned on me said simply, "I go." And as we went, he leaned no more, but his back straightened, his limbs carried him swiftly and surely, and he went on alone. So, too, the others. They began to run and leap and shout, laughing with each other over the lifting of their curse, and hurrying off to the priests and their loved ones.

And I? I, too, felt the miracle of newborn health within me. A great gratitude for this, my undeserved blessing, welled up within me. For I had not looked for this cleansing. Of Jesus of Nazareth, I had known little and believed less. . . but I must know more of Him. Truly God, this Man must be, and I must worship Him and thank Him and love Him.

So I hurried back to the highway. I pushed my way through the crowd, no longer was I unclean. When I reached Jesus, I fell on my face at His feet, and poured out my thanks and my devotion before Him.

Jesus looked about Him and said, "Were there not ten cleansed? But where are the nine?" "There are none found that returned to give glory to God, save this stranger." Then gently He lifted me to my feet. He laid His hand upon me in blessing and said, "Arise, go thy way: thy faith hath made thee whole."

So, because He bade me, I went my way, and was declared clean by the priests of Mt. Gerizim. I did not go to Ruth, nor have I yet seen my growing boys, because my task must be accomplished first.

"Were there not ten cleansed?" Jesus asked. "Should not all give glory to God? But where are the nine?" I must find them!

So I have come to you, this day. Help me. Are there among you some who have received His blessings and have not bowed down in Thankfulness? Are. . .there. . . nine, perhaps? Could. . .one of them. . .be you?

-- Dorthy Charlemagne

* * * * *

# HAPPINESS

Whatever hour God has blessed you with, take it with grateful hand, nor postpone your joys from year to year, so that, in whatever place you have been, you may say that you have lived happily.

-- Horace

* * * * *

Happiness is much like a butterfly. The more you chase it, the more it may elude you. But if you go about other things, it will come and sit on your shoulder.

* * * * *

There'll always be something in life for the person who can take his lunch outside -- and call it a picnic!

* * * * *

## Gospel Brings Happiness

"If you were arrested and charged with being a Christian, would there be enough evidence available to convict you?" asked Elder Marion D. Hanks, Assistant to the Council of the Twelve.

"The Answer," he said, "will determine how happy you are."

"Happiness is the object and the real purpose of our existence," Elder Hanks said.

He pointed out that happiness is not a product of circumstances or of conditions and that it does not come with the indulgence of appetites.

"Happiness comes with good conduct, sweet relationships with those dear to us, understanding and sensitive relationships with all men, and a measure of confidence in the presence of God."

* * * * *

## Beauty And The Day's Work

There was once a young man who took an unusual view of work. He was given a job in a stone quarry, facing with chisel and hammer the rough blocks that were to form the foundation for a temple.

"You must face ten of these blocks each day," said the foreman, "but you need not be too careful about how they look, since they are to be buried in the earth."

When the young man had finished the first day's work, he stood for a while and looked down on what he had done. The stones were roughly square, to be sure, but every one was ugly and uneven. The youth, loving beauty, seized his hammer and chisel and went to work again, smoothing the rough places and running a straight line along each edge.

Every morning and evening the youth spent an extra hour or two adding form to blocks that he well knew were to be buried deep in the earth.

Now it happened that the chief architect came one day to the quarry. His trained eye noted the beauty in the pile of foundation stones, and he said to the youth, "I suppose you know that these stones will never be seen again by the eyes of men?"

The youth hung his head, for he thought the great man was angry with him. At last he raised his eyes and said, "The extra work has cost my master nothing. I have done it on my own time and for my own pleasure."

The next day the architect came again and sat where he could look down into the quarry without being seen. An hour before the other men arrived, the youth came and the ring of his hammer sounded fresh and clear in the crisp dawn. The architect smiled. "Here is a labor of love in the cause of beauty," he said to himself. "The boy is of a noble nature. This day shall he drop his chisel and come with me as an apprentice in the sacred task of temple building."

Years later, when the youth of the stone quarry was fashioning a great amphitheater in a far-distant city, a young man came to him and said, "Sir, what must I do to succeed? I am about ready to begin my life's work."

The boy of the stone quarry smiled. "There is no recipe for success," he said, "but I can open for you the door to happiness. Add beauty to your day's work, whatever that may happen to be!"

* * * * *

## The Singing House

I tied the napkin around Fred's neck and placed before him his glass of orange juice, his cereal, his big glass of foamy milk. In my opinion I classified myself among the superior mothers whose children are brought up in the approved manner of an enlightened day.

Fred ate it all dutifully and then slipped down from his chair.

"Now can I go over to Jim's Mother?" he asked.

"But Fred," I remonstrated, "You were over there yesterday and the day before. Why not have Jimmy come here today?"

"Oh, he wouldn't want to." Fred's lip quivered in spite of his six years of manhood. "Please, Mother."
"Why do you like Jimmy's house better than ours, Son?" I pursued. It came to me suddenly that Fred and all his companions were always wanting to go to Jimmy's house."

"Why," he explained hesitatingly, "It's cause, it's cause Jimmy's house is a singing house."
"A singing house?" I questioned. "Now what do you mean by that?"

"Well," Fred was finding it hard to explain. "Jim's mother hums when she sews; and Annie-in-the-kitchen, she sings when she cuts out cookies; and Jimmy's daddy always whistles when he comes home." Fred stopped a moment and added. "Their curtains are rolled clear up and there's flowers in the windows. All the boys like Jimmy's house, Mother."
"You may go, Son," I said quickly. I wanted him out of the way so I could think.

I looked around my house. Everyone told us how lovely it was. There were oriental rugs. We were paying for them in installments. That was why Fred's daddy didn't whistle when he came into the house.
I put on my hat and went over to Jimmy's house, even if it was ten o'clock and Saturday morning. It came to me that Mrs. Burton would not mind being interrupted in the middle of the morning. She never seemed to be in a hurry. She met me at the door with a towel around her head.

"Oh, come in. I have just finished the living room. No indeed, you are not interrupting. I'll just take off this head-dress and be right in."

While I waited, I looked around. The rugs were almost threadbare; the curtains, dotted Swiss, ruffled and tied back; the furniture, old and scarred but freshened with new cretonnes. A table with a bright cover held a number of late magazines. In the window were hanging baskets of ivy and wandering Jew, while a bird warbled from his cage hanging in the sun. Homey, that was the effect.

The kitchen door was open and I saw Jerry, the baby, sitting on the clean linoleum, watching Annie as she pinched together edges of an apple pie. She was singing; singing "Springtime in the Rockies."

Mrs. Burton came in smiling, "Well," she asked, "What is it? For I know you came for something; you are such a busy woman."

"Yes," I said abruptly. "I came to see what a singing house is like."

Mrs. Burton looked puzzled. "Why, what do you mean?"

"Fred says he loves to come here because you have a singing house. I begin to see what he means."

"What a wonderful compliment!" Mrs. Burton's face flushed. "But of course, my house doesn't compare with yours. Everyone says you have the loveliest house in town."

"But it isn't a singing home," I objected. "It's just a house without a soul. Tell me how you came to have a singing home."

"Well," smiled Mrs. Burton, "if you really want to know. You see, John doesn't make much. I don't think he ever will. He isn't that type. We have to cut somewhere, and we decided on nonessentials. I am not a very strong person and when Jerry came, we decided Anne was an essential if the children were to have a cheerful mother. Then there are books, magazines, and music. These are things the children can keep inside. They can't be touched by fire or reverse so we decided they were essentials. Of course, good wholesome food and clothing are other essentials; but we don't buy things out of season, and our bills are not large. The children's clothes are very simple and I make them myself. But when all these things are paid for, there doesn't seem to be much left for rugs and furniture. But we find we get as much joy from our long country walks, as we would in a car, especially if we had to worry about financing it. We don't go in debt if we can avoid it. Moreover we are happy," she concluded.

"I see," I said thoughtfully. I looked over at Jerry and Fred in the corner. They had manufactured a train out of match boxes and were loading it with wheat. They were scattering it a good deal, but wheat is clean and wholesome.

I went home. My Oriental rugs looked faded. I snapped my curtains to the top of the windows, but the light was subdued as it came through the silken draperies. The overstuffed couch looked bulky and not nearly so inviting as Mrs. Burton's old day-bed with pillows you were not afraid to use. My home didn't sing. I determined to create a singing house.

-- May Morgan Potter

* * * * *

## Why Christmas Is Nice

Once upon a time in the days before anything much was organized and when people were all pretty much alike and had not learned to be Doctors and Bookmakers and Husbands or Milkmen there were never any holidays because everyone was too busy.

What they were busy doing was --taking stuff.

They spent all of their time either taking stuff, or trying to take stuff, or planning to take stuff from each other, or fixing the walls and fences and bobwire in their section of the jungle so no one could take stuff from them.

In those days it was considered most necessary to have a lot of stuff and taking it gave people a stimulating feeling. When they took something especially good (I. E. big) the feeling started in the back of their backs and spread down across their back and made a tingle in their left foot. This feeling was the only feeling anyone ever had except maybe being scared or being hungry.

Several techniques were used, first: swiping. This was the most difficult because naturally few people were foolish enough to leave any of their stuff unguarded.

The second, and most popular method was to find someone smaller than you, give him an unexpected bash. Then you could grab his stuff and run. This method, although dangerous, had the advantage of being healthful, as the bashing and running promoted deep breathing and kept the waistline down.

Now, in time, the smaller people learned to be very clever, hiding and swiping, and the larger developed a protective layer of bone across the back of their skulls, and some of the medium sized discovered that they could tell big lies about the amount of stuff they had hidden and this was about the same as actually having the stuff.

And so a status quo came to exist. It balanced out pretty well for everyone, that is, except Marvin Ouk.

Marvin Ouk lived in a rather provincial section of the jungle, and his only neighbors were named Gloog, Howk, Murdleigh and Lester.

Now Gloog, Howk, Murdleigh and Lester had each accumulated exactly the same amount of stuff. They were all of about the same size, and they had equally excellent walls, and so it became difficult for them to increase their stuff. One day Murdleigh would bash Gloog and take his shirt and eggbeater, but the next day Howk would bash Murdleigh and take his shirt and a fountain pen, and so on.

They were all getting bashed a great deal and in the long run there was no percentage in it. So after a while they all concentrated mostly on taking stuff from Marvin, which wasn't easy.

Marvin was the smallest, the most simple-minded and the least devious of all the people. He didn't even have a proper wall or fence and as a result he had no stuff. In fact, Marvin never had anything. He didn't even have a pair of pants (which slowed him down socially). He lived on a diet of toadstool (these being the only thing he could depend on not being taken) and the only feeling he ever experienced was not getting hit, which he considered enjoyable.

So it wasn't long before Gloog and Howk and Murdleigh and Lester even gave up trying to take stuff from Marvin. It wasn't worth the trouble it took to bash him because although he bashed easily, Marvin was concussion prone and merely fell quietly face forward and didn't yell or holler or do anything fun.

And so in this part of the jungle the status quoed more than suitable. Actually the status became over-quoed and Gloog and Howk and Murdleigh and Lester sat being their walls and got restless.

"It is not right to not take stuff," Murdleigh said, "One should get more stuff. It is the way things are." He would then go out and try to sneak up on Gloog or catch Howk or swipe something from Lester. But he never would.

Then he would go back home and fret some more. "I will forget how to take stuff," he would tell himself. "I will lose my technique." And one day he added, "I must keep in practice or my know-how will desert me."

So he rushed out and found Marvin Ouk and in his mind he pretended that Marvin was carrying a double armful of stuff. He then gave Marvin an excellent bash and pretended to take the imaginary stuff away from him, but it didn't work. He didn't get any feeling or tingle at all.

He went back home and fretted some more. "It was not playing the game to pretend," he told himself, and he began to think. After a bit he had an idea. "Umm," he said, "If I'm going to practice on Marvin, I must play the game. He must have something to take, so I will go out and. . .he paused and made up a word to express the odd idea he had in mind. "Give," he said, "I will give Marvin something first. Then I can take it."

When Marvin saw him he sighed and looked about for a soft spot to fall forward on. He was, of course, surprised, even shocked, when Murdleigh stopped in front of him and made no bashing gestures. "Ouk," said Murdleigh, making a peculiar and frightening grimace (which men later learned to call a "smile"), "Ouk, I have some stuff here I want to give you." He pushed a spoon toward Marvin. Marvin backed away. "Murdleigh has sprung a gasket," he thought. "I shall carefully go away as he may become dangerous."

But Murdleigh anticipated Marvin's escape and seized him by the arm. "Here," he said, and placed the spoon in Marvin's hand, "I want you to have this."

Then he stepped back and prepared to give Marvin a bash and take the stuff in the approved manner, but before he could move, he felt a strange new feeling! A feeling ten times more powerful than the feeling he had when he took stuff. If started in the back of his chest and spread, not only through his back and his left foot, but all over. He began to tingle in both feet and both hands and on top of his head. The new feeling was so pleasant and so powerful that Murdleigh caught his breath and sat down on the ground.

"Ha," he said and again made the terrible grimace in Marvin's direction. Marvin turned and raced away.

"Who would have suspected?" said Murdleigh. Giving stuff is. . ." He searched for a noise he could use, another new word. "Ooser?" he said, and then "Meepy?" Then he tried "Misser" and then "Nice r."

Nicer sounded exactly right. "Giving stuff," Murdleigh said, "Is nicer than taking stuff."

Murdleigh soon found out that part of the new feeling was a desire to tell other people about it and he did; and so another great discovery was made.

The secret of the new feeling has been passed down from century to century to now, and although sometimes we don't see too much evidence of it, people seem to remember it very clearly at Christmas time, and instead of taking and bashing, they give. And it feels very nice.

* * * * *

# HONESTY

To the members of the Church everywhere I say, live honest, sincere lives! Be honest with yourselves, honest with your brethren, honest with your families, honest with those with whom you deal -- always honest. The very foundation of all character rests upon the principles of honesty and sincerity.

-- David O. McKay

* * * * *

To believe in something, and not to live it, is dishonest.

-- Mahatma Ghandi

* * * * *

There are ninety-nine men who believe in honesty for every honest man.

-- N. Eldon Tanner

* * * * *

Every man takes care that his neighbor shall not cheat him. But a day comes when he begins to care that he does not cheat his neighbor. Then all goes well. He has changed his market cart into a chariot of the sun.

-- Ralph Waldo Emerson

* * * * *

## He Is My Son

"Steve," I asked, "where are you going?"

He scowled, "To see Betty," he said, "I'll be back soon."

Betty was his girlfriend. She lived a few blocks away, near the park. A nice girl. Good parents.

Steve is my son - tall, with a broad back and thick, dark hair. When I held him in my arms, proud of our only son, I told my wife: "He is a gift to the world." And his mother shared my pride with her soft, lovely smile.

For seventeen years he is our son - and a mystery. We do not know him - strong and headstrong, and maybe a gifted artist. He works at it in spurts of fury. He will draw a laughing bunch of boys and girls, trees in bloom, kids playing in the snow. Gentle things like that. He has promise.

"Come home early," his mother said. "Tomorrow is a school day."
He said, "I'll be back soon, Mom. You worry too much."
"Before ten-thirty," I called.
"Okay," he said and left. It was nine-thirty.
"I don't like those friends he has," she said.

We had tried to talk to him about his new friends, but we were in two different worlds. The boys a few blocks away were tough. Steve seemed to want to prove that he was just as tough, that he could hold his own. We tried to talk to him about those friends, about living with purpose. It didn't help.

How do the walls get so high between a parent and a child? Steve used to share the music we loved. We would all go to the park and to the concerts together to hear it. Two years ago he got his own record player, money he saved from a summer job helping commercial artists. He liked his own kind of music and laughed at ours.

He used to share our faith. A year ago he stopped going to church with us. Maybe we didn't know how to make it a real live thing for him. Every Sunday we asked: "Coming with us, Steve?" And he would shake his head.
"You have to be at least thankful."
"Sure, Pop, I'm very thankful."
And then he began lying. . .first little lies, then bigger ones.
"Steve you can't lie and live with yourself," I said. "You can't lie no matter how the truth hurts. It's against God and it's against man. Lying is stealing with your mind."

"You're making a big thing out of nothing," he said. "If you don't lie now you will one day."

"Never," I told him. "No matter how it hurts. I couldn't live with myself."

My own wife and I don't know him. What could I do or say to show him the meaning of God and truth? How many parents are there like us?

We went on worrying and hoping and praying.

At ten-thirty my wife said, "I won't phone Betty's house. He'll think I'm treating him like a baby."

"You lean over backwards not to treat him like a baby," I said.
I went to find him.

Betty was standing in front of her house. "Where's Steve?" I asked.
"He went to the park with the other boys a few minutes ago," she said.
"He told me he'd be back soon to say good night. He'd better hurry.
My mother called me twice already."

"I'll find him," I said.

I took the first entrance into the park. Why would they go into the park. It was almost eleven. I hurried, searching the darkness for a movement, a sound.

A few seconds later, a man's voice suddenly shattered the silence: "Help!" Help!" I rushed toward the noise. Just beyond the glare of the street light four figures were bent over a fifth figure on the ground. Racing footsteps were coming down the walk. A flashlight swept the darkness. A cop's shrill whistle blew. The four figures leaped up and ran in my direction. As they rushed into the lamp light I saw their faces clearly and my blood froze. . . One of them was Steve.

Someone came sprinting from behind me. A second policeman moved toward us holding the other two boys. They forced all four to a bench. With guns drawn they made them sit down. One policeman stood behind the bench, the other in front.

I was standing at one end of the bench. Steve sat at the other.
We did not look at each other.
The man on the ground hobbled over to us, cursing.
"They mugged me!" he yelled. "One of them has my watch!"
The policeman in front of the bench quickly searched all the boys.
He found the watch in one boy's pocket. He found a switch blade in another boy's pocket.
The man who had been mugged looked at them one by one, in a blind cursing rage.
He stared at me.
"Who's this guy?" he asked.
The second policeman pointed to the spot under the light where I had been standing.
"He was there."

They asked me questions - my name, address, what I did for a living, and finally the question that drained the blood from my heart.
"Did you see them?"
I tried to speak. No words came out. My mouth was dry with the taste of ashes.
I was trembling. I shut my eyes to shut out the ugliness before me. I couldn't.
I was there. I had seen it all.

To myself I said, "No officer, I live just a few blocks away. I was just taking a walk. I heard a man yell "Help!" But I saw nothing. Nothing."

"Steve, you can't lie and live with yourself. . .It's against God and against man. . .Lying is stealing with your mind. . .You can't."

"Did you see them?" the first policeman asked again.

"Look mister," the second policeman said, "This is important. You let a few punks away with this and they laugh at the law and go on mugging, and worse. Tomorrow it might be your wife, or even your kid."

My wife! What would I say to her? Where were the words for that? My mind was an agony. My words came out hoarse.

"I saw them."

The policeman behind the bench pointed his ungunned hand at the first boy, "Was this the one?"

I nodded. He pointed to the second boy, then the third. I nodded. He reached the end of the bench. I looked away.

"Was this one, too?"

I couldn't turn my head toward Steve. I nodded.

"You're not looking at him," the second policeman said. "Look at him, look at him good."

"Steve, you can't lie and live with. . ."

My heart was weeping. I was numb with pain.

"Come on over here!" the second policeman ordered Steve. He waved him in front of me with the gun. The policeman behind the bench flashed the light full in Steve's face. I looked up slowly. Steve's eyes were filled with dread.

"Steve," I said, "Steve."

"Steve!" the policeman said, "You know him!"

"He's my son."

They were the most painful words I would ever mutter. Both policemen stared. The mugged man's mouth dropped open in disbelief. Steve glared at me, hate and tears filling his eyes.

"Steve," I said, "one day you'll know you can't lie. . .Steve!"

He turned his back on me. . .

Steve and the other three boys have now served two years of a three year sentence. Here is part of a letter Steve sent his father from jail:

"Dear Dad, I thought about what you did for the thousandth time and hated you for it. But what I see here in prison made a lot of that hatred go. All of the guys here are full of hate and I don't want to hate. . .

"I know now that life has to have truth. Without it, it's no life here or hereafter. . .

"You asked me to forgive you for saying those words that terrible night in the park, 'He is my son.' You wrote me that those words were not your last words, that the last words would have to come from me, from what I make of myself. I ask you and mother to forgive me. I pray God that He will, too, so the final words will be good words, and you can say, not with pain and shame, but with pride and love, 'He is my son."

* * * * *

An error which has to be corrected is a heavier burden than the truth.

-- Dag Hammarskjold

* * * * *

If you tell the truth you don't have to remember anything.

-- Mark Twain

* * * * *

# HUMAN RELATIONS

God does notice us, and He watches over us. But it is usually through another person that he meets our needs.

-- Spencer W. Kimball

* * * * *

The art of acceptance is the art of making someone who has done you a small favor wish that he might have done you a greater one.

-- Russell Lynes

* * * * *

The mass of men worry themselves into nameless graves, while here and there a great unselfish soul forgets himself into immortality.

-- Ralph Waldo Emerson

* * * * *

Quarrel not at all. No man resolved to make the most of himself can spare time for personal contention. Better give your path to a dog than be bitten by him.

-- Abraham Lincoln

* * * * *

Get someone else to blow your horn and the sound will carry twice as far.

-- Will Rogers

* * * * *

"If you treat a man as he is, he will remain as he is, but if you treat him as if he were what he ought to be, and could be, he will become what he ought to be, and should be."

-- Goethe

* * * * *

Challenge:

1. Resolve to write a note at least once a week to someone about an accomplishment.

2. Give a compliment to at least one individual a day, in person or on the telephone.

* * * * *

Every now and then you run across radiantly attractive people and you're delighted to find they adore you, till you realize that they adore just about everybody--and that's what's made them radiantly attractive.

-- Mignon McLaughlin

* * * * *

The most important part of leadership is to pick good men to lead, and have self-restraint enough not to meddle in what they are doing.

-- Theodore Roosevelt

* * * * *

"Don't be down on that you're not up on"

-- Harold B. Lee

* * * * *

He who accepts the help of a child is helping a child to grow.

* * * * *

. . .one cannot deny the humanity of another without diminishing his own.

* * * * *

"Harmony is the ability to differ, not to disagree."

-- Mrs. Nixon

* * * * *

Folks And Me

It is a funny thing, but true,
That folks you don't like, don't like you.

I don't know why this should be so,
But just the same I always know
If I am "sour," friends are few;
If I am friendly, folks are too.
Sometimes I get up in the morn
A-wishin' I was never born.
I make of cross remarks a few,
And then my family wishes too
That I had gone some other place
Instead of showin' them my face.
But let me change my little tune
And sing and smile, then pretty soon
The folks around me sing and smile
I guess 'twas catchin all the while.
Yes, 'tis funny, but it's true,
That folks you like will sure like you.

* * * * *

Lincoln was once taken to task by an associate for his attitude toward his enemies. "Why do you try to make friends of them? You should try to destroy them," advised the friend. . . "Am I not destroying my enemies," Lincoln gently replied, "when I make them my friends?"

* * * * *

Forgetting

If you were busy being kind,
Before you knew it you would find
You'd soon forget to think 'twas true
That someone was unkind to you.

If you were busy being glad
And cheering people who seem sad,
Although your heart might ache a bit,
You'd soon forget to notice it.

If you were busy being good,
And doing just the best you could,
You'd not have time to blame some man
Who's doing just the best he can.

If you were busy being true,
To what you know you ought to do,
You'd be so busy you'd forget
The blunders of the folks you've met.

If you were busy being right,
You'd find yourself too busy quite
To criticize your brother long,
Because he's busy being wrong.

* * * * *

## My Prayer

LORD, THOU KNOWEST BETTER than I know myself that I am growing older and will some day be old. Keep me from the fatal habit of thinking I must say something on every subject and on every occasion. Release me from craving to straighten out everybody's affairs. Make me thoughtful but not moody, helpful but not bossy. With my vast store of wisdom it seems a pity not to use it all, but Thou knowest, Lord, that I want a few friends at the end.

KEEP MY MIND free from the recital of endless details; give me wings to get to the point. Seal my lips on my aches and pains. They are increasing and love of rehearsing them is becoming sweeter as the years go by. I dare not ask for grace enough to enjoy the tales of others' pains but help me to endure them with patience.

I DARE NOT ASK for improved memory but for a growing humility and a lessening cocksureness when my memory seems to clash with the memories of others. Teach me the glorious lesson that occasionally I may be mistaken.

KEEP ME REASONABLY SWEET; I do not want to be a saint -- some of them are so hard to live with -- but a sour old person is one of the crowning works of the devil. Give me the ability to see good things in unexpected places and talents in unexpected people. And give me, Lord, the grace to tell them so. AMEN.

-- Anonymous

* * * * *

## Ten Commandments Of Discipline

1. Thou shalt use no emotion which you do not wish to see reflected in the child. An angry mother makes an angry child. Don't punish while you are emotionally upset.

2. Thou shalt encourage, not repress the natural curiosity of the child. Guide him in unfamiliar situations.

3. Thou shalt condemn the deed, not the child.

4. Thou shalt consider the child's reasoning, his motive and his experience before you condemn.

5. Thou shalt punish swiftly so that the error and the punishment are linked in the child's mind. (Don't punish without proof.)

6. Thou shalt make the punishment relate to the crime and be sure that the child understands the connection. (Don't magnify small annoyances.)

7. Thou shalt avoid cruel and unusual punishments and never embarrass the child before others. (Don't punish the whole family for one.)

8. Thou shalt not be a nagging parent. (Don't threat or make challenges.)

9. Thou shalt provide direct activity for the child that his curiosity about the world may be answered and the temptation to waste activity be avoided.

10. Thou shalt, above all, be sensitive to the child's successes and praise the child for his accomplishments. (Praising is the most effective; blaming can satisfy hunger for attention but should be avoided; ignoring causes lifelessness.)

* * * * *

## Thoughts

A few months after moving to a small town a woman complained to a neighbor about the poor service at the local drug store. She hoped the new acquaintance would repeat her complaint to the owner.

Next time she went to the drug store, the druggist greeted her with a big smile, told her how happy he was to see her again. He said he hoped she liked their town and to please let him know if there was anything he could do to help her and her husband get settled. He then filled her order promptly and efficiently.

Later the woman reported the miraculous change to her friend. "I suppose you told the druggist how poor I thought the service was?" she asked.

"Well, no," the woman said. "In fact -- and I hope you don't mind -- I told him you were amazed at the way he had built up this small town drug store, and that you thought it was one of the best run drug stores you'd ever seen."

* * * * *

## The Excuse We Should Never Use

Pause a moment. Look back on your life.
Haven't you been greatly helped by someone? By a parent whose concern and

continuing care shaped your character, by a teacher who was enough of a friend to show you how to continue when you were already to give up, by an employer whose awareness of your talents opened the way for your success, by a neighbor whose respect for you and your family made you feel at home where you live -- perhaps even by a stranger whose unexpected help came just when you needed it?

When you remember such people who made a difference in your life, isn't it clear that you also can make a great difference wherever <u>your</u> life touches someone else -- within your family, where you live, wherever you go? Why do we so frequently feel: "What I do doesn't really make a difference?"

We fall into a familiar error, using the wrong yardstick with which to measure goodness. We think that good actions are really important only in times of crises, only when an extraordinary demand calls for extra ordinary effort. Yet the time of crises is but a small part of the opportunity given each of us to contribute to other people's lives.

We need only remember how much and how often and in how many different ways our individual act of understanding, or encouragement, or guidance, of personal concern can enlarge the life of someone else, even as enduring good was done for us. And we need only remember there is no such thing as a <u>small</u> good act!

Surely we can take the initiative in extending to anyone we meet, anywhere, the friendship we would like from him. We can respect and be enriched by his differences, as he can be by ours. This is but to recognize that he also is made in the image of God, and that the brotherhood of man is everywhere becoming the neighborhood of men.

In our changing world, there are fundamental realities which do not change. That is why we can never use the excuse: "But what I do doesn't really matter."

-- Bernard Mandelbaum
Victor M. Ratner

* * * * *

'Tis the human touch in this world that counts,
The touch of your hand and mine,
Which means far more to the fainting heart
Than shelter and bread and wine;
For shelter is gone when the night is o'er
And bread lasts only a day,
But the touch of the hand and the sound of the voice
Sing on in the soul alway.

-- Spencer M. Free



* * * * *

We're here to make people feel like a million dollars, not two cents.

* * * * *

Bobby had been playing by the duck pond for several minutes when father called for him to come in the house. Bobby approached his father slowly, looking down at muddy feet and wet pant legs. When Bobby's father saw the mud and the wet, he said in a stern voice, "Well, Bobby, how many times must you be told to stay out of the mud and water? Go get me a willow, maybe a willowing will help you remember." Bobby was gone for several minutes before he slowly approached his father again -- this time with his hands behind his back. His father's voice was again stern as he said, "Well, I'm waiting, give me the willow." Bobby drew both hands around and produced not a willow but several rocks in each hand. Then he said in a meek little voice, "I couldn't find a willow, but here are some rocks you can throw at me."

-- Jean Larsen

* * * * *

A week after my son started first grade he came home with the news that Roger, the only Negro in the class, was his playground partner. I swallowed and said, "That's nice. How long before someone else gets him for a partner?" "Oh, I've got him for good," replied Bill. In another week I had the news that Bill had asked if Roger could be his desk partner.

Unless you were born and reared in one of the white-supremacy states as I was, you cannot know what this means. I went for an appointment with the teacher. She met me with tired, cynical eyes. "Well, I suppose you want a new desk partner for your child, too," she said. "Can you wait a few minutes? I have another mother coming in right now."

I looked up to see a woman my age. My heart raced as I realized she must be Roger's mother. She had a quiet dignity and much poise. But neither could cover the anxiety I heard in her questions. "How's Roger doing? I hope he is keeping up with the other children. If he isn't just let me know." She hesitated as she made herself ask, "Is he giving you any trouble of any kind? I mean. . .what with his having to change desks so much?"

I could feel the terrible tension in her, for she knew the answer. But I was proud of that first-grade teacher for her gentle answer; "No, Roger is not giving me any trouble. I try to move all the children around the first few weeks until each has just the right partner."

I introduced myself and said that my son was to be Roger's new partner and I hoped they would like each other. Even then I knew it was only a surface wish, not a deep-felt one. But it helped her. I could see that.

Twice Roger invited Bill to come home with him, but I found excuses. Then came the heartache I will always suffer. On my birthday Bill came home from school with a grimy piece of paper folded into a very small square. Unfolding it, I found three flowers and "HAPPY BIRTHDAY" crayoned on the paper and a nickel. "That's from Roger," said Bill. "It's his milk money. When I said today was your birthday he made me bring it to you. He said you are his friend, 'cause you're the only mother that didn't make him get another desk partner."

* * * * *

## Too Busy To Listen

Dear Folks,

Thank you for everything, but I am going to Chicago and try and start some kind of life. A new life for me.

You asked me why I did those things and why I gave you so much trouble, and the answer is easy for me to give you, but I am wondering if you will understand.

Remember when I was about six or seven and I used to want you to just listen to me? I remember all the nice things you gave me for Christmas and my birthday and I was really happy with the things at the time I got them, but the rest of the time during the year I really didn't want presents, I just wanted all the time for you to listen to me like I was somebody who felt things too, because I remember even when I was young I felt things. But you said you were busy.

Mom, you are a wonderful cook, and you had everything so clean and you were tired so much from doing all those things that made you busy; but you know something, Mom, I would have liked crackers and peanut butter just as well if you had only sat down with me a while during the day and said to me: "Tell me all about it so I can maybe help you understand."

And when Donna came I couldn't understand why everyone made so much fuss because I didn't think it was my fault that her hair is curly and her skin is so white, and she doesn't have to wear glasses with such thick lenses. Her grades were better too, weren't they?

If Donna ever has children, I hope you will tell her to just pay some attention to the one who doesn't smile very much because that one will really be crying inside. And when she's about to bake six dozen cookies, to make sure first, that the kids don't want to tell her about a dream or a hope or something, because thoughts are important too, to small kids even though they don't have so many words to use when they tell about what they have inside them.

I think that all the kids that are doing so many things that grown-ups are tearing out their hair worrying about, are really looking for somebody that will have time to listen a few minutes and who really and truly will treat them as they would a grown-up who might be useful to them you know---polite to them. If you folks had ever said to me: "Pardon me" when you interrupted me, I'd have dropped dead.

If anybody asks you where I am, tell them I've gone looking for somebody who has time because I've got a lot of things I want to talk about.

Love to all,

Your Son

-- A boy with a record as
a juvenile delinquent

* * * * *

## Direction By Love

You can't force your boys nor your girls into heaven. You may drive them to hell by using harsh means in the efforts to make them good when you yourselves are not as good as you should be. The man that will be angry at his boy and try to correct him while he is in anger is in the greatest fault; he is more to be pitied and more to be condemned than the child who has done wrong. You can only correct your children by love, in kindness, by love unfeigned, by persuasion, and reason.

When I was a child, somewhat a wayward, disobedient little boy -- not that I was wilfully disobedient, but I would forget what I ought to do -- I would go off with playful boys and be absent when I should have been at home, and I would forget to do things I was asked to do. Then I would go home, feel guilty, know that I was guilty, that I had neglected my duty and that I deserved punishment.

On one occasion I had done something that was not just right and my mother said to me, "Now, Joseph, if you do that again, I shall have to whip you." Well, time went on, and by and by I forgot it, and I did something similar again; and this is the one thing that I admired more, perhaps, than any secondary thing in her; it was that when she made a promise she kept it. She never made a promise, that I know of, that she did not keep.

Well, I was called to account. She said: "Now, I told you. You knew that if you did this I would have to whip you, for I said I would. I must do it. I do not want to do it. It hurts me worse than it does you, but I must whip you.

Well, she had a little rawhide, already there, and while she was talking or reasoning with me, showing me how much I deserved it and how painful it was to her to inflict the punishment I deserved, I had only one thought, and that was, "For goodness' sake whip me; do not reason with me," for I felt the lash of her just criticism and admonition a thousandfold worse than I did the switch. I felt as if, when she laid the lash on me, I had at least partly paid my debt and had answered for my wrong doing. Her reasoning cut me down into the quick; it made me feel sorry to the very core!

I could have endured a hundred lashes with the rawhide better than I could endure a ten-minute talk in which I felt and was made to feel that the punishment inflicted upon me was painful to her that I loved -- punishment upon my own mother!

-- Joseph F. Smith

* * * * *

## Hyacinths To Feed The Soul

When I was a student nurse, I baby-sat during off-duty hours to help pay my way. One day I got a call to sit for a whole weekend. All I knew when I headed for the job was that the couple wanted to "get away" from their two kids for a few days. Expecting that only rich people would be able to do that, I was surprised when the address turned out to be a tiny house.

Ted, the husband, had just joined an architectural firm. His wife, Ardeth, looked terribly tired. They waited, obviously anxious to be off, while I got acquainted with the children, two years and ten months old. I held the baby against my shoulder while Ted gave me the name of their hotel. "You'll be there the whole time?" I asked.

"That's headquarters," Ted answered. "We'll sleep late, prowl around town, eat when we get hungry, visit the art galleries. . ."

Mentally, I added up the cost of all that, plus my fee -- ten dollars. "But won't that be terribly expensive?" I blurted. I had adopted them already.

"Why, yes, I guess it will," Ted said. "But it's important. We're both tired and snapping at each other. Ardeth, especially, needs to get away."

Ardeth smiled at me. "Don't you know about hyacinths to feed the soul?" She took a volume from the bookcase and opened it to a poem called "Gullistan," by Muslih-uddin Sadi, a sheik who lived more than 700 years ago:

If of thy mortal goods thou art bereft,
And from thy slender store two loaves alone to thee are left,
Sell one, and with the dole buy hyacinths to feed the soul.

That poem taught me a good deal. Those two didn't have enough money for the trip, but they were tuned in on a set of values I'd never even thought of. Sunday night, when they came back, they looked like teen agers who'd just discovered love. And my ten dollars was tucked under the ribbon on a pot holding lavender hyacinth.

Over the years since, I've made a hobby of noticing people and whether or not they know about using nonessentials and extravagances occasionally to feed the soul. The happiest people do.

A no-nonsense mother I know lets Christmas and family birthdays release her usual tight lid on frivolity. "When I was a child," she explains, "gifts were always sturdy shoes, warm gloves, underwear. After I got married, I decided that we'd somehow manage the essentials, that the special occasions would be for fun. Now my husband and I give each other and the kids wild things we'd never dare include in the budget." Her idea of zingy gifts: tickets to a far-out play, a white-velvet coat she has worn twice and had cleaned twice but which makes her feel positively elegant; for the children, redeemable coupons for gooey treats at the ice-cream store.

Flowers given on birthdays or other predictable occasions are hardly hyacinths. But when bouquets are offered to celebrate Monday, or "the anniversary of the day we got the car paid off," or simply as "thank you for putting up with me so long" -- what a different matter! When our stomachs are empty, we get hungry. Symptoms of soul starvation are subtler. Tomorrows and tomorrows are rolling by. Paychecks are being spent on bread and shoes and rent, while the walls of the souls are often bare. If this matters to us, we can do something: we can buy hyacinths.

-- Carol Amen

* * * * *

# HUMOR

Job wasn't really tested -- he never had to contend with a stuck zipper.

* * * * *

Sign on a temporary sheetrock wall during construction of library addition at BYU, spring, 1976: If the Dress Code is against cut-offs, does that make it anti-Nehi-Levi?

* * * * *

If we could kick the person that is responsible for most of our troubles, we wouldn't be able to sit down for six months.

* * * * *

Adam and Eve had many advantages, but the principal one was that they escaped teething.

-- Mark Twain

* * * * *

## Answering Service

One father of a dozen children admits to a little difficulty keeping track of them. Take the night when the telephone rang after the family was asleep. Father answered the phone and heard a request for John. He called upstairs and heard a growing hubbub as young voices relayed the request from room. Father got a little impatient. "I don't want a riot. Just tell John to come down and answer the phone!" he shouted.

Finally a tiny voice penetrated the noise: "John is married. He doesn't live here anymore."

* * * * *

The story is told of a fourth grade school teacher who was supervising her class during an afternoon water painting session. She wandered around the classroom observing a variety of scenes on each student's easel and made appropriate comments and suggestions. But she stopped in curiosity as she saw what little Suzie was painting. On her paper Suzie had illustrated a lush landscape with tall trees, flowering bushes, and expanses of manicured lawns. This was clearly the most artistic and imaginative painting of any in the class. But the teacher asked Suzie to explain the long black limousine with a chauffer and two passengers which dominated the center of the picture. "Oh," explained Suzie simply, "this is God driving Adam and Eve out of the Garden of Eden."

-- told by Brent Hunter

* * * * *

## Discipline

I often wonder why parents worry so much. Bringing up children is perfectly simple, providing you don't have a nervous system. If you are the high-strung, sensitive type, but find it impractical to switch from parenthood to a less nerve—racking job, you need some rules of behavior. Take these ideas my husband and I worked out for our offspring. To make our rules work, you merely have to get good at the art of "strategic retreat." Here are the rules we use, with our successive lines of defense.

### On Neatness

1. Children are to put away their own things.
2. Children must help Mother put away their things.
3. Well, after Mother has put away their things, they are not to complain that she messed everything up.

### On Eating Between Meals

1. Children are never to eat between meals.
2. Only fruit or milk between meals.
3. When they eat candy between meals, they must brush their teeth.

### On Mealtime

1. Children must clean their plate.
2. No dessert for those who don't.
3. Absolutely no SECOND dessert!

### On Bedtime

1. Eight o'clock sharp.
2. Not one minute past 8:30 p.m.
3. Children who fall asleep while staying up late will not be carried to bed.
4. Unless they won't wake up.

### On Playing in the Living Room

1. Children must not play with glue or paint in the living room.
2. When playing with glue or paint in the living room, they must spread newspaper to catch spills.

3. Must say "I'm sorry" when they don't spread a paper, and spill glue or paint on the living room rug.

## On Evening Guests

1. Children must not get out of bed when guests arrive.
2. May get up only to say "Hello."
3. Must say, "Goodbye," nicely as guests leave.

## On Watching TV

1. Children shall not watch scary TV programs.
2. After watching scary programs, they cannot come in to sleep with parents.
3. Children who must sleep with parents after a scary program cannot bring the dog to bed with them.
4. Oh well. . .

That's our plan and it works. We're almost sure to be obeyed somewhere along the line. If you are worn down to a skeleton after trying this plan, don't blame us. Your children may be different!

* * * * *

## The Childless Couple

There's nothing sadder than a childless couple. It breaks your heart to see them all stretched out relaxing around swimming pools in Florida, trotting off to Europe like lonesome fools, it's an empty life. Everyone should have children. The happy memory of those baby days, the coughing spells, debts, diaper deliveries and never ending crisis. But eventually comes the real fulfillment as the child grows like a little acorn and becomes -- a real nut!

The wonder of watching your overweight ballerina make a fool of herself in a leotard. The warm smile of the small lad with the sun glittering on five-hundred bucks worth of braces ruined by peanut brittle. Ah, but children are worth it. Think back to the night of romantic adventure when your budding, beautiful daughter eloped with the village idiot. Remember your wife as she tried to fling herself out of the bedroom window? It takes a father's stature to stand by, ready and resolute, to jump after her.

The childless couple fills its lonely days with vacation trips, tranquillity, and leisure. You just have to look at them to see what the years have done----He is boyish, unlined and rested. She is slim, well-groomed and youthful. It isn't natural. If they had kids they'd look like the rest of them, tired, gray, wrinkled and sagging. In other words, like parents!

* * * * *

# JUDGING

Even the Lord does not propose to judge a man until the end of his days.

-- Kenneth L. Higbee

* * * * *

When the one great Scorer comes
to write beside your name,
He marks not that you won or lost,
but how you played the game.

* * * * *

## Count Down

The huge room is hushed and every eye is focused on the clock, every heart beating a little faster, realizing that the event is now at hand. Suddenly I wish I could retrace my steps and change several events in my life. . . not big changes but the little parts of living that make life take on its full meaning. Ten seconds. . .Nine seconds. . .

Like the time I was too quick to judge and I punished my son without getting the whole story. Seven seconds. . .Six. . .

Or like the day I came in from work and broke my daughter's heart by commenting in a teasing way about a blob of something on a plate in the middle of the dinner table. That blob was my daughter's first cake for her dad. Never before or since have I eaten a cake so terrible and yet so wonderful. five. . . Four seconds. . .

Just last week my youngest daughter came home from a party with a broken favor and I scolded her for her carelessness. The wonderful truth was explained to us a little later by way of a phone call. It seems that my daughter first had an unbroken toy but swapped gladly with a tearful owner of the broken one because "my daddy can fix anything." Three seconds. . .

My wife is here next to me. Just as she has always been. . .So many times I could have avoided an argument by realizing that in all the utter confusion of running the most important business in our lives, our home, she has three jobs. . .not one but three. . .one job is 11-years-old, one nine and one three. One second. . .

Now it happens. . .It's midnight. . .Happy New Year. . .We twirl our noise makers and blow our horns and shout with all the meaning we can muster. . .

Happy New Year! Through the miracle of time we are granted a new year to live again. . .a new lease on time to prepare for still another count down. Please, God, be with us in the days to come so that the days will count.

-- Stephen A. Joyner

* * * * *

## The Identification Of Jock Anderson

I am thinking in terms, at the moment, of an experience I had when returning from the First World War. I always hesitate to tell these experiences of the First World War because they definitely date me as approaching middle life. I was there in 1915 to 1918 and saw many things and experienced some things, but I'm thinking of a certain man who was known to us in the regiment as the "unsentimental cuss." He was a man apparently without any feeling, a man who was not touched by the things that affect most of us at times, a man who could stand by his comrades and see them shot down and never bat an eye. He was the kind of fellow that most of us as we noted his actions and his attitudes, heard his coarse language, and saw him in debauchery at times -- most of us became for the moment like the Pharisees of old and said in our hearts, though we didn't have the courage to say it out loud, "I thank thee, God, that I'm not like that." I felt that way. And I was as Pharisee.

We got over to France finally. And there it became the duty of the officers to read the incoming and outgoing mail. A very interesting assignment, incidentally. You learn a lot of things that way. This man was on duty reading the mail. He was a captain. He read a letter from a woman in Ontario, Canada, Mrs. Jock Anderson. She had written to her husband. It was impressed on my memory because of what happened subsequently. She said among other things, "My darling, Jock. I'm so happy to have you where you are. We're all so proud of what you're doing. The ten little bairns are coming along all right. I had to wean the baby because I have to work to help with the separation allowance the government gives us. But we're all right, Jock, and if God should see fit to take your life, we'll carry on. But, oh Jock, darling, won't you plead with God with me that he will never allow us to receive word that you are missing?" She said, "Poor Mrs. Johnson next door received that word two months ago, and she's almost frantic. She'd much rather have heard he was dead. Pray God with me Jock, that I may never get word you are missing."

That was the letter this "unsentimental cuss" read. And that night there appeared before him a sergeant and six men. They were to go out into no-man's land on a very dangerous mission. The sergeant read the roll, and the men responded to their names, and one of them was Jock Anderson. They went out, and in the early morning three of them came back with the sergeant. And again he called the roll. And they answered. But Jock Anderson was not among them. This unsentimental man -- of who I said I thank God that I'm not like him -- said, "Sergeant, do you know where Jock Anderson fell?"

"Yes, sir. He was on an elevated piece of land covered by a German machine gun."

"Would it be possible, Sergeant, for a man to go out and get his identification disc?"
You remember that each soldier had a disc around his neck, and there was a definite rule that unless you could produce his identification disc or his body, you could not report him dead no matter how many men saw him fall. And so the captain said, "Could you get his disc from where he is?"

The sergeant said, "No sir, it would be absolute suicide, but if you say so, I'll try."

The captain said, "No, I didn't mean that. I just wanted to know."

And that night the captain was missing. No one knew where he had gone. And the next morning there came a large envelope, a military envelope, and upon opening it we read, "Dear Major, I am enclosing herewith the identification disc of Jock Anderson. Will you please send word to Mrs. Anderson that God heard her prayer? Her husband is not missing. He's dead." And me, I'm off to Blighty in the morning. The doctor says it's an amputation case and may prove fatal. Cheerio."

And that was the man who had the intestinal fortitude to crawl out at night alone up to a dead man's body and get a disc from his neck in order that his wife could have the poor satisfaction of learning that her husband was not missing. Many times since then I have felt to say in my heart, "Help me, oh God, never to judge another man. However he may appear, there is something in him better than I.

* * * * *

## Crystal

Crystal entered our nineth grade math class, twenty minutes late as usual. There she stood in front of my desk, her blank blue eyes fringed with twiggy lashes, scanning the room for a place to sit. She was forced to scramble in the desk in front of me. It took her a full five minutes to get settled, but finally she reached up with pink polished finger nails and picked up a pencil from behind her ear, a signal that she was ready to begin. She used this pencil for scratching her bleached straw-like hair or tapping her glossed white lips or putting underneath her nose like a Hitler moustache, anything but for figuring out fractions, decimals, or story problems.

I always noticed her clothes because for me this was the high light of my day. Today she wore a black wool dress, sleeveless and with a plunging neck line, and short. I couldn't decide if it or her nylons were too short. It never failed, whenever she sat down the top of her nylons would peek out from under her skirt at me and the five guys who always managed to be sitting around Crystal.

I'd tried to talk to her but she would just bat her false eyelashes and smile. Once I asked her to explain a fraction problem to me but she acted so stupid and couldn't have cared less if I missed the problem or not.

She was definitely a snob. I'd sit and stare at all those tangled rats of bleached hair and think of how messed up Crystal was and how tangled up her morals probably were. Anyone who looked so cheap all the time certainly wouldn't have any morals. I couldn't imagine her doing any of the things my friends did.

My friends and I spent one afternoon a week candy striping at the Sacred Heart Hospital. This was our pet accomplishment and I was glad to do it, even though at times there were shows I wanted to see and parties I really wanted to go to.

One Friday morning the hospital called me and said that they needed a girl to work at 12:00 that noon. Usually I ate at 12:00 because that was just before my math class but I decided I'd go so that I'd have Saturday free.

I worked hard Friday and finally my hour was through. I knew I'd really have to run to make my math class even though the school was just a block away. I was rushing past the pediatric ward when I noticed a familiar scent among the pungent hospital odors. It was that darned perfume, "Allure", that Crystal always wore. I couldn't imagine anyone else wearing that stuff so I peaked in the little hospital room.

The blinds were pulled tightly shut and my eyes wouldn't focus for awhile. The first thing I saw when my eyes adjusted to the light was Crystal's tangled blond hair. She had her back to me and she was talking -- no -- reading to a tiny boy with large dark circles under his eyes laying in the far too big, starched hospital bed.

As Crystal finished "The Three Little Pigs," the little boy smiled and said in a voice that lacked the exhuberance and freshness usually found in someone so young, "I wish you'd stay with me forever, Crys, you're my very best friend."

"I'd love to stay longer, Joey, but I'll be terribly late for math and you wouldn't want that, would you? Now, you rest and I'll be back tomorrow."

Joey pulled at Crystal's sleeve as she got up to go. "Hey, Crys, I think you're the prettiest lady in the whole world."

Crystal blushed and then gently kissed Joey on the cheek. I quickly scrambled down the hall not wanting Crystal to see me. So that was why she was always late for math. Did she spend every noon hour with that little sick boy? How could she stand to be couped up in that stuffy room every day?

I slipped into my seat as the bell was ringing, and settled down, only half listening to the teacher. Crystal didn't come until the last few minutes of class. Her face was flushed and her tight fitting dress was all wrinkled and I noticed her eyes were red and puffy. She whispered something to Mr. Jenkins and he gruffly nodded as she sat down.

When the bell rang she just sat there dumbly staring at the book of fairy tales she held in her hands. I knew what had happened and I wanted to rush over and put my arms around her and shout, "I understand." But the words wouldn't come. I picked up my books and slowly walked out of the far too quiet room, out into the steady moving mass of students. While I walked along feeling secure among all these people like me, I kept hearing a soft, little boy's voice saying over and over, "Hey Cys, I think you're the prettiest lady in the whole world."

-- Vicki Hoffman

* * * * *

# KINDNESS

Kindness is a language which the deaf can hear and the blind can read.

-- Mark Twain

* * * * *

The greatest gifts you'll ever give
Though with them never part,
Are simply these: a helping hand,
And a selfless, loving heart.

* * * * *

The art of acceptance is the art of making someone who has done you a small favor wish that he might have done you a greater one.

-- Russell Lynes

* * * * *

If I can stop one heart from breaking,
I shall not live in vain;
If I can ease one life the aching,
Or cool one pain,
Or help one fainting robin
Unto his nest again,
I shall not live in vain.

-- Emily Dickinson

* * * * *

As I lay here in my quiet bed
I think this day
of the things I have said,
Have the words I've spoken
Been sweet and kind?
Or have I been harsh
With no love in mind.

Did I smile this day
though no song I did feel?
Did I pray to my Father
in paths I did kneel?

Did I help the one
in need that I found
Or did I leave him there
in silent sound.

* * * * *

## Christianity

In the home - it is KINDNESS
In the business - it is HONESTY
In Society - it is COURTESY
In work - it is THOROUGHNESS
In play - it is FAIRNESS
Towards the unfortunate - it is COMPASSION
Towards the weak - it is HELP
Towards wickedness - it is RESISTANCE
Towards sin - it is REPENTANCE
Towards the penitent - it is FORGIVENESS
Towards God - it is REVERENCE, LOVE AND
OBEDIENCE.

-- Anonymous

* * * * *

## Little Things

Oh, it's just the little Homely Things
The unobtrusive, friendly things,
The "Won't-you-let-me-help-you" things
That make our pathway light.

And it's just the Jolly Joking things,
The "Never-mind-the-trouble" things
The "Laugh-with-me-It's-funny" things
That make the world seem bright.

So here's to all the Little Things,
The "Done-and-then-forgotten" things
Those "Oh-it's-simply-nothing" things
That make life worth the fight.

-- Grace Haines

* * * * *

It takes a little muscle, it takes a little grit,
A little true ambition with a little bit of wit.
It's not the biggest things that count, and make
    the biggest show:
It's the little things that people do, that make
    this old world go.

A little bit of smiling, and a little sunny chat,
A little bit of courage to a comrade slipping back.
It takes a kindly action, and it takes a work of
    cheer,
To fill a life with sunshine, and to drive away
    a tear.

Great things are not the biggest things that
    make the biggest show;
It's the little things that people do, that make
    this old world go.

* * * * *

## A Neighbor Gives Thanks

Everyone knows her as just Grandma Twitchell. You ask most people what her first name is and they can't tell you. She lives alone (her husband died several years ago). She is a member of the Provo Community Church. She never attends the Provo 12th-13th LDS Ward Chapel, but she lives across the street from it - and when her grandson was killed in a parachuting accident, her friends of the Provo 12th Ward rallied round.

Grandma Twitchell sent out what might be called a "thank-you letter" after it was all over. I don't know how many received it, but when our family got one, I thought "This should be shared with more than just those who received it."

I would like to share it with you.

Here it is: "My warm and thoughtful friends, I thank you. For the beautiful azalea, the Richard L. Evans Quote Book, the Apples of Gold, and the money. For all these things I thank you."

"For all your friendly greetings on the street where I live.

"For your boys who have been my paper boys--the boy who sits and chats with me--the boy who was interested in my paintings--the boy who rode his Shetland delivering papers.

"For your girl who brought her valentine to me on a special Valentine's Day.

"For your boys who cut my lawn. They laughed and talked with me on hot summer days.

"For the girl who cut my lawn, really better than the boys.

"For your boys who had broken bikes for Grandpa to fix.

"For your children who want me to sing my Indian Song.

"For your little boy who ran home to get a muffin to give me 'cause she is so nice'.

"For your little girls who have brought me pussy willows and Autumn leaves.

"For your boy who brought me a fish when he went fishing, and also wanted me to meet the girl he was going to marry.

"For your little girl who rang my doorbell to tell me 'I am five years old now!'

"For the carolers at Christmas time.

"For all these things and more - I thank you.

"May there be just enough clouds in your life to make a beautiful sunset."

It was written in long-hand and signed, "Grandma Twitchell".

-- Theron H. Luke

* * * * *

## The Lesson Of The Gracious Heart

On the way to Inverness, Scotland, several years ago, a big, rawboned farm woman sitting beside me on the bus asked why an American should travel north in the dead of winter. "It's rocky weather in the Highlands."

I explained that I liked wild weather and that I was gathering material for a historical novel, talking to country people, soaking up sheep-lore and folkways that have changed little in four centuries.

She invited me to visit her overnight. "We've a wee croft, but warm, and I'd welcome your company, for it's lonely with my husband off to market."

It was raining hard when we reached her home, a dumpy stone cottage perched on a bleak slope. Collies welcomed us, and Mrs. McIntosh led me into a spotless, shabby parlor.

Suddenly the lights flickered and died. She sighed, "The power's out," and lit candles. While she was making a fire there was a knock on the door.

She opened it and a boy came in. She took his dripping coat and cap, and as he moved into the firelight I saw that he was about 12 years old -- and pitifully crippled.

After he caught his breath, he said, "My father tried to ring you, but your phone is dead. I came to see that you're all right."

"Thank you, John," she said, and introduced us. The wind rose, raving and screaming, battering the shutters. I told them how much I loved the drama of the storm and the real need for an open fire.

"You're not scared?" John asked.

I started to say no, but Mrs. McIntosh, though obviously afraid of nothing, quickly said what the boy longed to hear: "Of course she was scared, and so was I. But now we've got a <u>man</u> about."

There was a moment's silence. Then he rose. "I'll see that everything's snug," he said. And he hobbled out of the room with a little swagger.

I was touched by the incident, and weeks later it continued to haunt me. Why hadn't I answered his question as Mrs. McIntosh had -- tenderly, imaginatively? And how often before in my life, insensitive through self-absorption, had I failed to recognize another's need?

Perhaps my heart had been asleep for years, but now it was awakening, anxious to compensate for lost opportunities and avidly curious. By what magic had Mrs. McIntosh transformed a crippled boy into a confident man? Had it been an instinctive kindness, or deliberate? Was it, I wondered, compassion, tact or a combination of all these? Then I recalled an expression used by Dr. Norman Vincent Peale, pastor of New York's Marble Collegiate Church. Speaking of such generosity of spirit, he had termed it the "gracious heart."

Looking back, I realized how often I had been helped by such hearts, how often I, too, had been exalted by a single gracious phrase or act. My mother did this for me many times when I was young and vulnerable, conferring the precious gift of self-esteem by a thoughtful gesture.

The gracious heart is above all strongly understanding of the feelings of others. My teen-age brother taught me this the night he helped to create a popular girl. He had seen her at a dance -- a shy, unattractive little freshman. Nobody paid any attention to her, and she faded against the wall. My brother was moved by her predicament. He asked her to dance and a minor miracle occurred. She was so happy that she sparkled and was almost pretty. Another boy cut in; afterward she danced nearly every dance.

Gallantry like that deepens every relationship. It can polish a marriage to a new luster. My friend Marge told me that on her 40th birthday she was, like many women, deeply depressed. She knew that happy, productive years lay ahead, but in the excessive value placed on youth in our society, she had lost her perspective. She said nothing of this to her husband at breakfast, but after he left she gave way to tears. She foresaw graying hair, deepening wrinkles, a struggle to remain slender. By the time her husband returned from work she had regained a degree of calm, but the ache persisted. After dinner he said, "Come and look at your presents."

They had always exchanged practical gifts and she suspected he had sneaked in the new vacuum cleaner they needed. But to her amazement she unwrapped a pair of jeweled boudoir slippers and lace negligee with matching gown.

"He didn't explain why," she said, "and he didn't have to. I knew what he was trying to imply: "You're beautiful, you're glamorous." And the odd thing was, I began to feel that way."

The gracious heart is never too busy to reveal itself. I recall hearing of a lonely little boy who was devoted to a battered, one-eyed Teddy bear. When he was hospitalized for a tonsillectomy, he took Teddy along and was holding him close when the surgeon came to his bedside and announced that it was time for the operation. A nurse moved to take the bear, but the doctor said gravely, "Leave Teddy there. He needs some attention, too."

When the child regained consciousness Teddy was snuggled against the pillow -- and across his missing eye was the neatest bandage a skillful surgeon could devise.

Opportunities to put this rewarding talent to good use are all around us. I was shopping with a friend in New York's Italian section when she noticed a boy about eight helping his father sell vegetables from a pushcart. He proudly sold a cauliflower to a woman and waited for payment, but she reached past him and gave the money to his father. The little fellow's smile faded; his shoulders slumped. My friend realized that some how she would have to retrieve the child's pride. She called him over and selected tomatoes and scallions which he put in a bag. She could have given him even change; instead she gave him a dollar. For a few seconds he frowned, calculating; then he brightened and handed her the correct change.

"Thank you," she said. "I couldn't have figured that fast."

"Aw, it was nothin'," he said, looking at his father. But it was something to him, and suddenly all four of us were beaming, warmed by the glow that her imaginative act had created.

"The gracious heart protects and enlarges the self-respect of the other person, builds his ego," says Dr. Peale. "When you come home from work and your child races to greet you, asking excitedly, "Did you hear what happened on Main Street today?" Your gracious heart; somehow, has not heard the news -- it gives the child the pleasure of telling you. But if you say, "Oh, yes. I heard about it an hour ago," your heart is only building up your own ego. There is enormous love in this world -- unconscious, instinctive, eager for expression. Each of us can learn to unlock it with the thoughtful courtesies of a gracious heart!

-- Elizabeth Byrd

* * * * *

## The Girl

She was twelve years old. Funny, she somehow seemed older than that. An ungainly, awkward, embarrassing twelve years old. It was a painful age. Our family had just moved to El Sobrante and I was new, but even that very first day in class I noticed it. She was different than the other kids, somehow. I can remember watching her, very carefully, and wondering, why is it that she's different? She was slower, yes, in just about everything, but there were a lot of kids in the class who had just arrived at that stage in life when arms and legs were getting longer, and it took a while to gain control of the newly acquired length. That wasn't it. Somehow I could sense it -- sort of an unwritten law in the tightly woven society of that classroom, that ostracized her from the rest of the class. She was "different." Almost no one would have anything to do with her.

That was the year they put some of the fifth and sixth graders together in the same class. I remember a lot of muttering about "corresponding IQ's" and the "revolution in the elementary school system," but we didn't care too much about that sort of thing. All that mattered to us was that we had to go to school. In the middle of April that's not a very entertaining prospect.

At recess we would climb a rough dirt road that led to a huge field of long tickley weeds, sprinkled with wild yellow mustard flowers and tiny purple daisies and orange satiny poppies. It was a sin to pick a poppy, a brand of treason peculiar to Californians.

She would always trail behind us as we climbed up the hill. Sometimes I'd sneak a glance backwards. She wouldn't ever even touch a poppy -- she'd very carefully pick her way over to a clump of them, and reverently inhale. I never could understand that. I could never smell anything, but she could detect a fragrance, I know -- her face would betray the secret, as a slight smile would form momentarily across her face. Then it would vanish.

We would go running, hand in hand, across the field, or we would play catch or try to play baseball. We girls weren't too good at baseball, though, and would often have to settle for a modified game of kickball. She would always stay apart from us. Not because she wanted to, I'm sure, but because she had to. It was the unwritten law.

How she withstood the giggling and smirking behind her back I'll never know. I couldn't stand it. It was behind her back enough so as not to incriminate any of her assailants, yet blatant enough to sting. Isn't it amazing how cruel seemingly unsophisticated children can be. I could see it hurting her, yet what could I do? I rationalized. I couldn't help make it easier for her.

There was one other girl in the class who felt the same way I did about the situation. She was quiet. And I remember her eyes. They were very soft. Linda Sinclair. Linda would go over and talk to the other girl sometimes. She would smile at her. Heal over, just a little, the wounds of the day. She was good. And she didn't care about what the others thought. The other girl wouldn't ever say much to Linda, though. I think she was afraid. But every once in a while she would look at Linda and smile a little. Just a little.

I remember graduation time. That was the big event of the year. There would be graduation ceremonies for all the sixth graders; they would wear the choir robes, and all the fourth and fifth graders would watch, round eyed, and after the diplomas were handed out and all the handshaking finished, they would sing "I Believe." And the mothers would cry a little.

She was graduating that night. I was in the choir. I got to wear my pink flowered dress with the pink cumberbun and long bow that reached down the length of my dress, as the choir robes were already in use that night. Linda was sitting next to me. She was holding a small white package with a pink ribbon wrapped around it, and when we were ready to sing she inconspicuously slid it under her chair.

"I believe for every drop of rain that falls a flower grows. . ."
The mothers cried a little. We sat down again, and Linda picked up the package. I had just about gathered up enough courage to ask her what it was, when it was time for the benediction, and we all had to stand up. I wondered if God heard the minister better when we were all standing up than when we were sitting down.

It was over at last, the sixth grade class was a thing of the past, a memory, they were officially graduated. There were grins drawn across all their faces. Linda started walking across the room, and I followed, not knowing where else to go. She was looking for someone -- then she saw her and pushed her way over to the girl. Linda hesitated for a moment in front of the girl, then smiled a little, shyly, and handed her the present. "Happy graduation," she said, and walked away. I'll always remember the expression on that girl's face. At first it was puzzlement. I could painfully read her thoughts. Why did she give this to me? And then she started crying. Silently, to herself. And she walked out the door of the school.

That night I went home and cried. I didn't really know why. But it hurt to think of the girl, and I hoped with everything that was in me that I would be able to feel for people, like Linda did. And that things would get better for the girl. I wonder if she's still crying.

* * * * *

## Information Please

When I was quite young, my father had one of the first telephones in our neighborhood. I remember well the polished old case fastened to the wall. The shiny receiver hung on the side of the box. I was too little to reach the telephone, but used to listen with fasination when my mother used to talk to it.

Then I discovered that somewhere inside the wonderful device lived an amazing person -- her name was Information Please and there was nothing she did not know. Information Please could supply anybody's number and the correct time.

My first personal experience with this genie-in-the-bottle came one day while my mother was visiting a neighbor. Amusing myself at the tool bench in the basement, I whacked my finger with a hammer. The pain was terrible, but there didn't seem to be any reason in crying because there was no one home to give sympathy. I walked around the house sucking my throbbing finger, finally arriving at the stairway -- The telephone! Quickly I ran for the footstool in the parlor and dragged it to the landing. Climbing up I unhooked the receiver in the parlor and held it to my ear. Information Please I said into the mouthpiece just above my head.

A click or two and a small clear voice spoke into my ear. "Information."

"I hurt my finger. . ." I wailed into the phone. The tears came readily enough now that I had an audience.

"Isn't your mother home?" came the question.

"Nobody's home but me," I blubbered.

"Are you bleeding?"

"No," I replied. "I hit my finger with the hammer and it hurts."

"Can you open your icebox?" she asked. I said I could. "Then chip off a little piece of ice and hold it to your finger."

After that I called Information Please for everything. I asked her for help with my geography and she told me where Philadelphia was. She helped me with my math, and she told me my pet chipmunk -- I had caught in the park just the day before -- would eat fruits and nuts.

And there was the time that Petey, our pet canary died. I called Information Please and told her the sad story. She listened, then said the usual things grown-ups say to soothe a child. But I was unconsoled. Why is it that birds should sing so beautifully and bring joy to all families, only to end up as a heap of feathers, feet up on the bottom of a cage?

She must have sensed my deep concern, for she said quietly, "Paul, always remember that there are other worlds to sing in."

Somehow I felt better.

Another day I was on the telephone. "Information Please."

"Information," said the now familiar voice.

"How do you spell fix?" I asked.

All this took place in a small town in the pacific Northwest. Then when I was 9 years old, we moved across the country to Boston -- I missed my friend very much. Information Please belonged in that old wooden box back home, and I somehow never thought of trying the tall, shiny new phone that sat on the hall table.

Yet as I grew into my teens, the memories of those childhood conversations never really left me; often in moments of doubt and perplexity I would recall the serene sense of security I had then. I appreciated now how patient, understanding and kind she was to have spent her time on a little boy.

A few years later, on my way west to college, my plane put down in Seattle. I had about half an hour or so between planes, and I spent 15 minutes or so on the phone with my sister, who lived there now. Then without thinking what I was doing, I dailed my hometown operator and said, "Information Please".

Miraculously, I heard again the small, clear voice I knew so well, "Information".

I hadn't planned this but I heard myself saying, "Could you tell me please how to spell fix."

There was a long pause. Then came the soft spoken answer, "I guess that your finger must have healed by now."

I laughed, "So it's really still you, I said. "I wonder if you have any idea how much you meant to me during that time."

"I wonder, she said, if you know how much your calls meant to me. I never had any children, and I used to look forward to your calls."

I told her how often I had thought of her over the years and I asked if I could call her again when I came back to visit my sister.

"Please do, just ask for Sally."

Just three months later I was back in Seattle. . .A different voice answered Information and I asked for Sally.

"Are you a friend?" "Yes, a very old friend." "Then I'm sorry to have to tell you. Sally has been working part-time the last few years because she was sick. She died five weeks ago." But before I could hang up she said, "Wait a minute. Did you say your name was Paul?"

"Yes." "Well, Sally left a message for you. She wrote it down. Here it is I'll read it --Tell him I still say there are other worlds to sing in. He'll know what I mean."

I thanked her and hung up. I did know what Sally meant.

* * * * *

# LIFE

The Plan of Salvation is designed to make of this earth, a heaven; and of man, a God.

-- Bruce R. McConkie

* * * * *

What do we live for if not to make the world less difficult for each other.

-- George Eliot

* * * * *

All the water in the world, no matter how hard it tried, could never sink a ship unless it got inside. And all the evil in the world, the blackest sin and kind, can never hurt you one least bit, unless; you let it in.

* * * * *

A man would do nothing if he waited until he could do it so well that no one would find fault with what he had done.

* * * * *

Before you're baptized Heavenly Father writes in pencil. After you're baptized He writes in pen.

* * * * *

"To one man, the world is barren, dull and superficial, to another rich, interesting and full of meaning."

-- Arthur Schopenhauer

* * * * *

Life itself cannot give you joy unless you will it.
Life gives you time and space and you must fill it.

* * * * *

When I was young, I wanted everything and all at once, until our old Scottish minister explained things this way:

One night he dreamed he saw a new shop on High Street and, going in, he found an angel behind the counter. What did the shop sell? "Everything your heart desires," the angel said.

"Then I want peace on earth," cried the minister, "an end to sorrow, famine and disease. . ."

"Just one moment," smiled the angel. "You haven't quite understood. We don't sell fruits here -- only seeds."

-- M. L. Grassick

* * * * *

We are blind until we see
That in the human plan
Nothing is worth the making if
It does not make the man.
Why build those cities glorious
If man unbuilded goes?
In vain, we build the world, unless
The builder also grows.

-- Edwin Markham

* * * * *

The Recipe

If we want a sweet taste we can put in
more sugar,
For sour, more lemon will do, but what
shall we add to make citizens nobler;
more upright, more worthy and true.
There's many a sermon on character building,
there's much about learning in school,
Of all the great thoughts given man since
time's dawning, the best is the plain
golden rule.

* * * * *

Far better it is to dare mighty things, to win glorious triumphs, even though checked by failure, than to take rank with those poor spirits who neither enjoy much nor suffer much, because they live in that gray twilight that knows not victory nor defeat.

* * * * *

Life has a burden
for everyone's
shoulder

None can escape
from its sorrow
and care

Miss it in youth,
and it comes
when you're older

And fits you as
close as the
garment you wear.

* * * * *

## Little Town

So long this little town was my whole
world;
Deep sky, low-lying hills, and waters
purled.

My home now wears an unfamiliar face;
New owners always want to change a
place.

The faces that I loved are there no more;
A modern shop replaced the country store.

The small schoolhouse has long outgrown
its need;
New buildings stand where farmers planted
seed.

Beloved old church has fallen to decay;
The white spires of a new one greet the
day.

All is not changed; the hills remain the
same;
The sunset dies with well-remembered
flame.

The sun-baked slopes still yield the ripened
grain;

The cows trudge to the pasture, down the
lane.

And when the valley dons its cloak of
white;
The lights glow in the darkness of the
night;

But most of all, when lilacs drip with
rain,
My memories and my heartstrings they
enchain.

-- Leone E. McCune

* * * * *

Tomorrow is not promised us,
So let us take today
And make the very most of it,
The once we pass this way.

Just speak aloud the kindly thought
And do the kindly deed
And try to see and understand
Some Fellow creature's need.

Tomorrow is not promised us
Nor any other day
So let us make the most of it
The once we pass this way.

* * * * *

## Life's Highway

Today I walked the highway
With faltering step and slow;
My load seemed very heavy
And long the way to go.

A comrade walked beside me;
And as I glanced his way,
I saw that he, too, carried,
His burdens through the day.

I smiled and reached to help him,
I lifted half his load;
My own seemed strangely lighter
As we trudged down the road.

-- Letitia Morse Nash

* * * * *

Life is like an onion; you peel it off one layer at a time, and sometimes you weep.

* * * * *

Life is a journey not a camp.

-- Hugh B. Brown

* * * * *

"Life is a radiation; to live is to radiate."

-- David O. McKay

* * * * *

What God Hath Promised

God hath not promised skies always blue,
Flower-strewn pathways all our lives through,
God hath not promised sun without rain,
Joy without sorrow, peace without pain.

But God hath promised strength for the day,
Rest for the laborer, light on the way,
Grace for the trial, help from above,
Unfailing sympathy, undying love.

-- Anne Johnson Flint

* * * * *

Nine Requisites for Contented Living

Health enough to make work a pleasure;

Wealth enough to support your needs;

Strength enough to battle with difficulties and to forsake them;

Grace enough to confell your sins and overcome them;

Patience enough to toil until some good is accomplished;

Charity enough to see some good in your neighbor;

Love enough to move you to be useful and helpful to others;

Faith enough to make real the things of God;

Hope enough to remove all anxious fears concerning the future.

-- Goethe

* * * * *

## This Is Your Life

No matter what else you are doing
From cradle right down to the end
You are writing your life's secret story
Each Night a new page is penned.
Each Month is the end of a chapter,
Each year the end of a part.
And never a word is misstated
Not even a wish of the heart.

Each morn when you awake the book opens,
Revealing a page clean and white.
Each thought, each word, and each act,
Reveal on its pages by night.
God leaves that to you, you're the writer
And never a word will be dimmed
Until some day you write the word "Finish"
And give the book back to Him.

* * * * *

## Saving For A Rainy Day

My resolution is emphatic . . .
Today's the day I'll clean the attic.

To sentiment, I will not yield,
So here I go, emotion steeled.

I'll start out nobly with the worst --
This venerable trunk comes first.

Here's Grandma's treasured Persian shawl
I thought the Church got that last fall.

Oh yes, I gave it to the Fair
Then hurried back, and bought it there.

These shabby baby shoes are sweet . . .
Imagine them on Junior's feet!

Nobody else would want this stuff,
And I have had it long enough.

But what to do? I won't consent
To burn it up . . . I'm not cement.

It's fun to look at!! Furthermore,
What have I got an attic for?

-- Margaret Fishback

* * * * *

## Just A Thought For The Week

Just supposing we started THIS very day
To live our lives in a different way;
Just supposing we vowed and constantly tried
To help those in trouble on life's wayside;
If we showed by our doings a hint of His love,
Wouldn't Earth be a bit more like Heaven above.

### Monday

Look for a smile today & return it with one of your own,
Give someone new faith & hope - it's such a beautiful loan.

## Tuesday

Gather a thought that's kind - one that's sincere & deep,
But be sure to pass it along, for such are too precious to
keep.

## Wednesday

Forget yesterday's old sorrows, mistakes, sadness & pain,
Lift your heart with hope & a song, as flowers to sun & rain.

## Thursday

Offer a word of comfort & prayer to help someone in need,
A little thoughtful gift or a smile make us all rich indeed.

## Friday

You shall not pass this way again so do any good you can do,
Don't put it off till tomorrow or the chance may be lost for
you.

## Saturday

Today will soon be a memory, so don't let it come to an end,
Without a smile, a song, or just a word with a friend.

## Sunday

Don't let worry & care depress you, or brush the day's joy
away --
But rise & give thanks to God above for His love and
another "blest day".

* * * * *

## Change

I have resisted change with all my will,
Cried out to life, "Pass by and leave me still."
But I have found as I have trudged time's track
That all my wishing will not hold life back,
All finite things must go their finite way;
I cannot bid the merest moment, "Stay."
So finding that I have no power to change
Change, I have changed myself. And this is strange,
But I have found out when I let change come,
The very change that I was fleeing from
Has often held the good I had prayed for,

And I was not the less for change, but more.
Once I accepted life and was not loath
To change, I found change was the seed of growth.

-- James Dillet Freeman

* * * * *

## You Tell Me I Am Getting Old

You tell me I am getting old.
I tell you that's not so.
The "house" I live in is worn out,
And that, of course, I know.
It's been in use a long, long while;
It's weathered many a gale.
I'm really not surprised you think
It's getting somewhat frail.

The color's changing on the roof,
The windows getting dim,
The walls a bit transparent
And looking rather thin.
The foundation's not so steady
As once it used to be --
My "house is getting shaky,
But my "House" isn't me!

My few short years can't make me old.
I feel I'm in my youth.
Eternity lies just ahead,
A life of joy and truth.
I'm going to live forever, there;
Life will go -- It's grand!
You tell me I am getting old?
You just don't understand.

The dweller in my little "house'
is young and bright and gay!
Just starting on a life to last
Throughout Eternal Day.
You only see the outside,
Which is all the most folks see.
You tell me I am getting old?
You've mixed my "house" with me.

-- Dora Johnson



* * * * *

## The Journey

I started on a journey, not many years ago,
Just where the road would lead me, I really did
not know.
I left my Father's house that day; I was anxious
yet afraid.
I knew that I must leave him, for the plans had
now been made.
So I took myself a body and started on my way,
Down the road of Eternity and hoped I would not
stray.
At first the road was very clear, I walked along
with ease.
It wasn't going to be so hard. My Father would
be pleased.
Then I saw the path of pleasure, it looked so
nice and gay.
It wouldn't hurt to stop awhile, because I need
not stay.
There were paths in all directions, it was very
hard to choose.
"Why not try them all?" I thought, "I surely
could not lose."
I saw the path of evil that's laid out for the
weak.
I simply couldn't pass it by without a little
peek.
And then the path of worldly gain, it looked like
such high style,
I simply had to linger on for just a little while.
By now I was so weary I surely needed rest,
So I took the path of discouragement, to see
if it were best.
I rested there for a while, but found no peace
of mind,
And so I started on again to see what I could find.
And as I walked along one day, I was as weary as
could be.
I wondered why it was so hard, I simply could not
see.
I thought of all the steps I took and all the
paths I'd tried,
And wondered why it was so hard to find the path
to God.
Then suddenly I realized that the road was straight
and fine,

And all those little side trips were just a
waste of time.

* * * * *

## I Am A Child Of Royal Birth

I am a child of royal birth.
My Father is King of heaven and earth.
My spirit was born in the courts on high.
A child beloved, a princess am I.
I was nurtured there; I lived by His side
In a home where patience and love abide.
My mother was there in that glorious place
Blessing her children with queenly grace.

I grew to the stature that spirits grow.
I gained the knowledge I needed to know.
I was taught the truth and I knew the plan
That God and the Christ laid out for man.
I was there when the stars of morning sang.
I mingled my voice when the heavens rang.
I was there to rejoice, to praise and applaud
The shouts of joy from the sons of God.

I waited my turn and I came to earth
Through the wonderful channel of human birth.
Then the curtains were closed and the past was gone;
On the future too, the curtains were drawn.
I live on the earth, and God willed it so.
With freedom to choose the way I should go.
I must search for the truth, I must serve and obey;
I must walk by my faith or fall by the way.

Some day I'll go back; I will answer the call;
I'll return with my record to the Father of all.
The books will be opened and so will my heart.
There will be rejoicing if I've done my part.
My Father, the King, with His infinite love
Will welcome me back to the mansions above.
The curtains will part and eternity
In its light and glory will open to me.

-- Anna Johnson

* * * * *

## The Roller Coaster Ride

I caught my nerve
and paid my dime;
but still unknowing
I waited in line.

"It's too late now."
I couldn't back out.
The ride operator
called with a shout,

"Everyone on!"
I stepped up bravely,
bit my lip
and sat up stately.

"Hold on tight!",
he said with a scoff.
I gripped the rail
and soon, we were off!

-I am born-

We started around,
higher we traveled.
I looked out the car
down to the gravel.

"Tiny figures grow smaller
the higher we rise.
They're so far down there!"
I shut my eyes.

-I learn fear-

Then came curves,
more and more;
I held too tight
and looked to the floor.

"Relax, relax!",
I whispered out low,
"Lean with the turns,
don't look below!"

-I learn from experience-

Then, higher we climbed

and stopped with a bump;
then down, soaring faster.
My heart seemed to jump.

This was fun. I liked it --
the wind in my hair,
the feeling I got
riding high in the air.

-I learn joy-

I clutched my purse,
holding it tight
so it wouldn't fall.
We swerved to the right.

Then up my hands flew --
my purse was gone!
I leaned over to see
the rafter it hung on.

-I know grief-

More turns, more curves,
more thrills, more frights.
More ups and downs,
more lefts and rights.

I grew to know each curve
as it came --
If it was hard or good;
I made it a game.

-I know age-

We then rode slower;
the turns were smaller.
As we came towards the station
the people grew taller.

We were slowing to a stop,
and so was the day.
I stepped up dizzily
and walked away.

-I am passed-

I thought, in my leaving, about my ride.
I know now the thrills and fears,
I learned to be clever, quick, and wise;
I buried my griefs through the years.

But, now it is finished;
My station I've earned.
Yes, my life is over.
More take their turn.

-I live again-

-- Kimberly Wentz

* * * * *

## Live Each Day To The Fullest

Live each day to the fullest.
Get the most from each hour, each day, and each age
of your life.
Then you can look forward with confidence,
And back without regrets.

Be yourself -- but be your best self.
Dare to be different and to follow your own star.
And don't be afraid to be happy.
Enjoy what is beautiful.

Love with all your heart and soul.

Believe that those you love, love you.

Learn to forgive yourself for your faults,
For this is the first step in learning to forgive others.
Listen to those whom the world may consider uninteresting,
For each person has, in himself, something of worth.

Disregard what the world owes you,
And concentrate on what you owe the world.
Forget what you have done for your friends,
And remember what they have done for you.

No matter how troublesome the cares of life may seem to
you at times. . .
This is still a beautiful world. . .
And you are at home in it,

As a child is at home in his father's house.

When you are faced with a decision,
Make that decision as wisely as possible --
Then forget it.
The moment of absolute certainty never arrives.

Above all, remember that God helps those who help themselves.
Act as if everything depended upon you,
And pray as if everything depends upon God.

-- S. H. Payer

* * * * *

My Dearest Child,

How well I remember the day you left my side and ventured forth on your mission to earth. That day I clothed your spirit with a cloak of love and tenderly sent you off to school. My thoughts are with you always. How I love you. I know of the grief and pain as well as the joy and happiness you experience. I know your school is full of ugliness and temptation as well as beauty, but remember <u>all that I have is yours if you come back to me</u>.

Each of you went into your new adventure with talents buried deep inside. Bring forth those talents. Develop them and share them. Give what is yours to give with all your heart. Covet not one another's gifts.

You, my child of Zion, have many blessings that my other children do not have. You share my Holy Priesthood. You may go to the Sacred Temple to learn of my eternal truths. You bear your children with the knowledge that they shall be yours forever, if you live worthy to come back to me. But, remember, where much is given , much is expected.

There are many among you who hunger for food and need care. Give of yourselves until you are drained of your strength, and then give more. There are many among you who hunger and thirst for my words. Go forth with a humble spirit. Give my message in their homes. Pour out my good tidings. Restore faith where it has been lost. Give them my spoken words.

And so, my beloved child of Zion, let charity and love be your constant companions. Come to me often in prayer. Be humble and faithful. Be diligent in my work and my kingdom shall be yours forever .

I love you and miss you so very much; and oh how I am looking forward to your return to me and your Mother!

All my love,

Your Heavenly Father

* * * * *

## Laws Of Nature

I remembered one morning when I discovered a cocoon in the bark of a tree, just as the butterfly was making a hole in its case and preparing to come out. I waited a while, but it was too long appearing and I was impatient. I bent over it and breathed on it to warm it. I warmed it as quickly as I could and the miracle began to happen before my eyes, faster than life. The case opened, the butterfly started slowly crawling out and I shall never forget my horror when I saw how its wings were folded back and crumpled; the wretched butterfly tried with its whole trembling body to unfold them. Bending over it, I tried to help it with my breath. In vain. It needed to be hatched out patiently and the unfolding wings should be a gradual process in the sun. Now it was too late. My breath had forced the butterfly to appear, all crumpled, before its time. It struggled desperately and, a few seconds later, died in the palm of my hand.

That little body is, I do believe, the greatest weight on my conscience. For I realize today that it is a mortal sin to violate the great laws of nature. We should not hurry, we should not be impatient, but we should confidently obey the eternal rhythm.

I sat on a rock to absorb this thought. Ah, if only that little butterfly could always flutter before me to show me the way.

-- Nikos Kazantazakis

* * * * *

## The Radiant Spirit

In the Beautiful Kingdom lay a broad, white roadway running like a pearled ribbon from the Mountain of the Great Throne to the Silver Sea. Many people, young and old, traveled along the Highway, for it was the Road of Life. This is a tale of two men who journeyed thereon.

Now, there was a legend in the Beautiful Kingdom that when a man had traveled the Highway's length, even unto the shores of the Silver Sea, the Radiant One would take him by the hand, and lead him into an enchanted land, where his eyes would behold things too beautiful for mortal man to look upon. None had ever returned to tell of its wonder, for the law is that a traveler walked that way but once.

It was springtime when Jan and Justin began their pilgrimage. All the earth was made fair and lovely by the silvery sunshine that fell from happy skies. Buds and flowers grew in rich abundance, and birds' celestial music filled the air like a blessed benediction.

Jan was in ecstasy. Nothing, he thought could be as beautiful as this; no, not even the vision of the Radiant One.

Each day, each hour, brought new delight to his soul, and his feet tarried along the trail until Justin became impatient.

"Hurry," he would call to Jan, "These are only flowers, and trees, and birds which we can see every day. Why linger among these common things? Let us not stop until we have reached the Silver Sea."

He would have hastened ahead, but he could not, for it had been decreed that they journey together. He complained bitterly when Jan delayed while they listened to the rustling of moonlit pines.

"Angel whispers, they are," he told Justin, but Justin could only hear the branches scraping one against the other, and he fretted to be on his way, until his heart became filled with worry and resentment.

Summer came, and passed, then autumn and the earth was more beautiful than it had been in the springtime. To Jan, each scarlet leaf became a miracle, each golden tree more exquisite than the last, and where a green field had lain in lazy loveliness, now abundant harvests gave the promise of royal riches to all men. But Justin's impatience waxed more strong.

"The nights are becoming chilly," he complained, "It will soon be winter, and it is still a far journey to the Silver Sea."

"Yes, I know the nights are chilly," said Jan, "but the stars hang low and close like diamonds upon earth's pure breast, and I would drink of this beauty while I can, for we will pass this way but once."

So they tarried until the winter of life was upon them, and their footsteps faltered many times, for their bodies were tired from their long journeying. They knew now that they would soon reach the Silver Sea, and Justin railed his companion bitterly.

"See," he said, "You have wasted our strength and time along the way on transient trifles. Our eyes are dim and aged. Tell me, how can we now see the Radiant One?"

And Jan replied, "I am glad for the experience of the springtime, for summer's clouds and showers, for the recompense of the harvest. These things have given me power to understand the immensity of that which is to come."

Then the day came when they stepped beyond the sunset into the Silver Sea. With eager, expectant eyes they looked for the Radiant One, as the legend had told them.

Justin spoke first, "We are too late, or we have missed our way. This is only another sea, like the many we have passed, and the only one I see is a person standing in the sun."

But Jan did not hear, for his ears were filled with the chant of angel choirs, his eyes were filled with the beauty that was too great for mortal man to look upon. His soul stood singing, for it knew the ecstasy of immortality, the glory and the joy of heavenly things, the wonder of eternity.

The Radiant One took him by the hand.

"Only those who have known me as they journeyed along the way of life can see me here. I walk with all men, but there are those who will not see and some who will not hear. Blessed are you, Jan for you have seen me in the sunrise, and in the sacred silence of the night. You have known me when I manifested myself in acts of kindness by fellow travelers. You have felt my presence even when the storms of life obscured your vision. I bless you, Jan with eternal Joy. I am the one whose mission it is to give happiness to men.

* * * * *

## The Day We Flew The Kites

"String!" shouted Brother, bursting into the kitchen. "We need lots more string."

It was Saturday. As always, it was a busy one, for "Six days shalt thou labor and do all thy work" was taken seriously then. Outside, Father and Mr. Patrick next door were doing chores.

Inside the two houses, Mother and Mrs. Patrick were engaged in spring cleaning. Such a windy March day was ideal for "turning out" clothes closets. Already woolens flapped on back yard clotheslines.

Somehow the boys had slipped away to the back lot with their kites. Now, even at the risk of having Brother impounded to beat carpets, they had sent him for more string. Apparently, there was no limit to the heights to which kites would soar today.

My mother looked at the sitting room, its furniture disordered for a Spartan sweeping. Again her eyes wavered toward the window. Come on, girls!" Let's take string to the boys and watch them fly the kites a minute."

On the way we met Mrs. Patrick, laughing guiltily, escorted by her girls.

There never was such a day for flying kites! God doesn't make two such days in a century. We played all our fresh twine into the boys' kites and still they soared. We could hardly distinguish the tiny, orange-colored specks. Now and then we slowly reeled one in, finally bringing it dipping and tugging to earth, for the sheer joy of sending it up again. What a thrill to run with them, to the right, to the left, and see our poor, earth-bound movements reflected minutes later in the majestic sky-dance of the kites! We wrote wishes on slips of paper and slipped them over the string. Slowly, irresistibly, they climbed up until they reached the kites. Surely all wishes would be granted.

Even our fathers dropped hoe and hammer and joined us. Our mothers took their turn, laughing like schoolgirls. Their hair blew out their pompadours and curled loose about their cheeks; their gingham aprons whipped about their legs. Mingled with our fun was something akin to awe. The grownups were really playing with us! Once I looked at Mother and thought she looked actually pretty. And her over forty!

We never knew where the hours went on that hilltop day. There were no hours, just a golder, breeze now. I think we were all beside ourselves. Parents forgot their duty and their dignity; children forgot their combativeness and small spites. "Perhaps it's like this in the Kingdom of Heaven," I thought confusedly.

It was growing dark before, drunk with sun and air, we all stumbled sleepily back to the houses. I suppose we had some sort of supper. I suppose there must have been a surface tidying-up, for the house on Sunday looked decorous enough.

The strange thing was, we didn't mention that day afterward. I felt a little embarrassed. Surely none of the others had thrilled to it as deeply as I. I locked the memory up in that deepest part of me where we keep "the things that cannot be and yet they are."

The years went on, then one day I was scurrying about my own kitchen in a city apartment, trying to get some work out of the way while my three-year old insistently cried her desire to "go park and see ducks."

"I can't go!" I said. "I have this and this to do, and when I'm through I'll be too tired to walk that far."

My mother, who was visiting us, looked up from the peas she was shelling. "It's a wonderful day," she offered; "really warm, yet there's a fine, fresh breeze. It reminds me of that day we flew kites."

I stopped in my dash between stove and sink. The locked door flew open and with it a gush of memories. I pulled off my apron. "Come on" I told my little girl. "You're right, it's too good a day to miss."

Another decade passed. We were in the aftermath of a great war. All evening we had been asking our returned soldier, the youngest Patrick Boy, about his experiences as a prisoner of war. He had talked freely, but now for a long time he had been silent. What was he thinking of -- what dark and dreadful things?

"Say!" A smile twitched his lips. "Do you remember -- no, of course you wouldn't. It probably didn't make the impression on you it did on me."

I hardly dared speak. "Remember what?"

"I used to think of that day a lot in PW camp, when things weren't too good. Do you remember the day we flew the kites?"

Winter came, and the sad duty of call of condolence on Mrs. Patrick, recently widowed. I dreaded the call. I couldn't imagine how Mrs. Patrick could face life alone.

We talked a little of my family and her grandchildren and the changes in the town. Then she was silent, looking down at her lap. I cleared my throat. Now I must say something about her loss, and she would begin to cry.

When she looked up, Mrs. Patrick was smiling. "I was just sitting here thinking," she said. "Henry had such fun that day. Frances, do you remember the day we flew the kites?"

-- Frances Fowler

* * * * *

# LOVE

An Indian tribute:

May your mocassins make happy tracks in many snows,
And the rainbow always touch your shoulder.

* * * * *

"If we discovered that we had only five minutes left to say all we wanted to say, every telephone booth would be occupied by people calling other people to stammer that they loved them."

-- Christopher Morley

* * * * *

To love someone means to see him as God intended him.

* * * * *

Love . . .
is patient and kind; love is not jealous
or conceited, or proud, or provoked; love
does not keep a record of wrongs; love is
not happy with evil, but it is pleased with
the truth. Love never gives up: its faith,
hope and patience never fail.

* * * * *

My childhood's happiness was measured out in little things. Was yours? I bless my mother who knew so much about children and their joy in little things.

My mother's happy smile and appreciative and endearing words at finding the house all cleaned up when she returned from Relief Society meeting or from some duty connected with her office of president of the Relief Society, were little things that filled my childhood with real joy. What did it matter that every loose thing had been tucked in the machine drawer out of sight or that innumerable out-of-place things crouched shamefully beneath the bed, when mother knew that the IMPORTANT things for her little girls were HER SMILE and PRAISE.

-- Caroline Eyring Miner

* * * * *

## When Grandpa Looks At Grandma

When Grandpa looks at Grandma,
Somehow he doesn't see
Her wrinkled brow, her hair white now --
Her aged serenity.

When
He doesn't see her falter
When night its darkness brings.
That she is slow, he'll never know --
Or any of those things.

When Grandpa looks at Grandma,
Somehow he doesn't hear
The broken tones that she now owns --
Her voice seems firm and clear.

Her eyes that smile warmly then,
Are faded blue and dim.
Though time has ranged, they have not changed
They look the same to him.

When Grandpa looks at Grandma,
Forgetting she is old,
He sees his bride cling by his side --
Her hair is shining gold.

He sees her in the splendor
Of love that grows and grows.
If she is grey and bent today,
Grandfather never knows.

* * * * *

## Two Keys

A key unlocks, desire is born
an embryo -- but yet --
sure, as is the coming morn,
and waiting to be met
by like desires -- not yet set free
no evidence of how or when
we feel the hand of diety
writing truths with silken pen
guiding two keys near the lock

so sure and sweet the fit -- what?
Can one key fail to hear the knock
be gentle pen, she'll find the slot
and finding the light the dual fires
kindled in burning with the Son
giving, sharing, consuming, nay higher
eternal 'till heavens course is run.
Oh steward of her special keys
I pray thee stay a day
that God and you might hear my pleas
unlock her key -- so I can say --
I love her.

-- John Rogerson

* * * * *

"What Is Real"

What is real
asked the rabbit one day
when they were lying side by side.
Does it mean having things that buzz inside you
and a stuck-out handle
said the skin horse.
It's a thing that happens to you
when a child loves you for a long, long time
not just to play with, but really loves you --
then you become real.
Does it hurt? asked the rabbit.
Sometimes, said the skin horse for he was always
truthful.
When you are real you don't mind being hurt.
Does it happen all at once like being wound up,
or bit by bit?
It doesn't happen all at once. You become. It
takes a long time. That's why it doesn't often
happen to people who break easily, or have sharp
edges or have to be carefully kept. Generally
by the time you are real, most of your hair has
been loved off and your eyes drop out and you
get loose at the joints and very shabby.
But these things don't matter at all because
once you are real
you can't be ugly, except to people

who don't understand.

-- From the Velveteen Rabbit

* * * * *

The love between husband and wife is a warm, flowing, inspiring power. It is sure and strong and safe and satisfying to each of them, and the benefits of this love are felt by other people in a variety of ways. This kind of feeling inspires the participant to do his professional job with more enthusiasm and sensitivity, it tends to create a feeling of acceptance and kindliness in a person toward the world in general. It makes life's demands reasonable, its sacrifices tolerable, its rewards apparent and emphatic. It causes a person to want to be better makes smiling easy, makes aloneness unlonely and silence peaceful. It motivates, supports, encourages, rewards.

-- Mary Urban

* * * * *

## What Can I Give You

What can I give you, child, against the in-
truding years? What will keep each moment bright
to withstand all the tears?

I can give you laughter. . .It will not be enough.
I can give you courage for when the road is rough.

I can give you words of faith for when the
night is long. And for the songless moment, I
can give you a song.

I can give you promise of guidance from above:
And always, always, always, I can give you love.

## True Love

Let me not to the marriage of true minds
Admit impediments. Love is not love
Which alters when it alteration finds,
Or bends with the remover to remove;
O, no! it is an ever-fixed mark
That looks on tempests and is never shaken;
It is the star to every wandering bark,
Whose worth's unknown, although his height be taken.
Love's not Time's fool, though rosy lips and cheeks

Within his bending sickle's compass come;
Love alters not with his brief hours and weeks,
But bears it out even to the edge of doom.
    If this be error and upon me proved,
    I never writ, nor no man ever loved.

-- William Shakespeare

* * * * *

Woodrow Wilson to Ellen Axson
During Their Courtship

October 16, 1883
Baltimore, Maryland

. . .How I wish that I could write you tonight such a letter as I should like to write; but it seems as if my love for you were literally unspeakable. . .Thoughts of you fill my life. You seem to be in everything I read, in everything I do. I can't enjoy myself without wishing that you might share the enjoyment; I can't read anything that is stimulating or eloquent or instructive without wishing that I might share it with you. I involuntarily smile in sympathy with anyone who seems happy, because I am happy; I pity everyone who seems downcast because I imagine that they are not loved by those whom they love. I am fast losing all semblance of a reputation for dignity because of the way I frolic and joke and rejoice in the manufacture of light-hearted nonsense when I am with my friends. I fool as if I should like very much to repeat poetry all the time -- if I know any to repeat. I am in a fair way to be run away with by this love that has taken possession of me. If you continue to love me and write me such elating letters I don't know what will become of this thitherto respectable person!

* * * * *

"Righteous love comes so naturally and so beautifully that it is apparent that there is a special providence about it. "They were meant for each other," we say. While I am sure some young couples have some special guidance in getting together, I do not believe in predestined love. If you desire the inspiration of the Lord in this crucial decision, you must live the standards of the Church, and you must pray constantly for the wisdom to recognize those qualities upon which a successful union may be based. You must do the choosing rather than to seek for some one-and-only so-called soul mate, chosen for you by someone else and waiting for you. You are to do the choosing. You must be wise beyond your years and humbly prayerful lest you choose amiss.

How wise is the man who does not expect perfection, but looks for potential. How wise the youth who looks for a mother for his children, not for an ornament to be admired by his friends, but a girl who wants to be a woman -- a domesticated, feminine, motherly woman."

-- Boyd K. Packer

* * * * *

## A Syrian Legend

Three men stood, one stormy night, at the threshold of a wayside cottage. Their knock at the door was answered by a child who asked their names and the purpose of their visit.

One of the two spoke saying: "My name is Love. My companions are Luck and Riches. We are seeking places for rest and refreshment. One of us would be pleased to receive the hospitality of this home tonight, and the choice of who it is to be we leave with you." The girl was bewildered; she ran and called the other members of the family, who gathered quickly to decide which of the three distinguished callers they would receive. They learned and repeated over and over again the names of their three would-be guests, studied their characters, and listened again to the request that was made.

Wisdom ruled the family's decision, and the choice was soon made. In unison they exclaimed: "We will entertain Love!"

But the family was perplexed to find that Luck and Riches accompanied the invited Love to the proffered room. Observing their astonishment, Love turned to the kind hosts and said, with a divine smile: "Be not alarmed. Wherever I am made welcome, there my companions also will make their home."

And that home, so say the Syrians whose legend this is, was blessed forever more.

* * * * *

## Experience Of Thomas Moore

My favorite love story is also a true one. Soon after he was married, Thomas Moore, the famous 19th century Irish poet, was called away on a business trip. Upon his return he was met at the door not by his beautiful bride, but by the family doctor.

"Your wife is upstairs," said the doctor. "But she has asked that you do not come up." And then Moore learned the terrible truth: his wife had contracted smallpox. The disease had left her once flawless skin pocked and scarred. She had taken one look at her reflection in the mirror and commanded that the shutters be drawn and that her husband never see her again. Moore would not listen. He ran upstairs and threw open the door of his wife's room. It was as black as night inside. Not a sound came from the darkness. Groping along the wall, Moore felt for the gas jets.

A startled cry came from a black corner of the room. "No! Don't light the lamps!"

Moore hesitated, swayed by the pleading in the voice.

"Go!" she begged. "Please go!" This is the greatest gift I can give you, now."

Moore did go. He went down to his study, where he sat up most of the night, prayerfully writing. Not a poem this time, but a song. He had never written a song before, but now he found it more natural to his mood then simple poetry. He not only wrote the words, he wrote the music too. And the next morning as soon as the sun was up he returned to his wife's room.

He felt his way to a chair and sat down. "Are you awake?" he asked.

"I am," came a voice from the far side of the room. "But you must not ask to see me. You must not press me, Thomas."

"I will sing to you then," he answered. And so for the first time, Thomas Moore sang to his wife the song that still lives today:

> Believe me, if all those enduring young charms,
> Which I gaze on so fondly today,
> Were to change by tomorrow and flee in my arms,
> Like fairly gifts fading away,
> Thou wouldst still be adored, as this moment thou art --
> Let thy loveliness fade as it will.

Moore heard a movement from the dark corner where his wife lay in her loneliness, waiting. He continued.

> Let thy loveliness fade as it will,
> And around the dear ruin each wish of my heart
> Would entwine itself verdantly still --

The song ended. As his voice trailed off on the last note, Moore heard his bride arise. She crossed the room to the window, reached up and slowly drew open the shutters.

-- Galen Drake

* * * * *

## This Road Can Be Traveled

It was the last week in January, seven years ago, when my husband walked into the room and, without emotion or expression, without looking at me, said, "The doctor wants me in the hospital tomorrow for some tests. He is almost sure I have cancer." Then he looked at me, and I wished he hadn't. "He said that the growth is about the size of an orange and is low in the colon."

You have cancer, I thought? How can that be? You aren't sick. You aren't thin; in fact, you may be a little overweight. You aren't pale or sallow-looking. You do have circles under your eyes, but you've had them for a long time. We've had so much of happiness, of love, of fun and laughter. And I'm greedy; I want more -- years and years of tomorrows. But not alone. Never alone. I felt a gentle touch brush away the tears on my face, and I heard my husband ask, "Hey! Where are you?"

We went through the motions of eating a meal, avoiding any mention of the intruder who now sat with us and waited. The same intruder was reflected in our eyes as we looked at each other; he stood by our bed that night until there was no rest or sleep.

On the way to the hospital the next day, we made a small detour. My husband has a private pilot's license, and we have a small plane at the local airport. We went there, and stood by the wing -- wondering how long it would be before we could take off again, together.

My alarm went off at 5 a.m. The nurse had told me to be at the hospital at 6:15 if I wanted to see my husband before he went to surgery. It was still dark as I made my way to room 505. The sign on the wall read: "Patient -- Male. Age -- 45. Special orders: No liquids after midnight." For four days he had been in that bed, being poked and tested, having X rays taken -- which confirmed what had been suspected. Now he sat cross-legged in the middle of his bed. He'd had a sedative, but he wasn't calm -- he was mad. I couldn't blame him for being cross; he had a tube in his nose and a white towel wrapped around his head. I wanted to call him Tony the Turk, but in his mood I didn't dare. Then, before I could say a word, two orderlies pushed a cart into the room. "Would you please wait in the hall?" Who, me? I thought. I will not. I'm not ready to go. I wanted to tell this Turk how much I love him. Why is it that I can never think of the right thing to say at the right time? There he is, my love, my life, just looking at me. Why doesn't _he_ say something? I'll tell him I love him. I take a deep breath and say, "Be good."

With his turban slipping side-ways, he scowls and says to me, "You be good in that red dress." They push the cart away, and I follow it -- right to the elevator door. Just before it closes, our eyes meet. It's all right. We said the right thing.

The hands on my watch point to the 12:31. I am numb; I can't let myself think. Suddenly, the doctor comes into the waiting room, a kind-looking man dressed in street clothes. I listened attentively while the doctor explained what he had done and why. He looked at me expectantly, but I said nothing. What was there to say? My husband was in intensive care, not me. I walked down the hall and out toward the parking lot. The tears started, and I could not stop them. I couldn't raise my hands to cover my face or to wipe away the tears. I had to get back. Back to the closed door of the intensive-care unit, and there I was going to stay. He would know I was there. He would know, and I would know. I stood outside that closed door until a nurse said, "Go on in." Now the door was open, but I couldn't move. I was more frightened than I had ever been in my whole life.

"Hi, sweetie." It's his voice! He raised his head and looked out into the hall at me. He held out his hand to me, and he was no different. I am no different. We are still us. I bent down to kiss him, and tell him, "They got all the cancer; everything else was clear. No sign anywhere." True -- but I did not tell him that the necessary severance of the colon had been complete and low, with not enough left to rejoin. He now had a new method of body elimination. But I did not know the words to tell him that. Instead I resorted to words we both knew -- words that were true. "I love you. I love you."

Finally, I'm there beside his bed again. He is wide awake and talkative. "Hi, honey, how are you?" He doesn't wait for an answer, just goes on talking. "Look at what I've got." He pushes the sheet aside. I couldn't look. I couldn't. I looked at his face instead. I'd lived with this man for 26 years. We'd shared almost everything. I thought I knew him, but he was more than I ever thought. There was no self-pity in his face, no rebellion in his voice. There was curiosity, interest. And he wanted to share it with me. He had shown me, taught me, shared with me, and he hadn't changed. So, I looked. Just next to that terrible incision I knew they had made, there was a small, pink, petal-like opening, about the size of a quarter. That was all. No blood, no gaping wound. He'd had a colostomy, and it looked as if it had always been there; as if he might have been born with it.

He was smiling when I looked up, and he asked me, "Isn't that something?" Then his smile disappeared, and he frowned at me. "You look terrible." Thanks a bunch, I thought. "Go home, honey, and get a good night's sleep."

Always telling me what to do! They have cut him open, taken out a cancer the size or an orange, handled every organ they could reach, looked at the rest, re-routed one of his life-sustaining functions, made an opening in his side, pulled a section of his intestines through, sewed him up, and made a pin cushion out of him with needles. He has all kinds of tubes and plumbing fastened to him, is in intensive care -- but I should have known that just as long as he had a heart and a brain he wouldn't change. That body is just a house for the man I love. They can add to, ortakeaway from it, remodel the whole structure, and he will still be in there, intact, laughing out at me from those snapping hazel eyes.

-- Nellie Randall

* * * * *

## The Soldier's Reprieve

"I thought, Mr. Allan, when I gave my Bennie to his country, that not a father in all this broad land made so precious a gift -- no, not one. The dear boy slept only a minute -- just one little minute -- at his post; I know that was all, for Bennie never dozed over a duty. How prompt and reliable he was! I know he fell asleep only one little second -- he was so young, and not strong, that boy of mine! Why, he was as tall as I, and only eighteen! And now they shoot him because he was found asleep when doing sentinel duty! Twenty-four hours, the telegram said -- only twenty-four hours! Where is Bennie now?"

"We will hope with his Heavenly Father," said Mr. Allan, soothingly. "Yes, yes, let us hope; God is very merciful!"

"'I should be ashamed, Father!' Bennie said, 'when I am a man, to think I never used this good right arm' -- and he held it out so proudly before me -- 'for my country when it needed it'. Palsy it rather than keep it at the plow! 'Go then -- go, my boy.' I said, 'and God keep you! God has kept him, I think, Mr. Allan!" and the father repeated these last words slowly, as if, in spite of his reason, his head doubted them. "Like the apple of his eye, Mr. Owen; doubt it not."

Blossom sat near them, listening with blanched cheek. She had not shed a tear. Her anxiety had been so concealed that no one noticed it. She had occupied herself mechanically in the household cares. Now she answered a gentle tap at the kitchen door, opening it to receive from a neighbor's hand, a letter. "It is from him," was all she said. It was like a message from the dead. Mr. Owen took the letter, but could not break the envelope because of his trembling fingers. He held it toward Mr. Allan with the helplessness of a child. The minister opened it and read as follows:

"Dear Father, --When this reaches you I shall be in eternity. At first it seemed awful to me; but I have thought about it so much now that it has no terror. They say they will not bind me, nor blind me, but that I may meet my death like a man. I thought, Father, it might have been on the field of battle for my country, and that, when I fell, it would be fighting gloriously; but to be shot down like a dog for nearly betraying it -- to die for neglect of duty! Oh, Father, I wonder the very thought does not kill me! But I shall not disgrace you. I am going to write you all about it, and when I am gone you may tell my comrades. I cannot now.

"You know I promised Jemmie Carr's mother I would look after her boy, and when he fell sick, I did all I could for him. He was not strong when he was ordered back into the ranks, and the day before that night I carried all his luggage, besides my own, on our march. Toward night we went on a double-quick and though the luggage began to feel very heavy, everybody else was tired, too; and as for Jemmie, if I had not lent him an arm now and then, he would have dropped by the way. I was all tired when we came into camp. It was Jemmie's turn to be sentry, and I would take his place; but I was too tired, Father. I could not have kept awake if a gun had been pointed at my head; but I did not know it until -- well, until it was too late."

"God be thanked!" interrupted Mr. Owen, reverently. "I knew Bennie was not the boy to sleep carelessly at his post."

"They tell me today that I have a short reprieve -- given to me by circumstances -- time to write to you, our good Colonel says. Forgive him, Father, he only does his duty; he would gladly save me if he could; and do not lay my death up against Jemmie. The poor boy is brokenhearted, and does nothing but beg and entreat them to let him die in my stead.

"I can't bear to think of Mother and Blossom. Comfort them, Father! Tell them that I die as a brave boy should, and that, when the war is over, they will not be ashamed of me, as they must be now. God help me; it is very hard to bear! Good-bye Father! God seems near and dear to me; not at all as if he wished me to perish forever, but as if he felt sorry for his poor, sinful, brokenhearted child, and would take me to be with him and my Savior in a better, better life."

A deep sigh burst from Mr. Owen's heart. "Amen!" he said, solemnly; "Amen!"

Tonight, in the early twilight, I shall see the cows all coming home from pasture, and precious little Blossom standing on the back stoop, waiting for me: but I shall never, never come! God bless you all! Forgive your poor Bennie."

Late that night the door of the "back stoop" opened softly, and a little figure glided out and down the footpath that led to the road by the mill. She seemed rather flying than walking, turning her head neither to the right nor to the left, looking only now and then to heaven, and folding her hands as if in prayer. Two hours later, the same young girl stood at the Mill Depot watching the coming of the night train; and the conductor, as he reached down to lift her into the car, wondered at the tear-stained face that was upturned toward the dim lantern he held in his hand. A few questions and ready answers told him all; and no father could have cared more tenderly for his only child than he for our little Blossom. She was on her way to Washington, to ask President Lincoln for her brother's life. She had stolen away, leaving only a note to tell her father where and why she had gone. She had brought Bennie's letter with her; no good, kind heart, like the President's, could refuse to be melted by it. The next morning they reached New York, and the conductor hurried her on to Washington. Every minute, now, might be the means of saving her brother's life. And so, in an incredibly short time, Blossom reached the capital, and hastened immediately to the White House.

The President had but just seated himself to his morning's task of looking over the signing of important papers, when, without one word of announcement, the door softly opened, and Blossom, with downcast eyes and folded hands, stood before him.

"Well, my child," he said, in his pleasant, cheerful tones, "What do you want so bright and early in the morning?"

"Bennie's life, please, sir," faltered Blossom.

"Bennie! Who is Bennie?"

"My brother, sir. They are going to shoot him for sleeping at his post."

"Oh, yes," and Mr. Lincoln ran his eye over the papers before him. "I remember. It was a fatal sleep. You see, child, it was a time of special danger. Thousands of lives might have been lost for his culpable negligence."

"So my father said," replied Blossom, gravely; "but poor Bennie was so tired, sir, and Jemmie so weak. He did the work of two, sir, and it was Jemmie's night, not his; but Jemmie was too tired, and Bennie never thought about himself, that he was tired, too."

"What is this you say, child? Come here; I do not understand," and the kind man caught eagerly as ever, at what seemed to be a justification of an offense.

Blossom went to him; he put his hand tenderly on her shoulder, and turned up the pale, anxious face toward his. How tall he seemed, and he was President of the United States, too! A dim thought of this kind passed through Blossom's mind, but she told her simple and straightforward story, and handed Mr. Lincoln Bennie's letter to read. He read it carefully; then, taking up his pen, wrote a few hasty lines, and rang his bell. Blossom heard this order given: "Send this dispatch at once."

The President then turned to the girl and said, "Go home, my child, and tell that father of yours, who could approve this country's sentence, even when it took the life of a child like that, that Abraham Lincoln thinks the life far too precious to be lost. Go back or -- wait until tomorrow; Bennie will need a change after he has so bravely faced death; he shall go with you."

"God bless you, sir!" said Blossom; and who shall doubt that God heard and registered the prayer?

Two days after this interview the young soldier came to the White House with his sister. He was called into the President's private room. Mr. Lincoln then said, "The soldier that could carry a sick comrade's baggage, and die for the act so uncomplainingly deserves well of his country." Then Bennie and Blossom took their way to their Green Mountain home. A crowd gathered at the Mill Depot to welcome them back; and, as Farmer Owen's hand grasped that of his boy, tears flowed down his cheeks, and he was heard to say fervently, "The Lord be praised!"

* * * * *

## "Warm Fuzzies"

Once upon a time very long ago there lived two people named Tim and Maggie who had two children called John and Lucy. To understand how happy they were, you have to understand how things were in those days. You see, in those happy days, everyone was given, at birth, a soft fuzzy bag. Anytime a person reached into this bag, he was able to pull out a warm fuzzy. Warm fuzzies were very much in demand because, whenever anyone was given a warm fuzzy, it made him feel warm and fuzzy all over. People who didn't get warm fuzzies regularly were in danger of developing a sickness in their backs which caused them to shrivel up and die.

In those days, it was very easy to get warm fuzzies. Anytime that someone felt like it, they would walk up to you and say, "I would like to have a warm fuzzy."

You would then reach into your bag and pull out a fuzzy the size of a little girl's hand. As soon as the fuzzy saw the light of day, it would smile and blossom into a large shaggy fuzzy. You would then lay it on the person's head or shoulder or lap. It would snuggle up and melt right against their skin and make them feel good all over. People were always asking each other for warm fuzzies, and since they were always given freely, getting enough of them was never a problem.

There were always plenty to go around and as a consequence everyone was happy and felt warm and fuzzy most of the time.

One day, a bad witch became angry because everyone was so happy and no one was buying her potions and salves. This witch was very clever and she devised a very wicked plan.

One beautiful morning , she crept up to Tim while Maggie was playing with their daughter and whispered in his ear, "See here, Tim, look at all those fuzzies that Maggie is giving to Lucy. You know, if she keeps it up, eventually she's going to run out and then there won't be any left for you."

Tim was astonished. He turned to the witch and said, "Do you mean to tell me that there isn't a warm fuzzy in our bag every time we reach into it?"

And the witch said, "No! Absolutely not! And once you run out, that's it and you don't have any more." With this, she flew away on her broom, laughing and cackling disparagingly.

Tim took this to heart and began to notice every time Maggie gave a warm fuzzy to somebody else. Eventually, he got very worried and upset because he liked Maggie's warm fuzzies very much and did not want to give them up.

He certainly did not think it was right for Maggie to be spending all her warm fuzzies on the children and on other people. He began to complain every time he saw Maggie giving a warm fuzzy to someone else.

Because Maggie liked him very much, she stopped giving warm fuzzies to other people as often and reserved them for him.

The children watched this and soon began to get the idea that it was wrong to give up warm fuzzies any time you were asked or felt like it. They, too, became very careful. They would watch their parents closely and whenever they felt one of their parents was giving too many fuzzies to others, they begun to object. They began to feel worried whenever they gave away too many warm fuzzies, even though they found a warm fuzzy every time they reached into their bag. They reached in less and less and became more and more stingy.

Soon people began to notice the lack of warm fuzzies and they began to feel less and less fuzzy. They began to shrivel up and occasionally people would die from lack of warm fuzzies.

More and more, people went to the witch to buy her potions and salves, even though they didn't seem to work.

Well, the situation was getting very serious, indeed!

The bad witch, who had been watching all this, didn't really want the people to die, so she devised a new plan.

She gave everyone a bag that was very similar to the fuzzy bag, except that this one was cold, while the fuzzy bag was warm. Inside the witch's bag were cold pricklies. Those cold pricklies did not make people feel warm and fuzzy, but made them feel cold and prickly instead. But, they did prevent people's backs from shrivelling up.

So, from then on, every time someone said, "I want a warm fuzzy," people who were afraid of depleting their supply would say, "I can't give you a warm fuzzy, but would you like a cold prickly?"

Sometimes, two people would walk up to each other thinking they could get a warm fuzzy, but one or the other of them would change his mind and they would end up giving each other cold pricklies.

So, the end result was that while very few people were dying, a lot of people were still unhappy and feeling cold and prickly. The situation got very complicated because, since the coming of the witch, there were fewer and fewer warm fuzzies around. So, warm fuzzies which used to be thought of as free, became extremely valuable.

This caused people to do all sorts of things in order to obtain them. Before the witch had appeared, people gathered in groups of three or four or five, never caring too much who was giving warm fuzzies to whom. After the coming of the witch, people began to pair off and to reserve all their warm fuzzies for each other exclusively.

If ever one of the two persons forgot himself and gave a warm fuzzy to someone else, he would immediately feel guilty about it because he knew that his partner would probably resent the loss of a warm fuzzy.

Another thing which happened was that some people would take cold pricklies which were limitless and freely available, coat them white and fluffy and pass them off as warm fuzzies. The counterfeit warm fuzzies were really plastic fuzzies and they caused additional difficulties.

For instance, two people would get together and freely exchange plastic fuzzies which presumably should make them feel good. But they came away feeling bad instead. Since they thought they had been exchanging warm fuzzies, people grew very confused about this, never realizing that their cold prickly feelings were really the result of the fact that they had been given a lot of plastic fuzzies.

So, the situation was very dismal, and it all started because of the coming of the witch who made people believe that when they least expected it they might reach into their warm fuzzy bag and find no more.

Not long ago, a young woman came to this unhappy land, and she had not heard about the bad witch and was not worried about running out of warm fuzzies. So, she gave them out freely, even when not asked.

The people disapproved of her because she gave the children the idea that they should not worry about running out of warm fuzzies. The children liked her very much because they felt good around her and they too began to give out warm fuzzies whenever they felt like it.

The grown-ups became concerned and decided to pass a law to protect the children from depleting their supplies of warm fuzzies. The law made it a criminal offense to give out warm fuzzies ina reckless manner. The children, however, seemed not to care and, in spite of the law, they continued to give out warm fuzzies whenever they felt like it and always when asked.

Because there were many, many children, almost as many as grown-ups it began to look as if maybe they would have their way.

As of now, it is hard to say what will happen. Will the grown-ups stop the recklessness of the children? Are the grown-ups going to join with the children in taking a chance that there will always be as many warm fuzzies as needed? Will they remember the days their children are trying to bring back when warm fuzzies were abundant because people gave them more freely?

* * * * *

## A Picture Of God

One of the best pictures of God that I ever saw came to me in a simple incident. It was a man, a minister who lived in a New England town, and had a son about fourteen years of age going to school.

One afternoon the boy's teacher called at the home asking for the father, and saying:

"Is your boy sick?"

"No. Why?"

"He was not at school today."

"Is that so?"

Nor yesterday."

"You don't mean it!"

"Nor the day before."

"Well, well!"

"And I supposed he was sick."

"No, he's not sick."

"Well I thought I should tell you!"

The father said, "Thank you," and the teacher left.

The father sat thinking, by and by he heard a click at the gate, and he knew the boy was coming, so he went to the open door. And the boy knew as he looked up that his father knew about those three days. The father said:

"Come into the library, Phil." Phil went, and the door was shut. The father said: "Phil, your teacher was here this afternoon. He tells me you were not at school today -- nor yesterday -- nor the day before. And we supposed you were. You let us think you were. You do not know how badly I feel. I have always trusted you. I have always said, "I can trust my boy'. And here you've been living a lie for three days. I can't tell you how badly I feel about it."

Well, that was hard on Phil to be talked to quietly like that. If his father had spoken to him roughly, or had asked him out to the woodshed for a confidential interview, it would not have been nearly so hard.

Then, after a moments pause, the father said: "Phil, we'll get down and pray." The thing was getting harder and harder for Phil all the time. He did not want to pray just then, but they got down, and the father poured out his heart in prayer. The boy knew as he listened, how badly his father felt over his conduct. Somehow he saw himself in the mirror on his knees as he had not before. It is queer about that mirror of the knee joints. It does show so many things. Many folks do not like it.

They got up. The father's eyes were wet, and Phil's eyes were not dry. Then the father said:

"My boy, there's a law of life that where there is sin, there is suffering. You can't detach those two things. Where there is suffering there has been sin some where. And where there is sin there will be suffering. You can't get those two things apart."

"Now," he went on, "you have done wrong, and I am in this home like God is in this world; so we will do this. You go up to the attic, I'll make a pallet for you there. We'll take your meals up to you at the regular times, and you stay up there as long as you have been living a lie -- three days and three nights."

Phil did not have a word to say. They went upstairs, the pallet was made, and then the father kissed the boy and left him alone in the attic with his thoughts.

When supper time came, the father and mother sat down to eat. But they could not eat for thinking about the boy.

Then they went into the sitting room for the evening. He picked up the evening paper to read, and she sat down to sew. Well, his eyes were not very good. He wore glasses, and this evening the glasses seemed very blurred. So he took them off and cleaned them very deliberately, then found that he had been holding the paper upside down. By and by the clock struck nine, and then ten, their usual hour for retiring. But they made no move toward retiring. She said, "Aren't you going to bed?" He replied, "I'll wait a while, too." The clock struck eleven, and the hands worked around toward twelve. Then they arose, looked up, and went to bed, but -- not to sleep. Each one made a pretense to be asleep, but each one knew the other was not asleep. By and by she said, "Why don't you sleep?" He said gently, "How did you know I wasn't sleeping? Why don't you sleep?"

"Well, I can't for thinking of that boy up in the attic."

"That's what's the matter with me," he replied.

The clock in the hall struck twelve -- then one -- then two. Still no sleep came. At last he said, "Mother, I can't stand this any longer; I'm going upstairs with Phil." He took his pillow and went softly out of the room up the attic stairs, and pressed the latch softly so as not to waken the boy if he were asleep, tiptoeing across the attic floor to the corner near the window. He looked -- there Phil lay, wide awake, with something glistening in his eyes and what looked like stains on his cheeks.

The father got down between the sheets with his boy, and they put their arms around each other's necks, for they had always been the best of friends; father and boy, and their tears were mixed up on each other's cheeks. Then they slept.

The next night when bed-time came, the father said, "Good-night Mother, I'm going upstairs with Phil." So the second night he slept in the attic with his boy. The third night again he said: "Mother, good-night. I'm going up with the boy again." The third night he slept in the place of punishment with his son.

"Even as the Son of man came not to be ministered unto, but to minister, and to give his life ransom for many. Matt. 20:28.

"Repent ye therefore, and be converted, that your sins may be blotted out." Acts 3:19.

* * * * *

## The Woman

She came wearily into the little Northern village; an old woman in the somber dress of a widow. And because her body was bent and worn, because her eyes were filled with an agony of heartbreak, the villagers were very kind to her.

People were beginning to be more kind all through the Provinces of Palestine. Perhaps it was an outgrowth of the creed that a certain Man had preached, -- that not many years since a certain Man had died for. Travelers had spoken of His miracles, of His tenderness, of His power over disease, of His radiant smile, of His birth in a manger. And there were those among the older villagers who had glimpsed, upon that wintry night long before, at the glow of the star that had already come to be a great legend in that country.

And so they were kind to the old woman. It wasn't long before she was part of the village life. But although she was a part of them she never mingled, and seldom did she speak except in gratitude for alms. Perhaps, said one, "She was a great lady once." Who knows? And so the matter rested, until the brown-eyed girl fell fainting on the doorstep of the old woman's small cottage, and was helped inside that her child might be born.

The brown-eyed girl, months before, had come to the village, but the villagers had not been kind to her as they had to the old woman, and the wives of the villagers spoke sharply when their little children sought to answer the gayety of her smile.

The child was born. And the old woman, heating water, warming clothes, making broth, looked at him across her work as a desert traveler would stare at a mirage.

-- So pretty, -- ah, so pretty, his little legs, so fat and straight. Ah, but they will travel far in their time. -- His little hands, -- reaching after a happiness he may never find. -- So, so pretty, as pretty almost, almost as my own small son.

"You care for my baby," questioned the brown-eyed girl. "Why?"

"He is like my own little son of long ago."

"You loved your little son, -- loved him so much that all other babies are dear to you for his sake; and yet, in your old age this son has left you to the charity of strangers. Is this the world's way?"

"My son is dead."

As the brown-eyed girl grew stronger her curiosity moved along and she asked other questions.

"Was your son handsome? Was he clever? Did people like him? Was he a man of learning? A child of charm?" And to all these questions the old woman answered, "Yes." But when the brown-eyed girl asked, "And how did he meet his death?" The old woman shuddered and turned away an ashen face. "But I, -- I cannot tell you, I cannot; it was too dreadful, too hard. -- Oh, the shame of it, the agony. How could it have come to be? He was such a sweet little boy, -- how could it have happened to him whose child heart was so free of all guile?"

And then, at last when the day came that the brown-eyed girl was strong enough to sit in the doorway of the cottage, the old woman said, "It is long since I have been able to bestow a gift, but your baby shall have the infant clothes of my son. I put them on, his first little clothes, with such love. All through the waiting months I had worked over them. I knew that he would be a son. His name was written on my heart ere ever I saw his face. "See!" All at once her thin finger was tracing a line of the initial entwined with fine embroideries upon one of the garments.

The brown eyes were misted as she looked down at the exquisite work that the old woman's hands had done. -- When they were young and eager hands, and she saw among the small starlike flowers worked with linen thread, a letter, -- and the letter was J.

When the brown-eyed girl was finally able to go away from the cottage she walked straight down the narrow street that lead between the crowding of houses to the market place. "I will tell you," she said to the group in the market, "of a woman dwelling in your midst. The woman who took me in. She it was who nursed me back to health as gently as an angel. She it was, who during the hours of my convalescence talked with me of her son." The villagers were leaning forward for there was something in the tone of the girl that compelled their attention.

"Her son was born at the south of Jerusalem. He was a clever sweet child. He grew to be a man of great learning. She was proud of him, -- and then came his death, a death so tragic that it had weakened the mind of her, and left her trembling on the edge of madness."

"We have heard of one born to the south of us who died in a desperate way. Travelers from afar have carried tidings, but there have been no tidings of his kin, of their fate."

The girl suddenly was still, and the people listening read into the stillness that which she was thinking. "The woman gave me the swaddling clothes that she had made for her own son many years ago. You may read for yourselves the initial that is worked into their embroidery. -- See the little letter laying over my son's heart?"

One by one the villagers came to the small house that the old woman occupied. "You were not always alone?" they asked, "You had a family once?"

"I had a son, would you care to hear of him?"

And so the old woman told them of a baby who had come to bring her joy and happiness. "Even as a tiny child he spoke wisely. Many of our friends listened to the words he said; and as he grew up he was chosen for many honors. All over the country men and women looked to him for wisdom and truth, for he was wise and good, my little son grown older."

But there came a certain night in Jerusalem. Oh, the happenings of it pass my understanding. There were lights, and there were soldiers, that forced their way into the garden. The folk hurried to me and spoke of a betrayal, and told me that my son, -- that my son. -- Not only the loss of his smile, not only the death of his dear body. It was the shame and the bitterness. It was enough that he should have to die, but to die beneath a cloud of suspicion and wrong, -- leaving not even a lovely moment at the last for me to cling against. -- When I fled from Jerusalem, I had planned to go back to the land from which we came, I and my son. But I grew bewildered, and the caravans that helped me on my way were all northerly bound, and I found myself, without meaning, upon your quiet streets. For my son's mother, I had not dreamed there would ever be such rest.

The old woman was failing, as the winter came the villagers could tell that her days were numbered, and they did little things that they knew would please her.

And then came the time in the winter which was the anniversary of a star that hung, years before, above a stable. The weaver had finished a white shawl, and wine was spiced and bottled, and so the villagers together went toward the small cottage that had come to be the home of the old woman. The interior of the little house was dark but someone rubbed flint upon the stone, and some one lighted a candle, and in the glow of it they saw the old woman sitting upright upon the blanket that made her bed. She was speaking. . .

"They came to me and told me of the betrayal, but I would not believe them.

-- He will send me word, I kept thinking, to tell me they are mistaken. -- Why there was much between us two, -- But he did not send word, -- and then, -- and then they brought me word of his death. A death that proved their stories."

Suddenly the old woman fell silent, and the villagers crowded forward, and as they surrounded her with their gifts and the semblance of their love, the anguish was swept magically from her face, and for the only time since she had come among them, she smiled. And at first they thought she was smiling at them, -- but, no, she was seeing a long, long gracious countryside, and she was speaking to her son.

"The fields of Corinth are so green in the springtime, and soon he will be running home, -- Come home, my little one, for it is bedtime. -- Come home." Her voice was shrinking to the mere thread of a sound. A great silence filled the little cottage, -- she was speaking again, "C-o-m-e h-o-m-e --- J-u-d-a-s."

-- Margret E. Sangster

* * * * *

# MAN'S WORTH

We are building in sorrow or joy
A temple the world may not see;
Which time cannot mar or destroy --
We build for eternity.

--N. B. Sargent

* * * * *

The other morning, as my six-year-old daughter was watching me shave, she suddenly asked, "Daddy, where does God <u>really</u> live?" "In the well,"I answered absentmindedly. "Oh, Daddy!" Debbie voiced her disgust at such a silly answer.

At breakfast my wife asked, "What's this you've been telling Debbie about God living in a well?" "In a well?" I frowned. Now why had I told her that?

Then, all at once, a scene came to mind that had been hidden in my memory for 30 years. It had taken place in the small town of Kielee, in southeastern Poland, where I was born. A band of passing gypsies had stopped at the well in our courtyard. I must have been about five years old at the time.

One gypsy in particular, a giant of a man, fascinated me. He pulled a bucket of water from the well and was standing there, feet apart, drinking. Some of the water was running down his short-cropped, fiery beard, and his muscular hands held the large wooden pail to his lips as if it weighed no more than a teacup. When he had finished, he took off his multicolored silk scarf and mopped his face with it. Then he leaned over and looked deep into the well. Curious, I tried to pull myself up the well's stone rim to see what he was peering at. The giant noticed me. He smiled and scooped me up in his arms. "Do you know who lives down there?" he asked. I shook my head. "God lives there," he said. "Look!" And he held me over the edge of the well.

There in the still, mirror-like water, I saw my own reflection. "But that's <u>me</u>!" "Ah," said the gypsy, gently setting me down. "Now you know where God lives."

-- Ben Wakes

* * * * *

## <u>Love Thy Neighbor</u>

It is a serious thing to live in a
society of possible gods and goddesses, to

> remember that the dullest and most uninteresting person you talk to may be a creature which . . . you would be strongly tempted to worship, or else a horror and a corruption such as you now meet, if at all, only in a nightmare. All day long we are, in some degree, helping each other to one or other of these destinations. It is with the awe and circumspection proper to them that we should conduct all our dealings with one another, all friendships, all loves, all play, all politics. There are no ordinary people, you have never talked to a mere mortal. Nations, cultures, arts, civilizations -- these are mortal, and their life is to ours as the life of a gnat. But it is immortals whom we joke with, work with, marry, snub, and exploit -- immortal horrors or everlasting splendours.
>
> -- C. S. Lewis

* * * * *

## Our Responsibility To Forgive

A few years ago a boy came into class. (In the Utah State Prison) After class he said, "Brother Smith, can I talk to you for a minute?" We went into the old library where we could be alone. He said, "My name is Jim Jones. I am from a small town up north." And then he started to cry as I have never seen a man cry in my life. His whole body shook with sobs. When he could control himself he said, "What have I done? What have I done to my parents, to my Church, to my town?" He said, "My dad is superintendent of the Mutual in my home town; my mother is a teacher in the Sunday School. Why the bishop used to hold me up as an example to the boys of the ward and say, 'Why can't you be like Jim?'" Then this boy said, "What have I done?"

I said, "Jim, you are going to be here for some time. I hope you will come and study with us. I hope you will come to Church and take adventage of the time you have here." And he did. A year and a half passed, and the parole board said, "You can go back home on the thirteenth of November on parole" - three months distant.

That night as we went into the prison, he came up to me and said, "Ray, what am I going to do now?"

I said, "What are you going to do? This is the day we have waited for. You are going home on the thirteenth of November."

He said, "I can't go home. I am ashamed to go home. I have brought disgrace to my parents. My home town is just a little town; everyone there knows everyone else. What am I going to do?"

He was only a young fellow - nineteen years of age.

I wrote to the bishop of Jim's home town. I said, "Bishop, on the thirteenth of November, Jim Jones of your ward is going to be released from the Utah State Prison. I want to come down and talk in sacrament meeting the following Sunday, if you have an opening."

The bishop graciously wrote back and said, "The time is yours."

That Sunday my wife and I got in the car and started down for Jim's home. On the way she said, "This is a long way to go to Church." On the way back she said, "It was worth it."

We arrived about an hour early, found the family, had a little lunch with them. About a quarter to seven Jim started walking back and forth, fixing his tie, wondering, "What will happen? What will they say when they see me in Church? They all know where I have been."

Well, we went over to the chapel. I sat on the stand with the bishop, of course. The people came in; they filled the seats, they filled the aisles; they sat in the back. The bishop looked at me and said, "I don't know what has happened. We don't have a crowd like this even at conference." And he said, "All I said last Sunday was that a man from the penitentiary was going to bring one of our boys home."

I was very happy that all of the townspeople were there. I had something to say to them that night. "You know I believe that when a criminal goes to prison and those doors clang shut on him, they should stay shut forever. They should never open. He should die in prison. There is no place for a criminal outside of prison walls." I made that statement in the meeting that night. Then I said, "Jim, will you stand please." And this boy stood up and all eyes of his neighbors turned to look at him. I said, "Brothers and sisters, a year and a half ago this boy came to us in the Utah State Prison, branded as a criminal, convicted of a crime against the people of the State of Utah. I saw that criminal die. And this boy I am bringing back to you is not a criminal. He is just a humble, repentant boy, who wants another chance in his home town to prove that he is decent. I have brought him back home through the front door of your church. Now if you don't want him there, he will find companionship in the pool halls and the beer parlors, and after about three months I will have him back in prison again. Now it is all up to you."

It was a wonderful sight, when that meeting was over, to see the townspeople gather around that family. No wonder on our way home my wife said, "It was worth it."

* * * * *

# MARRIAGE

To keep your marriage brimming,
With love in the loving cup,
Whenever you're wrong, admit it;
Whenever you're right, shut up.

-- Ogden Nash

* * * * *

A marriage is a series of friendships. Love serves as its underlying theme. Friendships provide it with the new challenges around which the relationship further develops. Each type of friendship with one's partner comes into being, rises to a peak of enthusiasm, and then wanes away. It becomes an item tucked away in our "cedar chest of sentimental valuables." Every once in a while we go to the chest and draw out a friendship item to give us a shot in the arm. Then we put it away till another day.

* * * * *

## Inventory

In marriage his young hand held mine in a sacred vow,
In childbirth his kind hand caressed and soothed my brow.
In love his hands cared for each tiny one who came;
In Priesthood his hands humbly blessed and gave each name.
In parenthood his busy hands signed school cards,
In guidance his hands lifted chins and gave award.
In sorrow his strong hands console the ones in need.
With thoughtfulness his calloused hands perform each deed.
In wisdom his hands reassure our destiny.
In faith his hands will hold mine through eternity.

* * * * *

## Ten Contributing Factors To A Happy Home

1. You young folks - ever keep in mind that you begin to lay the foundation of a happy home in your pre-marital life. . . Chastity during young manhood and womanhood is the highest ideal you can cherish, having happy home life in mind.

2. Choose your mate by judgment and inspiration, as well as by emotion.

3. Approach marriage with the lofty view it merits. Live worthy to enter the House of God.

4. The noblest purpose of marriage is procreation.

5. Let the spirit of reverence pervade the home, so that if the Savior happened to call unexpectedly, He could be invited to stay and not feel out of His element.

6. Let husband or wife never speak in loud tones to each other, "unless the house is on fire."

7. Learn the value of self-control.

8. Foster home-ties by continued companionship. Don't sacrifice companionship with wife and children for that of business associates.

9. Make accesible to children proper literature, music, and appropiate moving pictures.

10. Finally by example and precept encourage participation in church activity, thus establishing life's two paramount ideals: First, to build character; and second, to render service.

-- David O. McKay

* * * * *

<u>The Art Of Marriage</u>

Happiness in marriage is not something that just happens. A good marriage must be created. In the art of marriage the Little Things are the BIG THINGS. . .

It is never being too old to hold hands.

It is remembering to say, "I love you," at least once each day.

It is never going to sleep angry.

It is forming a circle of love that gathers in the whole family.

It is at no time taking for granted; the courtship shouldn't end with the honeymoon, it should continue through all the years.

It is doing things for each other, not in the attitude of duty or sacrifice, but in the spirit of joy.

It is speaking words of appreciation and demonstrating gratitude in thoughtful ways.

It is not expecting the husband to wear a halo or the wife to have wings like an angel. It is not looking for perfection in each other. It is cultivating flexibility, patience, understanding, and a sense of humor.

It is having the capacity to forgive and forget.

It is giving each other an atmosphere in which each other can grow.

It is finding room for the things of the spirit. It is a common search for the good and the beautiful.

It is not marrying the right partner, it is being the right partner.

It is discovering what marriage can be, at its best, as expressed in the words of Mark Twain used in the tribute to his wife:
Wherever she was, there was Eden.

--Wilfred A. Peterson

* * * * *

## The Golden Key

It was on a beautiful celestial day in the month celestial and in the celestial year of our Lord as a little Angel, all wiggles with excitment and anticipation, watched carefully beside the Golden Gates of Heaven the procassions of people arriving from Earth. He saw one of his angel friends come running towards him shouting with such great joy.

"Mama is coming today! The Gatekeeper just sent me word." "My daddy is coming too!" replied the first little one." and I am so excited I can hardly breathe..."

Before the two small friends could exchange another word the second little Angel darted out shouting.

"Mama. . .Mama. . . and Daddy and Bill and Biff. . . you're all here! What happened?" "We didn't see that car coming son," answered the fine looking man. The little Angel couldn't help but watch and listen, so great was their joyful reunion. The Gatekeeper arose and approached them saying, "Welcome to Eternity. I will show you to your separate mansions." "But we are all together now we will need only one home," protested the alarmed father. "Do you have the keys to your eternal home?" asked the Gatekeeper. "What keys do you mean?" cried the young mother. "Why the keys you recieved the day you entered the Temple of our God to be sealed for all time and eternity. . .your names were written on the records of your worthiness for your endowments."

The faces before him were grave as they answered, "But we were so far from the temple when we were married!" "And after your children were born?" queried the Gatekeeper. "Well we intended to each month that the ward excusions went but somehow something always came up to keep us from it. Oh Jim, why did we ever put it off?"

Words could not express their sorrow and arousing fear. "Will there be another chance? Please tell us! Will there?" "My children, you know the words of our Lord, your chance on earth has passed." "Please. . .Oh Please. . ., but a cloud seemed to envelope each one and they were borne away to the separate mansions of the eternities to receive their further instructions.

The little Angel's heart was heavy with sorrow for his small friend. He had run sobbing, still alone, back to the shade of the eternal tree, where but shortly before he had so eagerly and joyfully waited. The little Angel wondered and searched his memory. . .Had he ever heard his family mention the Keys to their mansions? He could not recall and so deep in thought was he that he did not see a tall dark man approach him quickly and bend over him.

"My little son!!! I knew I'd find you waiting here!"

With a shout of gladness the little Angel sprang into the longing, waiting arms and as he saw his own father's hands reach out to pick him up he saw the flash of a Golden Key. . .and he knew, he knew his joy was just beginning.

-- Mrs. Keith B. Harmon

* * * * *

## Not Just For Time

Jeanette's voice was rough with tears she was too proud to shed. "I don't see why you ever asked me in the first place if you didn't intend to go through with it."

Neil reached for her hand, but she jerked away impatiently. "Jeanette," he said, "listen to me. Not just with your ears; listen with your heart. I do love you. I want you to be my wife. But my furlough would be over before we could possibly get to the temple and back. Wouldn't you rather wait a few months and be married the right way?"

"A few months! How do you know it won't be years? Or forever? Neil Ernstrom, if you want me to marry you, it will have to be now or never!" Jeanette's face was set and stubborn, but she couldn't stop the trembling of her hands.

"Don't say that, darling. Would you really be happy with a home wedding? Do you want to hear those words, "Until death do you part" to us? Jeanette, I just don't go makeshifts. I like real, sterling things -- like you -- and like marriage for all eternity. Sweetheart, look at me."

Reluctantly she turned and looked into brown eyes filled with an acute tenderness, and it swept over her an instant that he really loved her. Her voice came softly then, "I know Neil. That's what we've always planned, but this is your last leave before you go overseas. You might never- Oh, Neil, I love you too much. If I can't have a temple wedding now, then I'll take next best. I'd be satisfied just to know that I belong to you. I want to write to you letters that begin "My dear, dearest husband."

"I know darling; I feel the same things only more. But can't you understand, Jeanette? I just won't feel right. I want to know that our marriage is sanctified and pure. Sweetheart, I'll come back to you. The waiting won't be long."

When he said "the waiting," there rose in Jeanette's thoughts the staring loneliness of the months she had already waited for him. Waiting seemed to her then the most miserable word she had ever heard. Swift rebellion brought her to her feet. "I'm not going to beg you any longer. After all, I do have some pride. You'd better go now, then, because I won't wait."

The boy in uniform sat stunned as she turned to leave him, but on a sudden thought, he jumped to his feet. "Jeanette! Wait! Let's go talk to the Bishop. We'll each tell him our ideas and ask him to advise us."

Her steps hesitated, and then she turned back with a breath of relief. "Oh, yes, Neil! I'm sure the bishop will convince you that I'm right."

Bishop Jones stood tall in the lighted doorway, his silver white hair shining above his youngish face. A warm handclasp and the twinkle in his deep-set blue eyes assured them of welcome. Come in! Come in and sit down. You nice kids have something on your minds?"

Neil told him why they had come and then suggested that Jeanette be first to explain her ideas.

Bishop Jones listened intently to Jeanette's fervent words, as the tears she had strained before to control fell now unnoticed.

"After all," she finished, "it isn't as if we can't be sealed in the temple after Neil comes back from overseas. We have our whole life to do that in." Content with her logic Jeanette sank back on the couch.

The bishop sat gazing thoughtfully at the toe of his shoe. Then he turned to Neil. "My boy, let's hear what you have to say."

Neil told of having witnessed a Temple marriage just before leaving for his mission. "Bishop, I don't need to tell you because you already know. Somehow it seemed to me as if the heavenly Father himself could have been watching there beside the couple, smiling his approval. It was the most beautiful, sacred moment I've ever known. It seemed like every sound in the world, even the heavens, were hushed, listening to that simple, sweet ceremony. I've always hoped my marriage could begin like that. To me, there is only one right way, the Lord's way. Anything less is only legal, not holy. Besides I want to be sure my children will be born under the covenant."

The bishop sat with his head in his hands for so long after Neil finished that the young couple began to wonder if he intended to speak at all. At last he said, "I realize you want me to tell you which of you is right. Instead, let me tell you a story. Maybe it will help you with your decision."

"A number of years ago, before the Arizona Temple was built, there was a young couple in Arizona who had a problem a little like yours. The young man (we'll call him Hiram) was a farmer. The savings he had would pay for their trip to the Salt Lake Temple to be married, or, if they didn't go to the temple, they'd have just enough to build a small house. The girl (shall we call her Elvira?) wanted very much to be married in the temple, but her young man convinced her that they'd go as soon as the first crop was harvested. They were married by their bishop and begun at once on their little house. The walls went up and the roof was on, but their money didn't stretch far enough for windows and doors. Hiram comforted his young wife, 'Don't mind that, Dear. We'll put them right in when we harvest the crop.'

When the money for their year's work came in, Hiram was full of happy plans. They'd have enough for the windows and doors, a little furniture, and seed for the next year's crop. 'At last, sweetheart, you can take down that makeshift, and we'll have real doors in our house. We'll get a comfortable bed for you, too. No more restless nights on the lumpy straw tick.'

"A little disturbed to see no response in his wife's face, he said, 'Elvira, what's the matter?'

"'Hiram,' she replied quietly, 'there's something I want far more than those things.'

"'What is it, Dear? You know I'll get it for you if I possibly can.'

"'Hiram! Oh, how could you forget? I want to go to the temple to have our marriage sealed, so my baby can be born under the covenant. I never will feel that our marriage really has the approval of our heavenly Father until we go to the temple.'

"Hiram stood thinking over what she had said. It seemed to him Elvira wasn't being practical. After all it was more important that they have seed for the crop so that they could at least survive. And what about their soon-to-be-born baby? It would be a long hard trip over rough roads. What if she should get sick on the way? It wasn't that he didn't want to go, but . . .

"'Elvira,' he said, 'let's wait until next year. Our financial situation will be more secure. And we wouldn't be risking your life and the baby's if we wait till them.'

"'Oh, please don't say wait! I've waited already till every day seems like a year. I'm not afraid. Surely our Father in heaven will help us. Besides, maybe we'll never get there if we don't go now. Please, Hiram.'"

"They went to the temple. The trip was long, and it was hard, but she returned safely. And their baby was born under the covenant, in a house without windows or doors in a bed made of straw. And the baby's mother was happy. She sang as she cared for her baby boy. He was hers, now, and in all the eternities to come. The cold winds that whistled in around the blanket hanging at the door had lost a little of their sting.

"It happened that Hiram and Elvira had to move to a part of Arizona where they had no contact with the Church. There were six more children, and Elvira tried to teach them the gospel from their earliest years. They were obedient children as they grew and learned to love righteousness, all except the eldest. His parents spent many sleepless hours worrying about their rebellious son. (Shall we call him Allen?)

"This boy left home early and went away to California where he married, at last, a girl who was a blues singer for a night club. Allen's wife, Belle was gone from home a good deal, but she did take time off work to have several children. Belle was a good girl, really, but her interest lay outside her home. Allen tried to take care of the children as best he could. Often he would come home from his work to find them wandering in the streets, dirty and neglected.

"Late one night when Allen came home, he found his three-year-old daughter lying across her bed barely able to breathe, her fever raging high. The house was dark, and the two older children were nowhere to be seen. A half hour later he was sitting beside her hospital bed. The doctor had told him the child had a critical case of pneumonia with possibly one chance in three to survive the night. As Allen sat there in helpless desperation, he tried to remember how to pray, but somehow the words sounded like an empty cry in the room.

"' Father in heaven. . .Oh, God. . .I don't even know if you listen to people like me, but I sure do need some help. She means such alot to me that I. . .Please listen. Don't let my little girl die. I know I haven't been like I should. But, won't you please help me? Oh, Father. . .Please listen to me.'

"The door opened and a man looked in. He said, 'They told me I'd find Brother Miller here. Can you tell me where he is?'

"Why, no. I don't know anyone by that name. . .Say, if you don't mind my asking. . . You said Brother Miller. . .Are you. . .a Latter-day Saint?'

"It happened that the man was an L.D.S. bishop. At Allen's request, he brought a companion, and they administered to the little girl. The bishop, staying afterward to talk to Allen, heard the story of his wanderings into despair, and how he himself had come in answer to Allen's prayer even as it was being uttered.

"With humble gratitude Allen watched his little girl begin to breathe more easily. The relief brought a long sigh to his lips. 'Going back over my life, Bishop, I can see now where I got off the path into this swamp, but now I'm in it, how can I get out? It seems like my life is just one dark stumble after another.'

"The bishop told Allen, 'The first step is to renew your activity in the Church, and then we'll help you along from there.'

"And he did move along from deacon on up to elder. Although it wasn't easy, he got the children ready each Sunday and took them with him.

"The day came when Allen was asked to give a talk in sacrament meeting. Belle hadn't shown any interest in his religious activity beyond a little ridicule. When he told her he was to speak in Church, she laughed. 'You preach in Church? What a joke! Now tell me another funny one.'

"As the service began, however, he was surprised to see Belle slip into a seat near the door. She had come for the first time into the chapel her husband had grown to love.

"When Allen rose to give the first speech of his life, the sight of his own wife sitting there, a mocking stranger to this beautiful gospel, brought all his longing into his throat and he stood for long moments unable to utter a sound. At last the tears began to slide down his face and his voice was released with them.

"'My brethren,' he said, 'and my sisters: I had carefully prepared a speech for you this evening, but I've decided instead to speak from my heart.' Then he related to them the story his mother had told him when he was a boy. He described the little dark house with a flopping blanket for a door. He told of her yearning for a temple marriage so that her children could be born under the covenant, of her courageous journey to the temple so that he, especially could have that blessing. 'My dear friends,' he said, 'I who had wandered into darkness have been brought back.

"'They tell me my wonderful mother left this life years ago, still longing for her one sheep who had strayed away. I hope that somewhere tonight she can know how grateful I am for her, for the things she taught me, for the sacrifices she made for me. Sometime maybe I can take her in my arms and tell her.'

"The men and women listening had come to love this humble man and sitting there motionless, they were moved indeed in their hearts. His gaze shifted to his wife, and he said, 'What would I give? Oh, my brothers and sisters, what wouldn't I give if I could know that one day I would enter that sacred temple with my wife and children and be sealed with them as a family for eternity. You can't know how I. . .There's nothing. . .' Allen stood at the pulpit struggling to go on. At last, he mumbled 'Amen' and sat down.

"After the services were over, I found my wife in the car. Belle was crying in great sobs. When I put my arms around her, she clung to me. 'Oh, my darling! I've lost you, although I see now I never had you. Where can I begin so I can come where you are?'"

Bishop Jones cleared his throat and sat silent, his head bowed low on his chest.

The young couple before him now pressed his hand in thanks, and walked quietly out of his house and down the street in thoughtful silence.

"He didn't know, did he, Neil, that he slipped and said 'I' instead of 'Allen' there at the end of his story. Isn't he simply wonderful? And Sister Jones! My goodness, I can't imagine her crooning in some night spot, can you? This gospel really does change people, doesn't it?"

"Yes, darling, it does. And you? I'm almost afraid to ask what you've decided."

"Oh, Neil, whatever made me want any way but the right way? I guess a few months won't seem long when I know we'll have forever together after that. But Neil. . . what if you're gone a whole year? You'd forget all about me by that time."

His arms closed tenderly around her, and she heard a soft whisper against her hair, "Forget you? No, Jeanette. I'll love you. . .not just for time, my darling, but for all eternity."

-- Lorraine R. Manderscheid

* * * * *

# MISSIONARY WORK

Bless us with a desire to reach thy Kingdom, and to bring those that we love with us.

-- Rusty Clark

* * * * *

Dare to be a Mormon,
Dare to stand alone.
Dare to have a purpose --
Dare to make it known.

* * * * *

## A Mission: A Foreordained Privilege

A recently returned mission president was visiting at the home of one of his recently released missionaries. He had the privilege of meeting his missionary's younger brother. As he was introduced to young Fred he asked his usual question: "How soon do you go on your mission?"

The answer was startling but not uncommon in the Latter-Day Saint homes of today. He said, "I don't know whether I am going on a mission. You see, I'm in medical school and I don't want to interrupt my formal education; then, too, I am in love with the finest girl I have met in my life and I don't want to lose her."

The mission president asked him if he had been formally called on a mission by the bishop. He answered, "yes."

Then, the mission president used another approach and said, "What do your parents think about your decision?" The answer was all too familiar. "They say, 'You have your free agency. It is up to you to make your decision.'"

The mission president asked the young man if he would visit with him in his office one day soon. He promised he would and within a matter of days the mission president had Fred as his visitor.

The president began their discussion by outlining to Fred the fact that his going on a mission was not hampered by the draft. He had not as yet married and truly it was his choice as to whether he should go. But, said the mission president, "You and your parents are in error when you say you have your free agency."

Joseph Smith writes, "Every man who has a calling to minister to the inhabitants of the world was ordained to that very purpose in the Grand Council of Heaven befor this world was."

The mission president continued. "It seems to me if we were foreordained to serve in the Spirit World in the Grand Council of Heaven that we would have had to consent to that calling before being ordained. At the time we consented we used up our free agency and the choice was no longer ours to whether we would fulfill the terms of that calling or not.

"In fact, it seems to me that we often misinterpret the principle of free agency in our lives. For instance, Fred, you are unmarried. You now have the privilege of going with any girl your heart chooses until you make a final determination and take her to the Temple. Once you have made your choice and she is sealed to you for eternities you have used up your free agency as far as girls are concerned. No longer are you able to in any way 'shop around.' Your determination has been made, your free agency exercised and no longer is free agency yours in this respect.

"By the same token, Fred, I think when you accepted your calling in the Grand Council of Heaven to be assigned to the House of Israel and elected to accept the call to 'minister to the inhabitants of the world' that your free agency, unless due to circumstances beyond your control, has been used up as far as your mission call is concerned.

"Now, you might say to yourself, 'I have no memory of having such a calling, and therefore I am not responsible to fulfill that calling.' But there is ample evidence scripturally that such callings were foreordained. Inasmuch as we walk by faith in this life rather than by sight and rememberance, these scriptures are given to us in order that we might know of a certainty that such foreordinations were real and are a matter of record.

"For instance, in the Pearl of Great Price, Chapter 3 Verses 22 and 23: 'Now the Lord had shown unto me, Abraham, the intelligences that were organized before the world was; and among all these there were many of the noble and great ones; And God saw these souls that they were good, and he stood in the midst of them, and he said: These I will make my rulers; for he stood among those that were spirits, and he saw that they were good; and he said unto me: Abraham, thou art one of them; thou wast chosen before thou was born.'

"In the Old Testament the Lord reaffirms the practice of foreordination by revealing His word to Jeremiah (Jeremiah, 1:4-5) 'Then the word of the Lord came unto me, saying, Before I formed thee in the belly I knew thee; and before thou camest forth out of the womb I sanctified thee, and I ordained thee a prophet unto the nations.' "

The mission president continued, "When I was 28 years old, I was ordained a Seventy by the late Levi Edgar Young, who was a member of the First Council of Seventy. After the ordination, President Young said, 'Would you like my line of authority?' After a recital of a short chain of brethern, he traced his authority back to his grandfather, Joseph Young.

"Then he repeated the circumstances connected with the calling and ordination of his grandfather to the office of Seventy. He said, 'The prophet met my grandfather on the street one day and told him that it had been made known to him, the prophet, that my grandfather, Joseph Young, was to be the first President of Seventy in this dispensation. In fact, the prophet said, you were foreordained to this very office and calling in the Grand Council of Heaven before this world was and I don't know whether to re-ordain you or not. But, I will for the record's sake.'

"The apostles of Christ chronicle that Christ was foreordained to his calling as the 'Redeemer of Mankind': 1st Peter, Chapter 1, Verses 18-20: 'Forasmuch as ye know that ye were not redeemed with corruptible things, as silver and gold, from your vain conversation received by tradition from your fathers; But with the precious blood of Christ as of a lamb without blemish and without spot: Who verily was foreordained before the foundation of the world, but was manifest in these last times for you.'

"Now," continued the mission president to Fred, "It is my faith and my testimony that you were called in the Grand Council of Heaven to be a 'leavening influence' to the world. In fact, to be a missionary unto our Father's other children and gather together those who were foreordained to become members of the Kingdom of Christ and those who in this mortal sphere have made themselves worthy to be adopted into the House of Israel through baptism.

"Our Father in Heaven has fulfilled His promises to you. You have been born in the choicest of all times when the light of the Gospel is on the earth. You live under the direction of a living prophet. You have choice parentage and you have been born under the covenant. You have been assigned to the House of Israel. The only way you can show your appreciation to your Father in Heaven for these great blessings, which exceed all other blessings in this life, is to accept your mission call and be of service in our Father's eternal plan. You have even specifically been assigned to the House of Ephriam, which is the tribe of service. The Lord rarely speaks of the children of Ephriam but what He refers to them as, 'My servants', as is evidenced in the 133rd section of the Doctrine and Covenants where the Lord is telling of the gathering in the last days in the center place of Zion: 'And they shall bring forth their rich treasures unto the children of Ephriam, My servants. And the boundaries of the everlasting hills shall tremble at their presence. And there shall they fall down and be crowned with glory, even in Zion, by the hands of the servants of the Lord, even the children of Ephriam.'

"In the 12th chapter of Revelations, written by John, the Lord describes in detail to us the battle that took place in Heaven. Many of us think that when Satan and his angels were cast out of Heaven that the battle ended. However, the battle ground merely changed places and John records a warning to those who live on the earth in the 12th verse: 'Woe to the inhabiters of the earth and of the sea! For the Devil is come down unto you, having great wrath, because he knoweth that he hath but a short time.'

"Joseph Smith records in his writings, 'In relation to the Kingdom of God, the Devil always sets up his kingdom at the very same time in opposition to God.'

"Now, Fred," concluded the mission president, "let me put it to you 'cold turkey.' Are you going to fulfill your promises to the Lord or are you going to find an excuse and follow the enticings of the evil one, who in the battle in Heaven drew one third of the children of our Father in Heaven with him?'"

There was a long pause as the mission president waited for an answer. Then came the firm resolution, "I'm going to talk to my bishop and tell him if he will reissue the call, I intend to fulfill my foreordained privilege."

The rightness of his decision was evidenced one year later when Fred wrote to his concerned advisor: "Dear President, I first must thank you for your inspired and persuasive remarks in my indicisive moments of one year past. Having now completed one year of my mission, I can now gaze in retrospect and classify this as the most developing year of my life. I wrote Mom and Dad recently and told them that if ever I influence a younger generation I would hope to instill within them the vital importance of each young man fulfilling an honorable mission. I sometimes could weep as I think how nearly I overlooked the only value of lasting import in my life -- the Gospel."

--Submitted by David A. McDougal

* * * * *

# MOTHER

Let a mother counsel her children with love as well as with knowledge, for a proud youth may not heed his mother's words -- but he will not forget her love.

* * * * *

No matter to what heights God has attained or may attain, he does not stand alone; for side by side with him, in all her glory, a glory like unto his, stands a companion, the Mother of his children. For as we have a Father in heaven, so also we have a Mother there, a glorified, exalted ennobled Mother. That is a startling doctrine, I recognize, to some folks, and yet we ought to be governed by reason in giving consideration to this doctrine which is a revelation from God . . . Motherhood is eternal with Godhood, and there is no such thing as eternal or endless life without the eternal and endless continuation of motherhood.

--Melvin J. Ballard

* * * * *

## Miracles

God took the pureness of the lily,
Softness of the clouds above,
The strength of the mighty oak tree,
And he formed a mother's love.

He took calmness from the gentle brook
And patience for a start,
He added faith and gratitude
And made a mother's heart.

--Lois Ann Williams

* * * * *

What would you take for the soft little head
Pressed close to your face at time of bed;
For that white, dimpled hand in your own held tight,
And the dear little eyelids kissed down for the night?
What would you take?

What would you take for that smile in the morn,
Those bright, dancing eyes and the face they adorn;
For the sweet little voice that you hear all day
Laughing and cooing -- yet nothing to say?
What would you take?

What would you take for those pink little feet,
Those chubby round cheeks, and that mouth so sweet;
For the wee tiny fingers and little soft toes,
The wrinkly little neck and that funny little nose?
What would you take?

* * * * *

## When Mothers Sing

When mothers sing the home is sweet,
And peace and joy abound;
Troubles seem to fade away,
Before this happy sound.

Children smile and baby coos
And Dad forgets his care;
Faith and hope and harmony
Dwell securely there.

Singing mothers everywhere,
Patient, tender, strong,
Send to Heaven this daily prayer --
"Lord, make my life a song."

* * * * *

She mended a doll, and the washing waited.
The dust lay thick while a fishhook was baited.
When company attacked, her dinner was eaten up.
She made a bed for a straying pup.
A ten-year-old helped with the cookie dough.
Her ironing dries out while she plays in the snow.
Her neighbors whisper to one another,
But I just laugh and adore my mother.

--Gale Kamp

* * * * *

She came tonight as I sat alone
The girl that I used to be . . .
And she gazed at me with her earnest eye
And questioned reproachfully:

Have you forgotten the many plans
And hopes that I had for you?
The great career, the splendid fame
All wonderful things to do?

Where is the mansion of stately height
With all of its gardens rare?
The silken robes that I dreamed for you
And the jewels for your hair?

And as she spoke I was very sad,
For I wanted her pleased with me . . .
This slender girl from the shadowy past
The girl that I used to be.

So gently arising, I took her hand,
And guided her up the stair
Where peacefully sleeping, my babies lay
Innocent, sweet and fair.

And I told her that these are my only gems,
And precious they are to me;
That silken robe is my motherhood
Of costly simplicity.

And my mansion of stately height is love,
And the only career I know;
Is serving each day in these sheltering walls
For the dear ones who come and go.

And as I spoke to my shadowy guest,
She smiled through her tears at me;
And I saw that the woman that I am now
Pleased the girl that I used to be . . .

--Author unknown

* * * * *

Beatitudes for Women

Blessed is she whose daily tasks are a lobor of love; for her willing hands and happy heart translate duty into privilege, and her labor becomes a service to God and all mankind.

Blessed is she who opens the door to welcome both stranger and well-loved friend; for gracious hospitality is a test of brotherly love.

Blessed is she who mends stockings and toys and broken hearts; for her understanding is a balm to humanity.

Blessed is she who scours and scrubs; for well she knows that cleanliness is one expression of Godliness.

Blessed is she whom children love; for the love of a child is more to be valued than fortune or fame.

Blessed is she who sings at her work; for music lightens the heaviest load and brightens the dullest chore.

Blessed is she who dusts away doubt and fear and sweeps out the cobwebs of confusion; for her faith will triumph over all adversity.

Blessed is she who serves laughter and smiles with every meal; for her bouyancy of spirit is an aid to mental and physical digestion.

Blessed is she who preserves the sanctity of the Christian home; for hers is a sacred trust that crowns her with dignity.

--Author unknown

* * * * *

## Before It's Too Late

A Father, talking to his careless daughter, said:

"I want to speak to you of your mother. It may be that you have noticed a careworn look upon her face lately. Of course, it has not been brought there by an act of yours, still it is your duty to chase it away. I want you to get up tomorrow morning and get breakfast; and when your mother comes, and begins to express her surprise, go right up to her and kiss her on the mouth. You can't imagine how it will brighten her dear face.

"Besides, you owe her a kiss or two. Away back, when you were a little girl, she kissed you when no one else was tempted by your fever-tainted breath and swolen face. You were not as attractive then as you are now. And through those years of childish sunshine and shadows she was always ready to cure, by the magic of a mother's kiss, the dirty, little, chubby hands whenever they were injured in those first skirmishes with the rought old world.

"And then the midnight kiss with which she routed so many sad dreams, as she learned above your restless pillow, have all been on interest these long, long years.

"Of course, she is not so pretty and kissable as you are. Her face has more wrinkles than yours, and yet, if you were sick, that face would appear far more beautiful than an angel's as it hovered over you, watching every opportunity to minister to your comfort, and every one of those wrinkles would seem to be bright wavelets of sunshine chasing each other over the dear face.

"She will leave you one of these days. These burdens, if not lifted from her shoulders, will break her down. Those rough, hard hands that have done so many necessary things for you will be crossed upon her lifeless breast.

"Those neglected lips that gave you your first baby kiss, will be closed forever, and those sad, tired eyes will have opened in eternity and then you will forever appreciate your mother. Remember her before it's too late."

* * * * *

## Mother and her Secret

You hear a lot about kids fooling there mothers, but you hardly ever hear of a mother fooling her kids. But I know one who did. Mine. But in the end we found out the truth about her.

We grew up during the depression. Now kids today may not know what a depression means. It doesn't mean one car in the family and steak once a week, even if that is as ghastly a life as kids today can imagine. The depression meant no shoes, no meat, and barely enough shelter -- with a frightening chance that the whole family would be evicted into the street. That was the depression and it was still harder my father had left us.

Well, all through those years my mother managed to keep her four children fed, sheltered, clothed, and in school. Her hair turned white before she was thirty-five. She was cheerful enough, but her eyes had a sort of haunted look. She never had any pretty clothes or good times.

When we four kids grew up, we all did well enough to pool a fairly handsome hunk of cash to send to mom each week, so that whatever years she had left from about fifty on would be different from the years before. But we were all kind of disappointed in mom's new life. She didn't move into a new home; she said she was perfectly comfortable in the old one. She didn't hire any help to take her off her feet; she said she liked doing housework. She didn't buy any pretty clothes. She kept delaying the vacations to Florida or to Europe that we planned for her, until we finally gave up planning. Still, that weekly check came in, and, as we figured it, since she didn't spend more than a fraction of it each week she must have saved a considerable sum by the time she died, some twenty years later.

Well, when we went through her papers, we found out that mom was broke. Those checks had been spent the instant they arrived. On what? As soon as we kids were off her back, Mom had arranged with a refugee outfit to ship her four war orphans from Europe. She'd set them up in a home near ours, and for twenty years she'd educated them, seen them through sickness and teen-age problems, and in two cases, into marriage.

She never told us about the four new kids. I guess she wasn't sure we'd approve of her going through the whole mess all over again. I'm not sure we would have, either. You see, it isn't easy for kids who have grown up seeing their mothers knock themselves out half their lives to raise them to understand that motherhood is a sort of incurable condition.

* * * * *

"Mother, are there really angels?"

"Yes, darling, our Bible tells us there are."

"I want to find an angel, mother -- one that I can see and touch and talk to. If I have to go miles and miles, I am going to find a real angel."

"That is a good plan, son. I will go with you, for you are too little to go far alone."

So they started out. The child ran and leaped, and the little mother followed as bravely as she could, for she was lame, and the child forgot that she could not run, and he ran on ahead. Presently a chariot came along with a lovely woman in it, dressed in beautiful clothes. The child ran close to the carriage.

"Oh, are you an angel?" But the beautiful lady just stared at the child, said not a word, then motioned to the coachman. He whipped up the horses, and dust flew in the child's eyes. He gasped for breath, but his mother came along and wiped his eyes and soothed him.

"That was not an angel!" exclaimed the son.

"No, indeed, son. Nothing like one."

He ran on again. Soon he met a beautiful young girl all in white. "I am sure you must be an angel!" he cried. The girl blushed. "You are a sweet child. Someone else said that only last evening. Do I really look like an angel?" She took him up in her arms and kissed him tenderly. But suddenly her face changed. "Oh, there is my love coming to meet me, and you have mussed my dress and soiled it! Hurry away, child, and go home to mother!"

She put the child down hastily, so he tumbled and fell in the dusty road. As he sobbed, his mother came along and comforted him.

"I don't believe she was an angel either, Mother"

"No, son, but she is young. She may be some day."

"I'm so tired, mother. Will you carry me home?"

"That is why I came, son." She picked him up tenderly, and carried him the long way home, singing softly. Suddenly he put his arms tight about her neck, and looked into her face.

"Mother, I never really knew before how beautiful you are! Oh, could you -- are you an angel, mother?" The mother brushed away the tears. "Oh, foolish child, who ever heard of an angel in a blue gingham dress!" But she stepped along lightly until you could hardly have known she was lame.

The little boy smiled. He knew in his heart that he had found a real angel -- one that he could see and touch and talk to -- his mother!

--Author Unknown

* * * * *

## A Letter to Mother

I didn't understand, until later, the reason for the feeling of sadness that lay so heavily on my heart that particular morning. It had started early, even before I had risen from my bed. Indeed, it must have awakened me from a troubled sleep, and I remained awake, struggling with a feeling of such inexpressible sadness that I had the strangest desire to weep, but I did not know why.

During the remainder of those early hours I tried to recover from the emotional disturbance within me. After I arrived at my office, I closed the door and began sorting the papers on my desk that needed my attention: contracts and agreements to be studied, correspondence to be read, letters to be written. Letters! With a sudden twing of conscience I remembered a letter I had neglected to write, one that I had been telling myself I would write -- soon. How easy to promise, and how easy to forget. How natural to put off until a more convenient time that which did not demand the present time that which could be put off, I thought. Well, now was the time, and so I wrote:

Dearest Mom:

I have had such a feeling of loneliness this morning that I feel the need to tell you how much I love you and miss the close companionship I so much enjoyed when I was home with you and Dad. If I have neglected to tell you this as often as I should, I hope you will forgive me. And since you are the kind of mother you are, I know forgiveness is in your heart even before I ask for it.

As I think of the words I should write, I remember the years that have passed since my childhood years of your love and sacrifice that are now so vivid in my memory but which during those early years were so much taken for granted. And I know you would not have had it otherwise, for thoughts of obligation of child to parents would have taken away much of the happiness of that world in which I lived. However, if I had known then, or if I had been capable of fully comprehending your sacrifices, the depth of my gratitude and my acknowledgments of it might have been hastened.

For some reason my memory of these years is more vivid this morning than ever before. As I sit here it is as though you are very near to me. I almost feel your presence by my side. How wonderful is the truth revealed through Joseph Smith to our spirits, that eternal part of us, may commune with each other and ignore the distance that separates us!

As I grew older, I began to understand the meaning of the bits of conversation I heard concerning the story of my birth. I began to understand the great physical sacrifice you made that I might possess a body and enter into this phase of my probation. When I learned that for many days after my birth you hovered between life and death I wondered, and still ask the question: can anything I do in life compensate for such sacrifice?

I have been reasonably successful in my business affairs. Were it not that the thought is unkind, I could almost wish that you and Dad needed my help. But even as I think of it I can almost hear you say as you have said many times, "Son, your continued progress in the Kingdom of God is to us more than payment in full for all we have done." Such ties of indebtedness adds strength to seal that binds the children to their fathers and mothers in love and gratitude throughout eternity. There never fails to be an endearing relationship between the giver of the gift and the receiver, if spirits are in tune and hearts are filled with love and gratitude. I know it is so, for I have felt it in my life, and I have seen it in yours. It is one of the few enduring things we can cling to in this sadly mixed-up world.

I hope your understanding heart will fill in those words I hope for and cannot find. And I wish, oh so earnestly, there could be some way to hasten that time when a child begins to fully understand and appreciate the love that lies in mother's heart!

Your loving son,

Robert

I sat quietly for a moment and then folded that letter. I was placing it in an envelope when my secretary entered, a telegram in her hand. I opened it and read:

Dear Son:

Your mother passed away early this morning. We had not known of her heart condition. Her last words were, "Tell Robert I love him."

* * * * *

## OPPORTUNITY

The secret of success in life is for a man to be ready for his opportunity when it comes.

-- Benjamin Disraeli

* * * * *

No power on earth can keep a first class man down or a fourth class man up.

* * * * *

Try to put well in practice what you already know; in so doing you will, in good time, discover the hidden things which you now inquire about.

-- Rembrandt

* * * * *

When one door closes, another opens; but we often look so long and regretfully at the closed door, that we do not see the one which has opened for us.

* * * * *

# PRAYER

Prayer will change the night to day.

* * * * *

A man suffering from insomnia asked a friend how he managed to sleep so well every night. "Do you count sheep?" he asked.

"No," replied the friend, "I talk to the Shepherd."

-- Harold Taylor

* * * * *

When President Spencer W. Kimball was in Washington, D. C. for the opening of the Washington Temple for public tours, he was invited to give the prayer for the Senate one morning. Not all of the Senators show up in time for the prayer. The President of the Senate was apologizing to President Kimbal for not having many there to hear his prayer. President Kimball's comment: "Oh, that's all right. I wasn't praying to them, anyway."

-- L. Tom Perry

* * * * *

I don't know of a single foreign product that enters this country untaxed except the answer to prayer.

-- Mark Twain

* * * * *

## Prayer Is The Key

Prayer is the key that opens the door
To a storehouse of wonderful things.
From the feeling of joy that accompanies
good health
To the peace that a happy heart brings.
Prayer is the key that opens the door
To blessings, tremendous and small,
And the wonder, you see, is the fact
that this "key"

Is a privilege extended to all!

-- Lucille Boesken

* * * * *

It made me shiver. And I about made up my mind to pray and see if I couldn't try to quit being the kind of boy I was and be better. So I kneeled down. But the words wouldn't come. Why wouldn't they? It warn't no use to try and hide it from Him . . . I knowed very well why they wouldn't come. It was because my heart warn't right; it was because I warn't square; it was because I was playing double. I was letting on to give up sin, but away inside of me I was holding on to the biggest one of all. I was trying to make my mouth say I would do the right thing and the clean thing . . . But deep down in me, I knowed it was a lie, and He knowed it. You can't pray a lie — I found that out.

-- Huckleberry Finn

* * * * *

## Prayer

I got up early one morning
And rushed right into the day,
I had so much to accomplish
That I didn't have time to pray.

Problems came tumbling about me
And heavier came each task
Why doesn't God help me? I wondered
He answered, "You didn't ask."

I wanted to see joy and beauty
But the day dragged on, gray and bleak,
I wondered why God didn't show me
He said, "But you didn't see."

I tried to come into God's presence;
I used all the keys at the lock,
God gently and lovingly chided,
"My child, you didn't knock."

So I woke early this morning
And paused before entering the day,
I had so much to accomplish,
That I had to take time to pray.

* * * * *

He who prays as he ought will endeavor to live as he prays.

-- Owen

* * * * *

Prayer crowns God with the honor and glory due to his name and God crowns prayer with assurance and comfort. The most praying souls are the most assured souls.

-- T. Brooks

* * * * *

## Prerequisite

I prayed for strength when life pulsed low
Until God answered me:
"Go lift the load from weary ones,
Then I will strengthen thee."

I asked for courage when hope despaired,
Then came the voice benigh:
"Inspire with faith thy brother's soul,
And I'll inspire thine."

I longed for light when darkness made
Me stumble through the night:
"Thy lamp held high for others' feet
Will make thy pathway bright."

I prayed that wisdom, talent, skill
Increase their meager store:
"First share the portions that you have,
And I will give thee more."

At length I learned that blessings sought,
And help for which I pray,
Are only mine when shed abroad
And give, first, away.

-- Leila Grace Bassford

* * * * *

## A Child's Prayer

Dear God:

Sometimes
The whole day long-
I don't know why-
I do things wrong.

My mother calls
And I don't heed;
I turn my back
On friends in need.

I don't do work
I ought to do;
I even fail
To think of you.

I'm sorry, God,
For days like these
And hope you will
Forgive me please.
And grant me, God,
A chance I pray,
To do my best
Another day.

-- Anonymous

* * * * *

## I Knelt To Pray When Day Was Done

I knelt to pray when day was done
And prayed, "Oh Lord bless everyone.
Lift from each saddened heart the pain
And let the sick be well again."
And then I woke another day and
Carelessly went on my way.
The whole day long, I did not try
To wipe a tear from any eye;
I did not try to share the load
Of any brother on the road.
I did not even go to see
The sick man just next door to me.

Yet once again when day was done,
I prayed, "Oh Lord, bless everyone."
But as I prayed, into my ear
There came a voice that whispered clear
"Pause now, my son, before you pray.
Whom did you try to bless today?
God's sweetest blessings always go
By hands that serve him here below."
And then I hid my face and cried,
Forgive me, God, I have not tried;
But let me live another day
And I will live the way I pray.

* * * * *

## The Man Who "Prayed About It"

Anything of worth--he "prayed about it". . .
The stranger that I talked to now and then;
It was always at an unexpected moment
That I'd see him and we'd stop to chat again.

He always smiled, as if he'd found a secret
To peace within himself. . .and heart's content;
He'd say of some new thought, "I'll pray about it"
And that was just exactly what he meant--

He must've gone away--I never see him,
But I'll always have a special memory
Of the pleasant little man who "prayed about it"
And left a bit of extra faith with me.

The years have passed--yet I still "pray about it"
However large or small the matter seems. . .
Somehow it just works out a little better
When you "pray about" new tasks or special dreams.

'Cause life's not apt to be too much to handle. . .
No worthwhile thing's impossible to do
And there's no need or hope so complicated
So difficult that faith can't see it through--

So whenever I'm impatient or uncertain. . .
When the course seems long and I begin to doubt it,
I recall the cheerful stranger's special courage
Then I find a quiet place. . . and "pray about it."

-- D. A. Marcum



* * * * *

## Conversation At Eventide

"This morning, Lord, when first I met the day,
I prayed for patience. I said, 'Whatever way
The hours unfold, Lord, let me be
Calm and loving -- kind and wise like Thee.'

"Thus, Lord, I prayed, and as the moments mounted and the din
I said, 'Keep controlled; no problem; just let His presence in.'
The day is ended, Lord, I come on bended knees
To thank Thee for thy help this day,
Be with me again tomorrow, please."

-- Mabel Jones Gabbott

* * * * *

## Prayers Before Apricots

Recently, I came across a talk which had been given by one of my daughters to a group of mothers and daughters, in which she related an experience with her first-born son. In this talk she related this experience, and I quote:

"Many years ago when our oldest son was a very little boy I found myself, one warm summer night after supper, frantically trying to finish canning apricots. I am sure that you all know the scene, you young mothers. Everything has happened during the day to keep you from getting to that project and finishing it. And now with the baby settled for the night and your husband off to his meeting on time, your little three- and four-year-olds are all but finished getting their pajamas on and getting ready for bed -- you think well, now I will get to those apricots. You realize that they are just not going to last until morning.

"This was the situation I found myself in that night, so I was beginning to peel and then to pit them when my two little boys appeared in the kitchen and announced that they were ready to say their prayers. In desperation and not wanting to be interrupted for the umpteenth time, I said to them very quickly, "Now boys, why don't you just run in and say your prayers alone tonight and mother will just keep working with these apricots."

"But David, the older of the two, planted his little feet firmly in front of me and asked, not unkindly, "But mommy, which is more important, prayers of apricots?" Little did I realize then as a young mother and a busy wife, that in my life ahead there would be many such dilemmas that I would be faced with, large and small, as I carried out this role as wife and mother in my home, and that my success in this responsibility would be measured by the manner in which I was able to solve problems.

This was my challenge then, and this, as I see it, is your challenge as wives and mothers today. How do we meet that challenge? is the big question of our lives."

What a lesson in priorities that little boy taught his mother. Prayers should come before apricots!

-- Harold B. Lee

* * * * *

## The Faith Of A Child

I heard of a nine-year-old boy, an orphan, who was hurried off to the hospital where examination indicated that he had to be operated on without delay. He had been living with friends who had given him a home. His father and mother (when they were alive) had taught him to pray. Thus, when he came to the hospital, the thing he wanted was to have the Lord help him.

The doctors had decided to hold a consultation. When he was wheeled into the operating room, he looked around and saw the nurses and the doctors who had consulted his case. He knew that it was very serious and he said to one of them as they were preparing to give him the anesthetic: "Doctor, before you begin to operate, won't you please pray for me?"

The doctor, with seeming embarrassment, offered his excuse and said, "I can't pray for you." Then the boy asked the other doctor, with the same result.

Finally, something very remarkable happened. This little fellow said, "If you can't pray for me, will you please wait while I pray for myself?"

They removed the sheet and he knelt on the operating table, bowed his head and said, "Heavenly Father, I am only an orphan boy, I am awful sick. Won't you please make me well?" "Bless these men who are going to operate that they will do it right. If you will make me well, I will try to grow up to be a good man. Thank you, Heavenly Father, for making me well."

When he got through praying, he lay down. The doctors' and nurses' eyes filled with tears. Then he said, "I am ready."

The operation was performed. The little fellow was taken back to his room and in a few days they took him from the hospital, well on the way to complete recovery.

Some days after that, a man who had heard of the incident went to the office of the surgeons and said, "Tell me about the operation you performed a few days ago -- the operation on the little boy."

The surgeon said, "I have operated on several little boys." The man added, "This little boy wanted someone to pray for him."

The surgeon said seriously, "There was such a case but I don't know but that it is too sacred a thing for me to talk about."

The man said, "Doctor, if you will tell me, I will treat it with respect, I would like to hear it."

Then the doctor told the story as I have told it here, and added: "I would like to tell you, I have operated an hundreds of people, men and women, who thought they had faith to be healed. But never until I stood over that little boy have I felt the Spirit of God as I felt it then. That boy opened the windows of heaven and talked to his Heavenly Father as one would have talked to his friends face to face. I want to say to you that I am a better man for having had this experience of standing and hearing a little boy talk to his Father in Heaven."

* * * * *

## Can You Teach Johnny To Pray?

Ellen Blair sat motionless. Aimlessly her eyes followed the delicate patterns on the wall made by the first rays of the morning sun as it filtered through the glass doors on the hospital corridor. The sparrows in the cypress trees outside the window had begun their twittering, and she realized the long night's vigil had passed.

A deep ache filled her heart. She was grateful to have her husband, Michael, beside her. It was he who had answered the telephone call last night that had summoned them to Valley Hospital. The brief explanation was that there had been an automobile accident following the commencement exercises at the high school. Their son Robert, still in his cap and gown, had been seriously injured.

Ellen blinked as if to blot out the image of the still, white face of her oldest son, lying unconscious on the elevated pillows in the emergency room.

"Concussion, skull fracture," the doctor had said. "The spinal tap showed blood in it, so we must do a craniotomy right away to try to locate the bleeding. If we can stop the hemorrhage, there is a chance; if not --" But he had not continued.

They had sat in the waiting room through the long hours, each praying silently. Ellen trembled as the realization of her son's serious condition again enveloped her.

Suddenly an unexpected commotion broke the quiet of the early dawn. It was Johnny Hansen, Robert's closest friend, who dashed through the swinging door. His tousled brown hair showed a quick combing. His white shirt, not completely tucked in, gave evidence of his rush.

"I just heard about Bob! How bad --"

Seeing the anxiety in the faces before him, he did not finish his question. Ellen tried to explain the seriousness of Robert's injuries, but her voice broke and she gave way to quiet crying. Michael carried on.

As their whispering voices became a monotone, Ellen's thoughts drifted back over the years since that August day 18 years ago, when Robert was born in this same hospital. . .

He had been such a red-faced little mite, as scrawny as a baby bird. How quickly the time had passed! It seemed only yesterday that he was fumbling and struggling over his new tricycle, still tied with Christmas ribbons. Before there had been time to think about it, Robert had gone to his first day of school, a little frightened, perhaps, but quite grown up in new blue jeans and red corduroy shirt. How many times she had wanted to fix these pictures forever in her mind! But each new stage replaced the last, and Robert showed an eagerness for all sorts of activity. Primary classes provided new growth, and the Cub pack brought wider fields to explore.

About this time the Hansens moved next door. In a neighborly way she sent Robert over with a plate of cookies, and in return he brought Johnny home with him.

It was not until a few days passed that she realized how much Johnny's environment was unlike Robert's. The ideals and standards were quite the reverse in Johnny's home. Drinking, smoking, and foul language were commonplace, and religion played no part at all in their way of life. She was reluctant to have Robert cultivate this friendship, but the two boys seemed drawn together like magnets.

Since Johnny was three years older than Robert, he was more mature and became an ideal in the eyes of her eight-year-old. They were always together. Then, in a child's most natural way, Johnny began to go to Primary with Robert.

One day the two boys came racing home from Primary, Johnny in the lead until they reached the door. Then he shyly stood behind it while Robert anxiously grasped her hand, pulled her into the hallway, and whispered into her ear.

"Mom, can you teach Johnny to pray?"

The unexpected request brought a lump to her throat when she looked at this shy, sensitive boy who normally bluffed his way with a rough exterior. He had been asked to give the opening prayer in Primary the next Wednesday.

"Of course we will help Johnny."

She went into the living room, and the boys followed her.

"You know what prayer really is, don't you, Johnny?"

"Yeah, I guess so."

"Jesus said that whatever righteous desire we ask for in prayer, if we believe, we will receive it."

"He did?"

"Yes. Prayer is not only words; it is talking with our Heavenly Father. Have you heard the hymn we sing at church that says, 'Prayer is the soul's sincere desire'?" She hummed a few strains of the hymn.

"Yeah."

"You know, Mom, they sang it at Primary conference," Robert commented, wanting to help with this important project.

"There are certain words we use in praying to show reverence and respect, such as thee and thou, and thy and thine. One of the first things we express in prayer is our thankfulness for our many blessings. You know what your blessings are, I'm sure."

"I guess everything good is a blessing," Johnny answered.

Together they wrote out a very brief outline for a prayer, and Johnny agreed to work on it.

The following Wednesday when Robert came home from Primary, he was not his usual, exuberant self, and the absence of Johnny was noticeable. Ellen could not help asking, "Robert, how did Johnny get along with the opening prayer?" But Robert evaded the question. With a shrug he went to his room.

Although perturbed, Ellen did not pursue the subject, but she asked Sister Lindley, the Primary president, about it when she met her the next day at the market.

"Oh, he tried," she said, "but he was so frightened after muttering a few inaudible words, he turned and ran out the door."

Her thoughts drifted next to the summer evening when Johnny was at their home at dinner time. She and Michael gathered their children around the dinner table to kneel for family prayer. Since Johnny appeared reluctant to leave, she asked, "Would you like to join us?"

Johnny nodded and had just fallen to his knees beside Robert when Mr. Hansen's bellowing voice came through the open window. "Johnny! Johnny! Where is that good-for-nothing kid? He better get home or --"

She saw the red creep up the boy's neck as he murmured, "I gotta go."

Obviously dreading the encounter with his father, he slipped out the back door.

The summer Robert was ordained to the priesthood, Johnny asked if he might be baptized. The bond between the boys seemed stronger than ever, and soon Johnny was also ordained a deacon. She remembered when he asked her husband, Michael, to explain a quotation he had heard in his quorum meeting: ". . .no man taketh this honour unto himself, but he that is called of God, as was Aaron."

"Even Jesus Christ himself had to be called of God, Johnny. He left the priesthood on the earth with his apostles, and they used it until there was a great apostasy of Christ's Church." Michael had patiently explained.

"Then how come we have it now?" asked Johnny.

"You know the story of Joseph Smith?"

"Sure."

"Well, in 1829 the priesthood was restored to Joseph by a heavenly messenger," Michael had continued.

"You mean it was passed down to us from the Prophet?"

"From the Prophet Joseph Smith or Oliver Cowdery -- they both received it at the same time."

Michael had felt some reservation about the young boy's comprehension of the priesthood and its true purpose, but he appreciated the boy's concern for it. . .

Soon after Johnny had been ordained a priest, he was asked to administer the sacrament in Sunday School. When he refused, his priests quorum adviser told him it was very simple: the card with the prayer written on it would be on the sacrament table, and he could read it, so he finally reluctantly agreed.

The first young priest blessed the bread. Then it was Johnny's turn to bless the water. He began falteringly, then stopped. He had misread the words. Again he started, and again he misread the words. The bishop asked him to repeat it, and a third time he started, then faltered and stopped. There was a tenseness in the air that could be felt throughout the congregation. Then suddenly Johnny stood up, crimson-faced, and left the chapel, while the other priest quietly took his place and gave the blessing on the water. It was many weeks before Johnny came back to church.

The Blairs had wondered what changes would take place when Johnny was graduated from high school. Would the friendship that had developed between these two boys fade? But college life did not spoil the admiration Johnny held for his young friend, and it was during the first semester of his second year that he had written Robert of his thrill at meeting the girl he planned to marry. He had added, "She is a wonderful girl, Bob, and a member of the Church. We wonder if your parents would go with us when we are married in the temple."

Ellen and Michael did accompany Johnny and his young bride to the temple. And as she saw them kneeling at the altar, she heard again in her mind Robert's childish plea, "Mom, can you teach Johnny to pray?". . .

Ellen was snapped abruptly back to reality as the white stretcher was wheeled down the hall. Terrible fear gripped her again as she looked at Robert's still form, his head swathed in bandages. Helplessly she looked at Michael, then at Johnny. A tear was trickling down his cheek.

The stretcher was wheeled into a room and the door closed behind it. When it opened again the two men in white wheeled the empty stretcher out, and a nurse came to the door.

"Dr. Klein, the specialist, is still in surgery, but he'll be here soon to talk with you. Dr. Snow is coming now," she said, nodding toward the doctor coming down the hall.

Both the doctor and nurse stepped into the room and again closed the door, leaving Michael, Ellen, and Johnny waiting in the hall.

Time seemed to stand still; then Dr. Snow reappeared and indicated that they should come in. His deep voice, though hardly above a whisper, seemed like the roar of a lion when he said, "Your son is not responding. I will call Dr. Klein, but I'm afraid it might be too late."

"Why? Oh, why?" Ellen sobbed.

It was Johnny's voice she heard now, faltering, "Please, could I pray for him?"

Not knowing exactly what to do, Johnny knelt clumsily beside the bed. The words came from the very depth of his soul, direct and meaningful, in gratitude for all that Robert had meant to him and for the teachings that had found a place, bit by bit, in his life. With firm conviction, he pleaded for the life of his friend. ". . . but in all things, Father in heaven," he prayed, "even in this, we ask that thy will, not ours, be done, but give us the wisdom to understand. . ."

The door opened. It was Dr. Klein, still in his surgical gown. "Dr. Snow just talked to me. We have done all we can do. I'm sorry," Dr. Klein said softly.

From years of habit the doctor automatically placed his fingers on his patient's wrist. He hesitated, then hastily but gently pulled back the sheet and placed his stethoscope on the boy's chest. Several times he shifted the stethoscope. He looked puzzled and the furrows deepened between his shaggy brows.

For many seconds no word was spoken. Then he abruptly ordered the nurse, "Replace the oxygen tent."

Ellen heard in her mind once more, "Mom, can you teach Johnny to pray?"

-- Jane S. Jamison
Reprinted with permission
Improvement Era, June, 1968

* * * * *

# PREPARATION

Luck is what happens when Preparation meets opportunity.

* * * * *

Be sure you take an interest in the future. That's where you will spend the rest of your life.

* * * * *

If you start soon enough, you won't have to run so fast to catch up.

* * * * *

Dig a well before you are thirsty.

-- Chinese Proverb

* * * * *

We were born to prepare to live, and we live to prepare to die.

-- Sterling W. Sill

* * * * *

There is an urgency in this day for us to prepare for the coming of the Lord. For those who have heeded the warning and continue in their preparations to accumulate the oil of righteousness in their lamps, great blessings are theirs.

-- Marvin J. Ashton

* * * * *

To be educated is to realize the implications of one's own beliefs.

* * * * *

To be educated is to Think clearly, Do well in the worlds work and the Power to appreciate life.

-- Brigham Young

* * * * *

# PROCRASTINATION

Procrastination is the thief of eternal life.

-- Joseph Fielding Smith

* * * * *

Procrastination is telling the Lord: "I'm not interested today."

-- Robert G. Allen

* * * * *

Joshua didn't say to "Choose you next year whom you will serve."

-- Neal A. Maxwell

* * * * *

I was greatly impressed as I listened to the B. Y. U. alumni president Ernest S. Wilkinson, M.D. tell of an emergency call that took him to the Intensive Coronary Care Unit of the L.D.S. hospital (in Salt Lake City) where a close personal friend of his of several years' duration was in critical condition with a massive coronary thrombosis. He said, "As I approached his bedside he grasped my hand and through an oxygen mask, though gripped with pain and breathing in a labored manner, he muttered, 'Oh Doctor, can you save me? I have so many things I have been putting off and wanting to do.'

"As we labored into the hours of the morning, utilizing all of the modern electronic gadgetry that medical service can provide, and as it became increasingly evident that my friend would not survive, I was haunted by his comment and its inference. Are we thinkers or are we doers? How many of us procrastinate the really important decisions in life? Will we be found wanting when we too are at the crossroads of life and death?"

-- N. Eldon Tanner

* * * * *

# PROPHETS

No one in this Church will ever go far astray who ties himself securely to the Church Authorities whom the Lord has placed in His Church . . . And those people who stand close to them will be safe.

--Spencer W. Kimball

* * * * *

## A Boy's Prayer

As told by the Grandfather tree in the Sacred Grove

I am a gnarled old tree, and even I am not sure of my exact age. I've stood for generations on a small farm in Manchester, New York. My posterity stands tall and proud around me in a compact and beautiful grove. I have been a witness to many things in my life, but there is one experience that as long as I may live, I know I will not and can not forget.

It was late in the year of eighteen hundred and nineteen that the Smith family moved onto my farm. There were nine children, and I was instinctively drawn to them through my admiration for their love and kindness. That is how, early the next spring, I came to meet the most unusual and extraordinary person I ever expect to see. He was just a lad, but such a serious and intense youth for his tender age of fourteen. He was tall for his age and gave the appearance of being a little awkward at times, but within his face were the contours and attributes of great character. His strong chin, sensitive mouth, and keen but gentle eyes gave added depth to his every reflection. The problems of the world fell heavily on his shoulders, and he would often come to sit at my foot and lean against my trunk to read or meditate. A mere boy -- but one I will never forget. His name was Joseph Smith.

With each of Joseph's visits to my grove, my respect and admiration for him increased. A silent companionship grew between us and we soon became fast friends. As the spring days grew warmer, his visits became more frequent. After helping his father and brothers in the fields and with the farm chores, he would often stop in the grove to rest and read. He loved to read and found excitement with each new discovery he made in his quest for knowledge, from his few, but well-chosen books.

The foremost desire in Joseph's heart was to know truth. He had an unending thirst for spiritual and religious wisdom. He often brought his Bible with him from which he would read aloud. He was one day reading the Epistle of James when he came upon the verse which reads: "If any of you lack wisdom, let him ask of God, that giveth to all men liberally, and upbraideth not, and it shall be given him."

I sat motionless as I watched the impact of the meaning of those words fall upon Joseph's troubled heart. Then his eyes shone as if candles had been lighted from within, and we both knew he had found the way to learn the truth.

The sun arose the next morning warming the beautiful spring countryside, for April had come forth in her most becoming attire. The birds in my tree top, happily engaged with the affairs of their families, were singing and chirping harmoniously. The squirrels and chipmonks darting swiftly to and fro, seemed to sense something special about this morning -- and would sometimes stop short and listen intently as if waiting for something to happen. The beautiful wild flowers in full bloom marked the green countryside with vivid splashes of color, and cast their fragrance upon the gentle breeze which lazily stirred the air.

I looked often towards the farm house, not expecting -- yet hoping to see Joseph. I wondered if during the night he had asked of God, and if his mind was now at ease. Soon I saw him coming through the field in my direction. There was something different about him that morning! He was less carefree and more intent than I'd ever seen him before. He looked around cautiously before entering the grove; and as he came hear, I was shaken with an inner excitement. A feeling that could not be explained told me that something wonderful was about to happen.

As Joseph looked heavenward through my branches, I saw the perplexed look on his face. It was then I realized that he had come to the seculsion of my grove to pray. I trembled with the knowledge that I would be allowed to view such a sacred occasion. The troubled look on Joseph's face revealed his dilemma -- that he knew not how to pray aloud. After mustering all his courage, he knelt upon the grass and uttered his first prayer.

As he prayed, a dismal and depressing spirit enveloped the grove like a dark cloak. It centered on Joseph and I watched helplessly as he was overpowered and thrown to the earth by the evil spirit. Compassion welled within me and I wished desperately for the power to save him from this destruction, but I could do nothing. With his last strength he cried out for deliverence from that enemy.

At that moment I saw a pillar of light descending from the heavens, and the evil spirit departed. A light so bright I could scarcely see descended gradually until it was nearly touching my branches. A warm feeling of peace surged through my being and I drew my branches aside as the light entered the grove. The brightness penetrated leaf by leaf, sending a tremor through each branch until every fiber tingled to the tips of my roots.

Within the light I saw two personages whose brightness and glory defied all description -- standing in the air above Joseph. As the light fell upon him, wonderment of what he saw drew him to his knees. The glory reflected in his face cannot be described. As They spoke, I trembled and my pulse quickened at the immensity of Their voices.

There was a hushed stillness in the sacredness of The Grove. The breeze was calmed, and the birds silent. It seemed as if the entire world was suspended in the presence of God.

He spoke saying, "Joseph, this is My Beloved Son, hear Him." After Joseph had asked for spiritual knowledge, many great and glorious things were revealed to him. I heard Joseph converse with the Lord. As They were about to depart, with humility the realization struck me, I too, was standing before my Maker.

As the light died away, the impact of what I'd seen and heard left me weak and shaken. Slowly the world seemed to re-awaken, but an air of sacredness and reverence remained within my grove. Pale, and with barely enough strength left to stand, Joseph arose to his feet. He leaned against my trunk for support, and I felt an inner strength within him he had not possessed before.

I had been a witness to a miraculous vision. The answer to a boy's prayer that would change the entire world. I know Joseph was chosen by the Lord. Chosen to restore His Church, and to place again upon this earth, God's greatest plan. To bring to pass the immortality and eternal life of man.

* * * * *

The great hall was filled to overflowing, but the eager crowds kept surging in. Many paused to speak to a little gray-haired lady sitting in the audience. There was nothing assuming about her as she greeted her many friends with her quick, flashing smile. A radiance about her seemed to reach out and touch the hearts of those who passed by. She was small, with the look of fragility of a piece of Dresden china, but there was an inner strength that all felt who came into her presence. Her face reflected the serenity of a life well-lived. There were many who said, "Aren't you proud of your husband today, Ray?" Of course, she was proud of him, but there had never been a time when she wasn't proud of him.

She looked at her husband sitting on the stand. He was just as handsome as he had been the day she had married him -- over fifty years ago. His hair was white now, but there was the same gentle dignity that had so impressed her when she first met him.

Was it really fifty years ago they had started out together? She remembered as if it were yesterday the first time she had seen David.

Her mother had called, "Look, Ray, here come the new boys now. See how sweet and gentle they are with their mother. They'll make good husbands for some lucky girls."

Ray looked up to see two boys helping their mother up the winding lane. Both of the boys were tall and handsome, but Ray only had eyes for one, David. "Tall, dark and handsome," those were the words that would best describe David, for he was over six feet tall and had dark wavy hair. When he turned to speak to her, Ray found herself looking up into calm brown-gray eyes.

David and his brothers and two sisters rented a cottage from Ray's mother while they attended the university that year. Although Ray attended the university too, it seemed as if the only time she ever saw David was when she put on her oldest most faded dress and was down on her knees to weed the garden, then she would invariably look to see David smiling down at her. She hadn't known until years after they were married that David was walking behind her one day at the university, and had turned to his friend and said, "Someday I'm going to marry a girl just loke her." Marriage with David was the farthest thing from her mind. Ray was engaged to a fine young fellow. He wasn't as tall or as good-looking as David, but they had wonderful times together. Later she decided that while she had fun with him she didn't love him, so she broke the engagement.

David wasn't engaged, but it seemed to her as if he never went out with anyone but the most beautiful and popular girls at school. What hope was there for her? David was president of the senior class and took a very active part in the Normal Society.

One day as she was walking down the hall she passed room 28 where the Normal Society held its meetings. The door was open and, recognizing David's voice, she stopped to listen. She had never heard a young man speak with such power and sincerity. As she listened she thought to herself, "He is going to amount to something someday." This had been her only premonition of David's greatness.

Ray never had a real date with David before he left for his mission. The nearest thing to it was when David's sister invited her to stay with them and attend the farewell party they were giving David. She had a wonderful time at the party. How thrilled she had been when he held her hand all the way home, but all too soon the evening was over, and David was gone.

They had corresponded for six months. Then she became provoked at something he had written, so she stopped writing to him. Several months later she sent him a letter beginning with, "An indefinable something prompts me to write again." In the return mail he sent his picture.

How wonderful it was to see David again after two years. He had changed a little. He had a look of maturity about him that he had not had when he left. He had grown with responsibility. On their first date together they had gone to the theater. The play was wonderful, but Ray could never remember what it was about.

What a glorious two years they had together. Whenever David was about to leave the farm in the summer or on weekends in the winter when he wasn't teaching school, they had gone on hayride parties, bobsled parties, to the theater, or the beach. What wonderful memories Saltair held for them. They both loved dancing. Then there were the long train rides home when they could hold hands on the dimly lighted cars.

One Saturday in October, Ray packed a big basket lunch, and they went to Lester Park to spend the afternoon. It was a glorious Indian summer day. It was warm, yet with the brisk tang of fall in the air. The maples had already turned a brilliant scarlet, and the poplars had changed from green to brightest yellow. The fragrance of burning leaves was in the air, and hung in a purple haze over the valley. They had been sitting under a big umbrella tree watching the sun go down. The birds had hushed their singing, and there was a peace and tranquility all about them. There, in the beautiful autumn, David asked Ray to marry him.

January 2, 1901 -- the beginning of a new century and of a new life for Ray and David. How proud she had felt riding beside David to the Salt Lake Temple! Inside the carriage she was snug and warm with the robes David carefully tucked about her. Outside the whole world seemed in a blaze of white glory as the sun reflected back the light from a million diamonds concealed in the snow that blanketed the earth. That day had been symbolic of their whole life together -- exquisitely being beautiful and glorious. And so Ray and David were married in the temple of God, for time and all eternity -- not for just a year or six or a lifetime -- but for eternity. The beauty and solemnity of that wonderful ceremony was something to be cherished forever. They had thought then that they could never be happier; and yet the years had brought an even deeper love and happiness than they could ever have imagined.

Before they were married, they never spoke of having children or the number of children they would have. Each had assumed that they would be grateful to receive as many choice spirits as God would see fit to give them. It was with joy, therefore, that they awaited the birth of their first child. Ray wore her approaching motherhood with glory and dignity, and when David placed the tiny dark-haired son in her arms, she rejoiced in her motherhood. Yet strangely enough that motherhood had nearly brought about their first quarrel.

Like all mothers then, she had had her baby at home. They had engaged a nurse, but the first night the nurse left them alone, David had to go to a meeting. As he started to put on his hat and coat, Ray had thought "Surely you aren't going to a meeting tonight." As if reading her thoughts David turned and looked at her for a moment then said, "Have you forgotten that it is Sunday School Board meeting tonight?" There was no warmth in her kiss as she bade him goodby. The closing door awakened the baby. Still weak, she sat and rocked the crying baby while tears of weakness, frustration, and hurt rolled down her cheeks. As she rocked the baby, she seemed again to hear her mother's voice saying, "Don't cry over spilled milk." When she was little, Ray had said, "If I can't cry before I'm hurt, and I can't cry after I'm hurt, when can I cry?" Her mother answered, "Don't cry at all. Just take things as they come and do the best you can."

Ray was suddenly ashamed of her pettiness. David had a job to do, and he was doing it. She had a job to do, too, and she would do it without complaint. No matter how long David left her again to act in the Service of God, Ray never felt any resentment toward him or toward the Church that occupied so much of his time.

Looking back Ray had tried to think what had been the best years of her life, but she could never make a decision. With a smile she remembered the time she, with her cousin Parley, had made a leaky old tub into a boat and sailed to the mainland from a small island of the Great Salt Lake to meet David when he returned from his mission, and the time she had driven to Franklin with David and had mistaken the governor of Idaho for a waiter. With a large family of children there were always funny things happening, and yet it hadn't all been easy. Still she wouldn't have changed any of it if she could. In the early days of their marriage they had had their share of financial worries too, but Ray would never embarrass David by complaining. She knew he would work out their problems somehow, and he always did. Then she remembered when one of their children came down with pneumonia. The doctor said she wouldn't live another hour, but he had not reckoned with the powers of the Priesthood. David had administered to her and she was healed.

When the children were little, they had been so sweet and precious. How she had hated to see them grow up, and yet she would not have had it otherwise. She and David had very firm convictions about the ways a child should be treated. Every child should be treated with the same courtesy and consideration they would show a favored guest. They felt the children were God's gift to them to be loved and cherished for all too short a time. How grateful she was that there were no regrets about the way they had treated their children. It made their sorrows a little easier to bear when they lost their beautiful two-and-a-half year old baby. "Some spirits are too beautiful, too pure, to have to be treated by mortal life," David had explained, and they had both been able to say with Job of Old, "The Lord giveth and the Lord taketh away, blessed be the name of the Lord."

It was strange the way you never forgot the little one who was gone. Maybe it was because you had so few memories that you cherished them more closely. She could still feel those little arms around her neck and that sweet little voice saying, "I love you, mama." But if she at times cried into her pillow, David and the children never knew.

In the evening when David was home, how he had loved to romp and play with the children! A rug never seemed to last very long in their house. Then when the babies were in bed, David would read the older children "The Lady of the Lake," "The Little Minister," or some of Burn's poems in his beautiful Scottish dialect. David had the gift of story telling, and Ray never tired of hearing him tell the same stories over and over again.

When David was thirty-two he had been requested to come to an opening session of conference. They had thought perhaps he would be called to be superintendent of Church Schools, and so they were completely unprepared for the announcement of his calling to one of the highest positions of the Church. When someone asked her later what her first thought was, she had said, "Now he will never be home," and started to cry. And so David went forth at home and abroad in the service of his Master. Whenever possible Ray went with him. David said so many times, "It helps to look down and see you sitting there."

When the children grew up and were old enough to get married, Ray and David worried about whether or not they would pick suitable mates, but they all did very well for themselves. Each of their children finished university, three with doctor's degree; and each had chosen a university graduate for a mate. Each of the boys went on foreign missions and the girls married returned missionaries. All of them were married in the temple.

The years went by all too quickly. The children were married and had children of their own. And once again she was free to go with David. Now today would bring the climax of their fifty years together; their working, planning, striving upward, always together.

The music stopped, and the little lady started from her reverie. She must start listening now. The speaker rose, and at his side stood David. Dear, wonderful David. His eyes caught hers just for a moment as they had done so many times before -- a brief reassurance of love and confidence.

A hush fell over the audience. The man was speaking now. "It is proposed that we sustain David Oman McKay as prophet, seer, and revelator. All those in favor will make it manifest by raising the right hand."

The silence was broken only by the rushing sound of ten thousand hands lifted in a sustaining vote.

As she looked at her husband standing before the vast assembly, a phrase from the Bible flashed through her mind: "David, beloved of God!"

--Zella Farr Smith

* * * * *

# REGRET

It's queer, the things you remember. When life has crumbled suddenly and left you standing there alone. It's not the big, important things that you remember when you come to that; it's not the plans of years, not the hope you worked so hard for. It's the little things that you remember then; the little things you hadn't noticed at tht time. The way a hand touched yours, and you too busy to notice; the hopeful little inflection of a voice you didn't really bother to listen to.

John Carmody found that out, staring through the living room window at the cheerful Tuesday afternoon life of the street. He kept trying to think about the big important things, lost now -- the years and the plans and the hopes. And the love. But he couldn't quite get them focused sharply in his mind, just now. Not this afternoon.

They, those important things, were all a huge but nebulous background in his mind. All he could remember, now, was a queer little thing; nothing, really, if you stopped and thought about it in the light of the years and the plans and the -- the great love. It was only something his little girl had said to him one evening, perhaps two or three weeks ago. Nothing if you looked at it rationally. The sort of thing that kids are always saying.

But it was what he was remembering now.

That particular night, he had brought home from the office a finished draft of the annual stockholders report. Very important, it was. Things being what they were, it meant a great deal to his future; to the future of his wife, and his little girl. He sat down to re-read it before dinner. It had to be right: it meant so much.

And just as he turned the page, Marge, his little girl, came with a book under her arm. It was a green-covered book, with pictures pasted on it. And she said, "Look, Daddy." He glanced up and said, "Oh, fine. A new book, eh?"

"Yes, Daddy," she said. "Will you read me a story in it?" "No, dear, daddy can't just now," he said.

Marge just stood there and he read through a paragraph which told the stockholders about certain replacements in the machinery of the factory. And marge's voice, with timid and hopeful little inflections, was saying, "But, Mummy said you probably would, Daddy."

He looked over the top of the typed script. "I'm sorry," he said. "Maybe Mummy will read it to you. I'm busy, dear." "No," Marge said politely, "Mummy is much busier upstairs. Won't you read me just this one story? Look -- it has a picture, see! Isn't it a lovely picture, Daddy?" "Oh yes. Beautiful," he said. Now that has class, hasn't it? "But I do have work tonight. Some other time. . ."

After that there was quite a long silence. Marge just stood there with the book open to the lovely picture. It was a long time before she spoke again. He had read through two more pages, explaining in full detail, as he had directed, the shift in markets over the past twelve months, the plans outlined by the sales department for meeting these problems which, after all, could safely be ascribed to local conditions and the advertising programs which after weeks of conferences had been devised to stabilize and even increase the demand for their products.

"But it is a lovely picture, Daddy. And the story looks so exciting," Marge said.

"I know," he said. "Ah. . .Mmmmm. Some other time. Run along now."

"I'm sure you'd enjoy it, Daddy," Marge insisted.

"Eh? Yes, I know I would, but later. . ."

"Oh, Marge said. "Well, some other time, then. Will you, Daddy? Some other time?"

"Oh, of course," he said. "You bet."

But she didn't go away. She still stood there quietly like a good child. And after a long time she put the book down on the stool at his feet and said, "Well, whenever you get ready, just read it to yourself. Only read it loud enough so I can hear too."

And that was why, now, he put his hand on the book, from the corner table where they had piled some of Marge's playthings, picking them up from the floor where she had left them.

The book wasn't new anymore, and the green cover was dented and thumbed. He opened it to the lovely picture.

And reading that story, his lips moving stiffly with anguish to form the words, he didn't try to think anymore, as he should be thinking about the important things, about his careful and shrewd and loving plans for the years to come, and for a little while he forgot, even, the horror and bitterness of his hate for the half-drunk punk kid who had careened down the street in a stolen car -- and who was now in jail on manslaughter charges. He didn't even see his wife, white and silent, dressed for Marge's funeral, standing in the doorway, trying to make her voice say calmly, "I'm ready, dear. We must go."

Because John Carmody was reading: "Once upon a time, there was a little girl who lived in a woodcutters' hut in a black forest. And she was so fair that the birds forgot their singing from the bough, looking at her. And there came a day . . ."

He was reading it to himself, but loud enough for her to hear, too. Maybe.

* * * * *

# REPENTANCE

To obtain forgiveness one must be convicted of sin, bow the knee in monumental humility, forsake the sin and fortify himself against repetition . . . and when he has fasted enough, wept enough, prayed enough and suffered enough, and when his heart is right, he may expect that forgiveness will come and with it that glorious peace which passeth understanding.

--Spencer W. Kimball

* * * * *

It's no good to repent of your sins if you don't repent of sinning.

* * * * *

To really repent you must completely change your life style.

* * * * *

We all make mistakes. If our repentance is sincere, we have the right to approach Him for forgiveness, but remember we are not entitled to any quota of mistakes. It's always better that we don't make them. And surely we shouldn't go on stupidly or stubbornly repeating the same old mistakes over and over again.

One of the most devilish doctrines that anyone could advocate would be to say that because someone had made a mistake, it wouldn't matter if he made one more, or many more. The best time to repent is now, before the next time.

But don't let anyone tell you ever that you are beyond repenting, or that there is no point in repenting, or that it is all right to postpone repentance.

--Richard L. Evans

* * * * *

If a man has a desire in his heart to know the truth, the normal and positive reaction, as his faith expands, causes him to know that he has participated in volitional acts that are wrong and therefore sinful. In this respect, all are in need of repentance, which leads us to the covenant of baptism.

Repentance is inseparably associated with forgiveness; and when forgiveness, as a personal possession working two ways, flows through the thought and action of man, he experiences a feeling of great joy, a release of tension and frustration caused by the commiting of sin. Thus, there is produced personal security and assurance. Here is power that prepares for further life corrections.

It is probably true that sin is never forgotten when once committed. But the laws governing repentance provide a release of emotional stress caused by the sin, when that sin is acknowledged and forsaken. Through repentance and forsaking will come the peace of mind, a form a regeneration, that enables one to go on in life in pursuit of true happiness. Thus fits. . . the ennobling challenge of the Christ to become like unto Him.

Stephen L. Richards said, in essence: "Men may wonder why they are retarded in the Church and in life. Such should be invited to look into their lives, and if they are frank and honest with themselves, they will find the answer."

As sin is looked upon, we are led to conclude that not until man is humbled, not until the heart throbs with genuine sorrow for repeated violations of God's holy laws, not until the citadel of sin is surrendered, can man hope for forgiveness or expect exhaltation.

--Alvin R. Dyer

* * * * *

# REVERENCE

Reverence is the price required in inviting the Spirit of the Lord to attend us.

* * * * *

## A Stranger

A Stranger stood by the old Church door,
His clothes were old and worn;
His shoes were scuffed and the soles were loose,
His coat was ragged and torn.

I paused as I saw him standing there,
His hair was thin and gray,
And I wondered, "Should I ask this man
To come with me to pray?"

So I went to his side and softly asked,
"Old man, what is your name?"
Then he answered me and turned around
And I noticed he was lame.

His foot was red and swolen
And I thought of the pain he bore,
But he said not a word of his worry or pain
As together we stepped through the door.

We sat in the back of the old white Church
And bowed our heads to pray,
But he rose after staying less than an hour,
Explaining he could not stay.

I quickly rose to follow my friend,
But when I reached the door
The man was gone, He'd vanished from sight,
And I thought I would see him no more.

But there he was on the step of the Church
So I went to him and said,
"Old man, why can you linger not?"
And I watched as he bowed his head.

"This is a house of worship.
It's God's own house you say:
You teach that He is with you all,
That He listens while you pray.

"We love Thy House, O Lord," you sing
In loud and joyous strains,
But His sweet spirit does not dwell
Where such irreverence reigns.

"Folks giggle, whisper, laugh and talk
In God's own house of prayer,
And when the people act this way
His spirit is not there."

He rose and left me all alone,
And I watched as he walked the road,
And realized he'd come to Church
To ease his heavy load.

But once again he'd left unhelped
His sorrow even more,
And I thought how right that man had been
As I listened at the door.

The noise and whispers from within
Now reached my opened ears,
And suddenly I realized that
I hadn't listened in years.

I'll never forget the way that I felt
As I stood at the door on that day
And listened, while unknown to them
Through irreverence they drove God away.

Since that day forth I've asked this prayer
And maybe you should too,
"Dear Father in Heaven, please help us all
To show more reverence to you."

* * * * *

## SERVICE

No man has ever risen to the real stature of Spiritual manhood until he has found that it is finer to serve somebody else than it is to serve himself.

--Woodrow Wilson

* * * * *

Give a boy a fish and feed him for a day. Teach him how to fish and feed him for a lifetime.

* * * * *

Hands that help are holier than lips that merely pray; the combination, however, is unbeatable.

* * * * *

To ease another's heartache is to forget one's own.

--Abraham Lincoln

* * * * *

You can't lift anybody until you are standing on higher ground than he is.

* * * * *

There is part of an old Christmas poem that goes:

What shall I give Him, poor as I am?
If I were a shepherd, I'd bring Him a lamb.
If I were a wise man, I would do my part.
What shall I give Him? I'll give Him my heart.

* * * * *

Julia Ward Howe, who wrote the "Battle Hymn of the Republic," asked a distinguished Senator to interest himself in the case of a person who needed help. The Senator answered, "I have become so busy that I can no longer concern myself with individuals. She replied, "That's remarkable. Even God hasn't reached that stage yet."

* * * * *

If you would know the real joy of wervice -- try helping someone who can't pay you for it.



* * * * *

The Lord is willing to go half way. He'll take care of me and I'll take care of His work.

* * * * *

If you cannot do great things, do small things in a great way.

* * * * *

Only a life lived for others is a life worthwhile.

--Albert Einstein

* * * * *

"Thee lift me, and I lift thee, and together we ascend."

--John Greenleaf Whittier

* * * * *

Help me to make this day much brighter.
Help me to know a neighbor's need.
Help me to make one's burden lighter.
Help me to be a friend indeed.

What might I do this day for another?
Help all I meet feel peace and love.
How can I this day serve another?
Send thy spirit to direct from above.

Let me not think of worldly pleasures.
Help me to in thy footsteps trod.
Help me to know that real treasures,
Are only found in the service of God.

* * * * *

<u>Where shall I work today?</u>

Master, where shall I work today?
My love flowed warm and free.
He pointed out a tiny spot
And said, tend that for me.

I answered quickly, oh no, not there,
Not any one could see
No matter how well my work was done;
Not that little spot for me.

When He spoke He was not stern,
But He answered me tenderly,
Little one, search that heart of thine;
Are you working for them or for me?

Nazareth was just a little place
And so was Galilee.

* * * * *

I am only one,
But still I am one.
I cannot do everything,
But still I can do something;
And because I can not do everything
I will not refuse to do the something
That I can do.

* * * * *

I prayed for strength when life pulsed low
Until God answered me:
"Go lift the load from weary ones,
Then I will strengthen thee."

I asked for courage when hope despaired,
Then came the voice benign:
"Inspire with faith thy brother's soul,
And I'll inspire thine."

I longed for light when darkness made
Me stumble through the night:
"Thy lamp held high for others' feet
Will make thy pathway bright."

I prayed that wisdom, talent, skill
Increase their meager store:
"First share the portions that you have,
And I will give thee more."

At length I learned that blessing sought,
And help for which I pray,
Are only mine when shed abroad
And given, first, away.

* * * * *

## Cans

Do all the GOOD you can
By all the MEANS you can
In all the WAYS you can
To all the PEOPLE you can
At all the TIMES you can
For as LONG as you can
Helping comes in CANS not in Can'ts
May your cupboard be filled with CANS!

* * * * *

The God of the Great Endeavor
Gave me a Torch to Bear.
I lifted it high above me
In the dark and murky air.

And straight way with loud hosannas
The crowd acclaimed its light
And followed me as I carried my torch
Through the starless night.

Till mad with peoples praises
And drunken with vanity
I forgot 'twas the torch that drew them
And I fancied they followed me.

But slowly my arm grew weary
Upholding the shining load
And my tired feet went stumbling
Over the hilly road.

And I fell with the torch beneath me
In a moment the flame was out
Then lo, from the throng a stripling
Sprang forth with a mighty shout.

Caught up the torch as it smouldered
And lifted it high again
Till fanned by the winds of Heaven
It fired the sould of men.

And as I lay in the darkness
The feet of the trampling crowd
Passed over and far beyond me
Its praises proclaimed aloud.

While I learned in the deepening shadows,
This glorious verity,
Tis the torch that the people follow
Whoever the bearer be.

--Anonymous

* * * * *

## Have you earned one more tomorrow?

Is anybody happier because you passed this way?
Does anyone remember that you spoke to him today
This day is almost over and its toiling time is through
Is there anyone to offer a kindly word of you?

Did you give a friendly greeting to a friend who came along?
Or a sort of churlish howdy and then vanish in the throng?
Were you selfish pure and simple as you rushed along your way?
Or is someone mighty grateful for a deed you did today?

Can you say tonight in parting with the day that's slipping fast
That you helped a single friend of the many that you passed?
Is some heart rejoicing over what you did or said?
Does a man whose hopes were fading now with courage look ahead?

Did you waste the day or lose it? Was it well or poorly spent?
Did you leave a trail of kindness or a scar of discontent.
As you close your eyes in slumber do you think that God would say
You have earned one more tomorrow by the work you did today.

* * * * *

## Night Watch

A nurse took the tired, anxious serviceman to the bedside. "Your son is here," she said to the old man. She had to repeat the words several times before the patient's eyes opened. Heavily sedated because of the pain of his heart attack, he dimly saw the young man in the Marine Corps uniform standing outside the oxygen tent. He reached out his hand. The Marine wrapped his toughened fingers around the old man's limp ones, squeezing a message of love and encouragement. The nurse brought a chair so the Marine could sit alongside the bed.

Nights are long is hospitals, but all through the night the young Marine sat there in the poorly lighted ward, holding the old man's hand and offering words of hope and strength. Occasionally, the nurse suggested that the Marine move away and rest awhile. He refused.

Whenever the nurse came into the ward, the Marine was there, oblivious of her and the night noises of the hospital, the clanking of the oxygen tank, the laughter of night-staff members exchanging greetings, the cries and moans of other patients. Now and then she heard him say a few gentle words. The dying man said nothing, only held tightly to his son most of the night.

Along toward dawn, the patient died. The Marine placed on the bed the lifeless hand he had been holding and went to tell the nurse. While she did what she had to, he waited. Finally, she returned. She started to offer words of sympathy, but the Marine interrupted her.

"Who was that man?" he asked.

The nurse was startled. "He was your father," she answered.

"No, he wasn't," the Marine replied. "I never saw him before in my life."

"Then why didn't you say something when I took you to him?"

"I knew right off there had been a mistake, but I also knew he needed his son, and his son just wasn't there. When I realized he was too sick to tell whether or not I was his son, I knew how much he needed me. I stayed."

--Roy Popkin

* * * * *

Tribute to Relief Society Presidents

Relief Society Presidents come in assorted sizes and shapes. Bishops revere them, Stake Presidents honor them, husbands put up with them.

One of the prime requisites of her job is a strong back and a pair of willing hands. She is endlessly toting things like turkeys, boxes -- always full -- chairs, dishes, trees, casseroles, and occasionally, babies.

The trunk of her car rotates between looking like the inside of a supermarket, a moving van, a china closet, a junk collection, and a rag bag.

Some Relief Society Presidents are well-organized, some are half-organized, and some "play it by ear." All end up with approximately the same results.

Relief Society Presidents probably appreciate their families more than any other women on earth, because their moments are so precious. Each day is a challenge -- to accomplish the impossible and still be home in time to meet that 2:45 school bus.

All Relief Society Presidents are most comfortable on their knees. And few there are who are not on very intimate terms with their Heavenly Father.

Discouragement is her greatest enemy. Faith, her best friend.

She is qualified for nothing in particular and everything in general.

She is part business executive, janitor, teacher, psychologist, speech maker, counselor, cook and defender.

Her chief feminine virtues must be: compassion, wisdom, enthusiasm, and courage.

Relief Society Presidents never concern themselves with the prestige of the position. She is much too busy.

Relief Society Presidents are a peculiar breed of womanhood. To them, a confidence is a sacred trust, a problem, something she can overcome.

Once in a while, a Relief Society President gets tired. But she never allows it to show. To do so is fatal. Rather, she quietly finds a day off and spends it praying for strength.

Her rewards are treasures unperceived by others. These she stores in the very depths of her soul to draw out in quiet moments and enjoy. A sister's humble testimony, a project well done, a witness of renewed faith, a few grateful tears, the touch of a dear hand, the love she has earned from her faithful sisters.

--Lois Tanner

* * * * *

One cold winter day, a ragged little urchin stood on a street corner of a large city, selling newspapers. His feet were bare and he had no coat. As he stood there shivering, a woman walking past noticed the child. She approached him and said, "Come with me, Dear. I want to buy you a coat and some shoes."

A smile lighted his cold little face as he took her hand. She led him to a large, warm department store where she had him completely outfitted from head to toe in warm clothes.

The boy was putting on the last of his new clothing as the woman paid the bill and slipped quietly out the door. When he finished dressing, he looked for the lady to tell her thank you. But he was told by the clerk that she had gone.

He ran from the store, frantically looking up and down the street. He must find the lady to thank her. There she was, walking down the street! He ran quickly to her, took her hand and said, "Lady, why did you go? I wanted to thank you."

"You're most welcome, Dear," she smiled.

The little boy then looked up into her face and said solemnly, "Lady, who are you? Are you God's wife?"

"No," she softly replied. "I'm just one of His children."

"Oh, I knew it!" he smiled with tears in his eyes. "I just knew you were some relation!"

* * * * *

## Doc Brackett

Doc Brackett didn't have black whiskers. Nonetheless, he was a fine man. He doctored in our town for many years. He doctored more people than any other doctor in our town but made less money.

That was because Doc Brackett was always doctoring poor people, who had no money to pay. He would get up in the middle of the coldest night and ride twenty miles to doctor a sick woman, or child, or to patch up some fellow who got hurt.

Everybody in our town knew Dock Brackett's office over Rice's clothing store. It was up a narrow flight of stairs. His office was always filled with people. A sign at the foot of the stairs said:

DOCTOR BRACKETT, OFFICE UPSTAIRS

Doc Brackett was a bachelor. He was once supposed to marry Miss Elvira Cromwell, the daughter of old Junius Cromwell, the banker, but on the day the wedding was supposed to take place Doc Brackett got a call to go out into the country and doctor a Mexican child.

Miss Elvira got sore at him and called off the wedding. She said that a man who would think more of a Mexican child than of his wedding was no good. Many women in our town agreed with Miss Elvira Cromwell, but the parents of the Mexican child were very grateful to Doc Brackett when the child recovered.

For forty years, the lame, and the halt, and the blind of our town had climbed up and down the stairs to Doc Brackett's office. He never turned away anybody.

He lived to be seventy years old, and then one day he keeled over on the sofa in his office and died. By this time his black hair had turned white.

Doc Brackett had one of the biggest funerals ever seen in our town. Everybody went to pay their last respects when he was laid out in Gruber's undertaking parlors. He was buried in Riverview cemetery.

There was talk of raising money to put a nice tombstone on Doc Brackett's grave as a memorial. The talk got as far as arguing about what should be carved on the stone above him. Some thought poetry would be very nice. Doc Brackett hated poetry.

The matter dragged along and nothing whatever was done.

Then one day George Gruber, the undertaker, said that Doc Brackett's memorial was already over his grave, with an epitaph and all. George Gruber said the Mexican parents of the child Doc Brackett saved years ago had worried about him having no tombstone.

They had no money themselves, so they took the sign from the foot of the stairs at Doc Brackett's office and stuck it over his grave. It read:

DOCTOR BRACKETT, OFFICE UPSTAIRS

--Damon Runyon

* * * * *

# SMILING

Smile! If you can't raise the corners of your mouth, at least let the middle droop.

* * * * *

They might not need me, yet
they might,
I'll let my heart be just
in sight --
A smile so small as mine
might be
Precisely their necessity.

* * * * *

## Nothing On Earth Can Smile But Man

Nothing on earth can smile but man,
Not even the loveliest flower can
Nor bird, nor bee, nor butterfly,
Nothing, just nothing but you and I;

Nothing on earth that heals so much
As a simple smile its cheer and such
Nothing that heartens the soul of folk
When the day goes wrack, and the heart goes broke.

Nothing that lingers so tenderly
When lips that smile are a memory
Nothing that costs so little to give
Nothing so blest, for in smiles you live.

* * * * *

Actions speak louder than words, and a smile says, "I like you. You make me happy. I am glad to see you."

That is why dogs make such a big hit. They are so glad to see us that they almost jump out of their skins. So, naturally, we are happy to see them.

An insincere grin doesn't fool anybody, and most people resent it. The smile you need to have is the smile from within, the type that will warm the heart of those you meet.

What if you don't feel like smiling? There are two things you can do. First force yourself to smile. If you are alone, force yourself to whistle, or hum a tune, or sing. Everytime you pass a mirror, stop and smile at yourself. Second, act as if you were already happy, and that will tend to make you happy. Here is the way the late Professor James of Harvard put it.

"Action seems to follow feeling, but really action and feeling go together, and by regulating the action, which is under the more direct control of the will, we can indirectly regulate the feeling, which is not.

"Thus the sovereign voluntary path to cheerfulness, if our cheerfulness be lost, is to sit up cheerfully and to act and speak as if cheerfulness were already there. . ."

Abraham Lincoln once made the comment: "Most folks are about as happy as they make up their minds to be." And he is right.

We radiate how we feel, and that influences other people, so why not radiate happiness, and encourage them to be happy.

* * * * *

## The Value Of A Smile

It costs nothing, but creates much.
It enriches those who recieve, without impoverishing those who give.
It happens in a flash, and the memory of it sometimes lasts forever.
None are so rich they can get along without it, and none are so poor but are richer for its benifits.
It creates happiness in the home, fosters good will in a business, and is the countersign of friends.
It is rest to the weary, daylight to the discouraged, sunshine to the sad, and Nature's best antidote for trouble.
Yet it cannot be bought, begged, borrowed, or stolen, for it is something that is no earthly good to anybody till it is given away!
For nobody needs a smile so much as those who have none left to give!

So practice smiling.

* * * * *

# SUCCESS

Success is still operated on the Self Service plan.

* * * * *

Good luck is a lazy man's estimate of a hard-working man's success.

* * * * *

There is no comparison between that which is lost by not succeeding and that which is lost by not trying.

-- Francis Bacon

* * * * *

The height of a man's success is gauged by his self-mastery; the depth of his failure, by his self-abandonment.

-- Horace Greeley

* * * * *

On the plains of hesitation lie the bleached bones of men who, on the dawn of a great victory in their lives, lay down to rest.

* * * * *

He has achieved success who has lived well, laughed often and loved much; who has gained the respect of intelligent men, and the love of little children; who has filled his niche and accomplished his task; who has left the world better than he found it, whether by an improved poppy, perfect poem, or a rescued soul; who has never lacked appreciation of earth's beauty, or failed to express it; who has given the best he had; whose life was an inspiration; whose memory, a benediction.

* * * * *

<u>The Family of Success</u>

The father of Success is named Work.
The mother of Success is named Ambition.
The oldest son is called Common Sense, and some of the boys are called Stability, Perseverance, Honesty, Thoroughness, Foresight, Enthusiasm and Cooperation.

The oldest daughter is Character. Some of the sisters are Cheerfulness, Loyalty, Care, Courtesy, Economy, Sincerity and Harmony.

The baby is Opportunity.

Get acquainted with the father of Success, and you will be able to get along with the rest of the family.

* * * * *

## It's Up To Me

I get discouraged now and then
When there are clouds of gray,
Until I think about the things
That happened yesterday.
I do not mean the day before
Or those of months ago,
But all the yesterdays in which
I had the chance to grow.
I think of opportunities
That I allowed to die
And those I took advantage of
Before they passed me by.
And I remember that the past
Presented quite a plight
But somehow I endured it. . .and
The future seemed all right.
And I remind myself that I
Am capable and free
And my success and happiness
Are really up to me.

-- James J. Metcalf

* * * * *

"Hang on the walls of your mind the memory of your successes. Take counsel of your strength, not your weakness. Think of the good jobs you have done. Think of the times when you rose above your average level of performance and carried out an idea or a dream or a desire for which you had deeply longed. Hang these pictures on the walls of your mind and look at them as you travel the roadway of life."

-- by the artist Whistler

* * * * *

# TEACHING

No ray of sunshine is ever
lost but the green which
it awakens takes time to
sprout, and it is not
always granted to the sower
to see the harvest.

-- Schweitzer

* * * * *

An education system isn't worth a great deal if it teaches boys how to make a living and doesn't teach them how to live.

* * * * *

The creation of a thousand forests is in one acorn.

-- Ralph Waldo Emerson

* * * * *

The basic ingredient of teaching always has been and always will be LOVE. When love comes first, the rest will follow in proper order. Without love, we struggle in vain with all we do.

-- H. Burke Peterson

* * * * *

If a teacher influences but one, his influence never stops.

-- Greek

* * * * *

## A Visiting Teacher

A good loaf of bread must be "kneaded"
A VISITING TEACHER, too, is "needed."

The "dough" rises to perfection,
The "VISITING TEACHER" rises to each
situation.

A "Punch" of the dough collapses the
  mixture.
But the result is a loaf with finer
  texture.
Many times when we are "Punched down"
  by troubles or sorrow,
A visit from the "TEACHER" makes a
  happier tomorrow.

A "spoonful of sugar" adds to the dough,
A "little love" helps us all grow.

The "Staff of Life" is needed by all,
Let us heed the "VISITING TEACHERS"
  CALL;
That we may "rise again" to be. . .
With "HIM" for all Eternity.

* * * * *

## To Those Who Teach

You are called to be true under shepherds,
To keep watch o'er the lambs of the fold,
And to point out the way to green pastures,
Of more value than silver or gold.

Unto you is entrusted the children,
Priceless treasures from Heaven above,
You're to teach them the truth of the gospel
Let them bask in the warmth of your love.

Do you ask for the help of our Father
In teaching His children so dear?
Do you put forth a true, honest effort?
Is your message impressive and clear?

Are you living a worthy example?
Is your character what it should be?
When the children have gathered around you,
Can you say, "Come, Follow Me"?

Earnest effort is always rewarded,
Righteous lives are inspiring to all,

You can render your thanks to our Savior,
By making the most of your call.

-- Jane B. Terry

* * * * *

## The Hand

It was nearing Thanksgiving and the teacher had just given the children instructions to draw something for which they were very thankful.

As she looked at the children she thought in her heart: These poor little children have so very little to be thankful for -- half fed, half clothed -- what would they draw that they were especially thankful for?

Take David for instance. He was so thin and uncared for, and so very shy. He didn't enter into the games with the older boys for he wasn't able to hold his own with them. Always when she was on duty on the playground, David would follow her about like a shadow as she moved around and pressed very close to her as though for protection. What could he draw for which he was especially thankful?

The drawings were completed and she held them up for the class to see. There were the usual turkeys, tables laden with good foods, etc., about which these poor children know from pictures.

David had drawn a hand and when she held it up she got many responses from the children. One child said, "That is the hand of God, for he gives us everything." Another said, "That represents all of the hands that help us." But David had drawn only one. This drawing caused more comment than any of the others, but David offered no explanation.

The teacher was curious, so when the others were busy working on their next assignment she leaned close to David and said, "Whose hand are you especially grateful for, David?"

Looking up into her face he simply said, "Yours."

Then she remembered the numerous occasions when he had pressed closely to her and she had reached down and taken his hand in hers and pressed it warmly. She had given something of herself to this little boy that was most priceless to him and for which he was exceedingly grateful.

-- Author Unknown

* * * * *

## Ten Commandments For The Teacher

1. Thou shalt make the child the center of thy teaching. Five days each week shalt thou help him to develop the best in his own personality.

2. Thou shalt provide opportunities for experience learning, not doing difficult tasks for the child but rather helping him to do them himself.

3. Thou shalt set before him high attainable ideals, surrounding him with the things that inspire thought, and encouraging him to cultivate a love for the good and true.

4. Thou shalt help him to achieve success, attempting not those tasks which are beyond his mental and physical ability but rather discovering within his natural ability that which he can do well.

5. Thou shalt teach him to create, not copy, for thou knowest the pride that is in thine own breast when thou doest something original.

6. Thou shalt help him to develop the art of living happily with others, by being kind, courteous, and considerate of his friends and associates.

7. Thou shalt teach him to make wise choices, permitting him to decide many issues for himself and requiring him to live by his decisions.

8. Thou shalt talk with him as a friend, remembering that love correcteth better than anger.

9. Thou shalt speak kindly to him, for thou knowest that there can be kindness in firmness.

10. Thou shalt help him to find happiness in play, so that he will learn that those who play fair and enjoy playing are the real winners.

* * * * *

## Fable Of The Animal School

Once upon a time, the animals decided they must do something heroic to meet the problems of a "new world," so they organized a school. They adopted an activity curriculum consisting of running, climbing, swimming and flying, and to make it easier to administer, all the animals took all the subjects.

The duck was excellent in swimming, better in fact than his instructor, and made passing grades in flying, but he was very poor in running. Since he was slow in running, he had to stay after school and also drop swimming to practice running. This was kept up until his web feet were badly worn and he was only average in swimming. But average was acceptable in school, so nobody worried about that except the duck.

The rabbit started at the top of the class in running, but had a nervous breakdown because of so much make-up work in swimming.

The squirrel was excellent in climbing until he developed frustration in the flying class, where his teacher made him start from the ground up, instead of from the treetop down. He also developed Charley Horses from overexertion and then got a C in climbing and a D in running.

The eagle was a problem child and was disciplined severely. In the climbing class he beat all the others to the top of the tree, but insisted on using his own way to get there.

At the end of the year, an abnormal eel that could swim exceedingly well, and also run, climb, and fly a little, had the highest average and was valedictorian. . .

-- Dr. George H. Reavis
Reprinted by permission

* * * * *

<u>Timmy</u>

Timmy, a slow learner, was taken to an ungraded school. The teacher asked why he was sent to her. He said, "I was sent because I'm a moron." "Teacher, what is a moron?"

The teacher said, "A moron is one who does not know all the answers."

"I guess I'm a moron -- because there are alot of things I don't know. My father must be one too. Just this morning at breakfast my mother said to dad that he never would learn to eat like real folks ought to. I like my father though because he always says: 'Timmy, what do you think?' I sure like that."

The teacher inquired, "What do you think, Tim?!

"Just let a bird sing two notes and I can tell you what kind of bird it is -- I can tell its color, what the papa bird looks like, how many eggs the mother lays, and the color of the eggs, and how long it will take them to hatch. I know all the birds that stay here, when and where they go, I even know what birds are here and when they are going somewhere else."

The teacher said, "Timmy, you're a genius."

Timmy said, "Teacher, you know more about me already than my teacher did all last year. She never asked me what I thought. She always told me what I didn't know. She must be a moron."

-- Source unknown

* * * * *

**This Poem Was Written By A Grade 12 Student Who Committed Suicide Some 2 Weeks Later.**

He always wanted to explain things.
But no one cared.
So he drew.
Sometimes he would draw and it wasn't anything.
He wanted to carve it in stone or write it in the sky.
He would lie out on the grass and look up in the sky.
And it would be only him and the sky and the things inside him
    that needed saying.
And it was after that he drew the picture.
It was a beautiful picture.
He kept it under his pillow and would let no one see it.
And he would look at it every night and think about it.
And when it was dark, and his eyes were closed, he could still
    see it.
And it was all of him.
And he loved it.
When he started school he brought it with him.
Not to show anyone, but just to have it with him like a friend.
It was funny about school.
He sat in a square, brown desk.
Like all the other square, brown desks.
And he thought it should be red.
And his room was a square brown room.
Like all the other rooms.
And it was tight and close.
And stiff.
He hated to hold the pencil and chalk,
With his arm stiff and his feet flat on the floor,
Stiff.
With the teacher watching and watching.
The teacher came and spoke to him.
She told him to wear a tie like all the other boys.
He said he didn't like them.
And she said it didn't matter.
After that they drew.
And he drew all yellow and it was the way he felt about morning.

And it was beautiful.
The teacher came and smiled at him.
"What's this?" she said. "Why don't you draw something like
Ken's drawing? Isn't that beautiful?"
After that his mother bought him a tie.
And he always drew airplanes and rocket ships like everyone else.
And he threw the old picture away.
And when he lay alone looking at the sky, it was big and blue and
all of everything,
But he wasn't anymore.
He was square inside
And brown
And his hands were stiff.
And he was like everyone else.
And the things inside him that needed saying didn't need it anymore.
It had stopped pushing.
It was crushed.
Stiff.
Like everything else.

* * * * *

## The Gospel Path

There were two lovely children, a girl with blond hair, her cheeks a rosy pink, her eyes a bright blue, and a boy who was dark, his eyes were mischievious, and his smile captured your heart. I was the mother of these two lovely children. My responsibility was great for I must teach them to walk the gospel path. I must make sure they would know the way.

I must mark every stone making the path straight and true that they may follow, for I know that I could not be at their side to guide each step they took. But, I would watch and wait for my two precious children praying that I marked their pathway well. My heart sank as I thought of the muddy pond they would have to cross. Would they see the stones I so carefully placed there and labored so earnestly and long.

It seemed like an eternity as I waited for my two lovely children to walk the gospel path -- then, I saw my daughter, her blond hair softly floating in the breeze. She skipped along following my directions; she was so happy. When she reached the muddy pond, she stopped, "Dear God," I prayed, "Please let her see my stepping stones." Then, how carefully she stepped upon each one until at last she saw me and joyfully she ran and threw her arms around my neck. "I made it, Mommy" she softly said. Yes, eternal life was hers.

Arm in arm we waited for my son to come in sight. Fear grew in my heart as the shadows grew longer, but at last we saw him on the path sauntering slowly along, exploring each little crooked path that could lead him astray. When at last he reached the muddy pond, he seemed to have forgotten all that I had taught him, for the black mud seemed to entice him. I called to him, but he didn't hear me. "Dear God, please don't let me lose him." Then I saw him reach for something shining in the deep black mud. His outstretched hand was trying to grasp the object when he slipped and fell. It was then my prayers were answered. I saw a teacher stretch forth a helping hand and placed him upon the gospel path once again. His feet now were muddy and would slip off each stepping stone. But, the teacher walked beside him, guiding each step he took, until, safely back upon the gospel path once again. Then at last, he was beside me, tears of joy streamed down my cheeks and with these tears I washed the mud from his face and hands.

The gospel path had been so hard for him, but my heart was filled with gratitude and praise to God for that teacher who guided him so faithfully and well.

Yes, our task is great for parents, leaders, and teachers; but if we work together diligently, we can place each child's feet upon the stepping stones of the Gospel Path which leads to life eternal.

* * * * *

Lance was Problem Number One in my second-grade class. He seemed interested only in destruction: tearing a girl's new dress, cutting leaves off the plants or trampling somebody's notebook in the mud.

As any conscientious teacher does, I searched for motives behind such behavior, and discovered genuine and tragic ones.

Lance had lost both parents when he was four. Since then he had been shunted from one temporary home to another. Only his school had not changed. Because a wise welfare worker had insisted, the child remained in our school through kindergarten, first and now second grade, although his address changed nine times.

Finally he was adopted. Lance's behavior began to improve immediately and I rejoiced with him. Now, I felt, I would be able to teach this child.

Then his new mother came to school to arrange his transfer to another city. The next day Lance was worse than ever before. Incongruous reports reached me: The custodian caught him taking a towel from the supply room; a playground supervisor accused him of digging holes in the lawn with a ruler.

On Lance's last day with us I felt both relief and a deep sorrow. How I wished I could have reached his tortured little heart! Then school was over and he lined up for the bus with the other children. Under one arm he held the box in which all second graders carried their crayons and pencils. As he stepped onto the bus, however, he dropped the container and the contents spilled in all directions. I rushed to help him. Big tears ran down his freckled cheeks as we knelt together and scooped up the contents -- earth from the school yard where Lance had been digging these last days. It appeared he was taking to his new home the one thing that represented permanence to him.

In that moment I knew where I had failed this child. Everyone needs some sense of security. I had it through my faith in God. But I had not thought to share it with my pupils. As the bus drove off with Lance and his precious box of earth, I said a fervent prayer that someone else might teach him to know God's love, and that I might never again fail to show it in my classroom.

-- Alice K. Montin

* * * * *

# TESTIMONY

That sweet voice of Spirit that is akin to light, that has something to do with pure intelligence, affirmed to me that this was the prophet of God. I need not try to define that experience to Latter-Day Saints. That kind of witness is characteristic of this church. It is not something reserved for those in high office. It is a witness, not only available but vital to every member.

I have come to know that the witness does not come by seeking after signs. It comes through fasting and prayer, through activity and testing and obedience. It comes through sustaining the servants of the Lord and following them.

-- Boyd K. Packer

* * * * *

The underlying strength of the Church . . . is in the testimonies of its individual members.

Heber C. Kimball, a counselor to President Brigham Young, warned the saints in 1856 that many trials would come to test their faith; that the time would come that no man or woman would be able to endure on borrowed light. Each must gain a personal knowledge of the truth and be guided by the light within himself.

President McKay assured a group of young people that a knowledge of the truth and a testimony of the gospel could come to them even in their youth if they would learn one great lesson: "That purity of heart, and a sincere heart seeking after the Savior's guidance daily, will lead to a testimony of the truth of Christ's gospel." This counsel indicates that testimonies may be gained through clean living and prayer.

President Joseph Fielding Smith has said: "Therefore, seeing even the Savior, does not leave as deep an impression in the mind as does the testimony of the Holy Ghost to the Spirit . . . the impressions on the soul that come from the Holy Ghost are far more significant than a vision. It is where spirit speaks to spirit that the imprint upon the soul is far more difficult to erase."

The testimony of the still small voice whispering to our innermost beings is of more worth than outermost signs or manifestations.

-- Henry D. Taylor

* * * * *

A testimony is a priceless gift from God. But even though a person may recieve a witness through the Holy Ghost there is no guarantee that this testimony will remain steadfast unless the person exerts constant effort to keep that testimony alive. Testimonies gained may be lost through carelessness, indifference and/or neglect.

Testimonies need to be nourished and fed. President Lee wisely counseled: "If we are not reading the scriptures daily, our testimonies are growing thinner, our spirituality isn't increasing in depth."

-- Henry D. Taylor

* * * * *

## Living By The Spirit

I will here make a remark concerning my own feelings. After the death of Joseph Smith I saw and conversed with him many times in my dreams in the night season. On one occasion he and his brother Hyrum met me when on the sea going on a mission to England. I had Dan Jones with me. He recieved his mission from Joseph Smith before his death; and the prophet talked freely to me about the mission I was then going to perform. And he also talked to me with regard to the mission of the Twelve Apostles in the flesh, and he laid before me the work they had to perform; and he also spoke of the reward they would recieve after death. And there were many other things he laid before me in his interview on that occasion. And when I awoke many of the things he had told me were taken from me, I could not comprehend them. I have had many interviews with Brother Joseph until the last 15 or 20 years of my life; I have not seen him for that length of time. But during my travels in the southern country last winter I had many interviews with President Young, and with Heber C. Kimball, and George A. Smith, and Jedediah M. Grant, and many others who are dead. They attended our conference, they attended our meetings. And on one occasion, I saw Brother Brigham and Brother Heber ride in a carriage ahead of the carriage in which I rode when I was on my way to attend conference; and they were dressed in the most priestly robes. When we arrived at our destination I asked President Young if he would preach to us. He said, "No, I have finished my testimony in the flesh. I shall not talk to this people any more. But (said he) I have come to see you; I have come to watch over you, and to see what the people are doing. Then (said he) I want you to teach the people -- and I want you to follow this counsel yourself -- that they must labor and so live as to obtain the Holy Spirit, for without this you cannot build up the kingdom; without the spirit of God you are in danger of walking in the dark, and in danger of failing to accomplish your calling as apostles and as elders in the church and kingdom of God . . .

-- Wilford Woodruff

* * * * *

## The Bible Holds True

Recent amazing developments in the space program show by computer that the sun really did stand still as the Bible says. Mr. Harold Hill, president of the Curtis Engine Co. in Baltimore, Maryland, and a consultant in the space program relates the following.

"I think one of the most amazing things that God has for us today happened recently to our astronauts and space scientists at Green Belt, Maryland. They were checking the position of the sun, moon, and planets out in space where they would be 100 years and 1000 years from now. We have to lay out the orbits in terms of the life of the satellite, and where the planets will be so the whole thing will not bog down.

"They ran the computer measurement back and forth over the centuries and it came to a halt. The computer stopped and put up a red signal, which meant that there was something wrong with the information fed into it or with the results as compared to the standards. They called in the service department to check it out, and they said, 'It's perfect!' The head of operations said, 'What's wrong?' 'Well, they have found there is a day missing in space in elapsed time.' They scratched their heads and tore their hair. There was no answer.

" One religious fellow on the team said, 'You know, one time I was in Sunday School and they talked about the sun standing still.' They didn't believe him, but they didn't have any other answer so they said, 'Show us.' He got a Bible and went back to the book of Joshua where they found a pretty ridiculous statement for anybody who has 'common sense.' There they found the Lord saying to Joshua, 'Fear them not for I have delivered them into thine hand; there shall not a man of them stand before thee.' Joshua was concerned because he was surrounded by the enemy, and if darkness fell they would overpower them. So Joshua asked the Lord to make the sun stand still! That's right -- the sun stood still and the moon stayed . . . and hasted not to go down about a whole day. (Joshua 10: 8, 12, 13) The space men said, 'There is the missing day!' They checked the computers going back into the time it was written and found it was close, but not close enough. The elapsed time that was missing in Joshua's day was 23 hours and 20 minutes -- not a whole day. They read the Bible and there it was --'About, (approximately) a whole day.'

"These little words in the Bible are important. But they were still in trouble because if you cannot account for 40 minutes you'll still be in trouble 1,000 years from now. Forty minutes had to be found because it can be multiplied many times over in orbits. This religious fellow also remembered somewhere in the Bible where it said the sun went backwards. The space men told him he was out of his mind. But they got the Book and read these words in Kings: Hezekiah, on his deathbed, was visited by the prophet Isaiah who told him that he was not going to die. Hezekiah asked for a sign of proof. Isaiah said, Do you want the sun to go ahead ten degrees? Hezekiah said, It's nothing for the sun to go ahead ten degrees, but let the shadow return backwards ten degrees. (2 Kings 20: 9-11) Isaiah spoke to the Lord and the Lord brought the shadow ten degrees backward. Ten degrees is exactly 40 minutes! Twenty-three hours and 20 minutes in Joshua, plus 40 minutes in 2 Kings make the missing 24 hours, the hours the space travelers had to log in the logbook as being the missing day in the universe! Isn't that amazing? Our God is rubbing their nose in His truth!"

-- Tom Anderson

* * * * *

# TIME

Waste is unjustified, and especially the waste of time -- as limited as that commodity is in our days of probation. One must live, not only exist: he must do, not merely be: he must grow, not just vegetate.

-- Spencer W. Kimball

* * * * *

It takes less time to do a thing right than to explain why you did it wrong.

-- Henry Wadsworth Longfellow

* * * * *

How you spend your time is more important than how you spend your money. Money mistakes can be corrected, but time is gone forever.

* * * * *

. . .But now there is time -- each day, one by one,
Measured and charted by shadows and sun,
Small bits of learning, large blocks of love,
For loving and learning are what time is made of;
And this day is endless as it comes to be
Time no longer, but eternity.

-- Mabel Jones Gabbott

* * * * *

Time is too slow for those who wait,
    too swift for those who fear.
Time is too long for those who grieve,
    and too short for those who rejoice and are happy.
But for those who love, time is not.

* * * * *

The most impressive example of tolerance is a golden wedding anniversary.

* * * * *

I can hardly wish any man better, than that he would seriously consider what he does with his time; how and to what ends he employs it; and what returns he makes to God.

-- Benjamin Franklin

* * * * *

Time, indeed, is a sacred gift, and each day is a little life.

-- Sir John Lubboc

* * * * *

A little too late is much too late.

* * * * *

Yesterday is an outlawed debt;
Tomorrow is a risky promissory note.
Today is real money. Invest in it.

* * * * *

Tomorrow: One of the greatest labor saving devices of today.

* * * * *

Don't be fooled by the calendar. There are only as many days in the year as you make use of. One man gets only a week's value out of a year while another gets a full year's value out of a week.

-- Charles Richards

* * * * *

The best preparation for the future is the present well seen to, the last duty well done.

-- George MacDonald

* * * * *

How you use today will determine how tomorrow will use you.

* * * * *

There is not a single moment in life that we can afford to lose.

-- Edward M. Goulburn

* * * * *

Waste of time is the most extravagant and costly of all expenses.

-- Theophrastus

* * * * *

Lost wealth may be replaced by industry, lost knowledge by study, lost health by temperance, but lost time is gone forever.

-- Smiles

* * * * *

Make time serve you, not you it.

* * * * *

Tomorrow is often the busiest day of the year; therefore, do all you can today.

* * * * *

Don't let yesterday use too much of today.

-- Will Rogers

* * * * *

Our days are like identical suitcases, all the same size but some can pack into them twice as much as others.

* * * * *

Time is money. We have no right to waste it.
Time is power. We have no right to dissipate it.
Time is influence. We have no right to throw it away.
Time is life. We must value it.
Time is sacred trust from God. We must answer for every moment.
Time is preparation for eternity. We must redeem it.

* * * * *

I have only just a minute,
Only sixty seconds in it,
Forced upon me - can't refuse it,
Didn't seek it - didn't choose it,
But it's up to me to use it.
I must suffer if I lose it,
Give account if I abuse it.
Just a tiny little minute -
But eternity is in it.

-- Christine Warren

* * * * *

God has given me this day
to use as I will,
I can waste it or use it for good.
What I do this day is very important,
because I'm exchanging it
for a day of my life.
When tomorrow comes,
this day will be gone forever, leaving
something in its place I have
traded it for, I want it
to be gain not loss; good not evil;
success not failure: in order that
it shall be worth the price
I paid for it.

* * * * *

## Today And Time

TODAY is here. I will start with a smile and resolve to be agreeable. I will not criticize. I refuse to waste my valuable time.

TODAY in one thing I know I am equal with all others. . .time. All of us draw the same salary in seconds, minutes and hours.

TODAY I will not waste my time because the minutes I wasted yesterday are as lost as a vanished thought.

TODAY I refuse to spend time worrying about what might happen. . .it usually doesn't. I am going to spend time making things happen.

TODAY I am determined to study to improve myself, for tomorrow I may be wanted, and I must not be found lacking.

TODAY I am determined to do the things that I should do. I firmly determine to stop doing the things I should not do.

TODAY I begin by doing and not wasting my time. In one week I will be miles beyond the person I am today.

TODAY I will not imagine what I would do if things were different. They are not different. I will make success with what material I have.

TODAY I will stop saying, "If I had time. . ." I know I never will "find time" for anything. If I want time, I must make it.

TODAY I will act toward other people as though this might be my last day on earth. I will not wait for tomorrow. Tomorrow never comes.

* * * * *

# VALUES

The best things in life are not things.

* * * * *

The highest kingdom I can find
Is in the confines of my mind.

* * * * *

The most natural beauty in the world is honest and moral truth. For all beauty is truth.

-- Shafteshevey

* * * * *

Talent is wanting something so much that you are willing to work for it.

* * * * *

We all are tools in the hands of God just like the mechanic who needs tools to repair a car. Each tool is different, each tool, however, is necessary. Do we know what tool we are and which parts we were meant to prepare?

* * * * *

The beauty seen is partly in he who sees it.

* * * * *

As a society we tend to love things and use people, rather than the reverse.

-- Eric Fromm

* * * * *

Self-pity is too clear a picture of the past and too dim a view of the future.

-- Robert Pederson

* * * * *

To seek the truth, for the sake of knowing the truth, is one of the noblest objects a man can live for.

-- Dean Inge

* * * * *

When a man has no design but to speak plain truth, he may say a great deal in a very narrow compass.

-- Bonald

* * * * *

Good better best --
never let me rest
until my good is better
and my better best.

-- Mark Jensen

* * * * *

Count your garden by the flowers,
    Never by the leaves that fall.
Count your days by golden hours,
    Don't remember clouds at all.
Count your nights by stars, not shadows.
Count your lives by smiles, not tears.
    And with joy throughout your lifetime
Count your age by friends, not years.

* * * * *

A wealthy lady was one day visited by two who desired to see first-hand of her wealth and riches, the glory of which they had heard many times. After several minutes of conversation with her in her home, they asked if they might please see some of her most precious jewels.

She excused herself from the room and was gone several minutes. When she returned, she had with her two small children. She explained, "Of all the gems and all the wealth which it may be my privilege to enjoy, these two jewels are by far my most precious."

* * * * *

I who am blind can give one hint to those who see: Use your eyes as if tomorrow you would be stricken blind. And the same method can be applied to the other senses. Hear the music of voices, the song of a bird, the mighty strains of an orchestra, as if you would be stricken deaf tomorrow. Touch each object as if tomorrow your tactile sense would fail. Smell the perfume of flowers, taste with relish each morsel, as if tomorrow you could never smell and taste again. Make the most of every sense; glory and beauty which the world in all the facets of pleasure reveals to you through the several means of contact which Nature provides. But of all the senses, I am sure that sight is the most delightful.

-- Helen Keller

* * * * *

## My Prayer

Give me this day the thoughts which make me know
Each hour what thou would have me do:
To patient be, tender, ever kind to those I love,
And conscious be of thee the whole day through.
What would thou have me do dear Lord?
Please tell me as I wait on thee.
I lift my heart, my very soul to thee.
Please tell me how to know thy will, thy perfect
plan for me.
Keep me to play my part and take my place
With other souls to whom thou also gives
A part to play in thy great plan.
Keep me to tread with joy the way
Thy wisdom sweet hath planned for me.
To murmur not, nor seek myself to please
But walk with thee in true humility.
To harmless be, not critical, dear Lord,
Of other souls who different paths are set by thee
to tread,
But just to walk with joy the way thou hast for me
And leave the rest to thee.

-- Emily Powell

* * * * *

## Twelve Things To Remember

The value of time
The value of perseverance

The pleasure of working
The dignity of simplicity
The worth of character
The power of kindness
The obligation of duty
The virtue of patience
The wisdom of economy
The improvement of talent
The joy of originating
The influence of example.

* * * * *

## Salutation Of The Dawn

Look to this day!
For it is life, the very life of life.
In its brief course be all the verities
And realities of your existence.

The glory of action
The bliss of growth
The splendor of beauty

For yesterday is but a dream
And tomorrow is only a vision;
But today, well-lived, makes
Every yesterday a dream of happiness
And every tomorrow a vision of hope.

Look well, therefore, to this day.
Such is the Salutation of the Dawn.

* * * * *

## Wealth

WEALTH is not the things we own, a stately house upon a hill, paintings and tapestries or servants taught to do one's will. In luxury a man may dwell as lonely as in a prison cell.

WEALTH is not a plentive purse, the bonds that one has stored away, boastful balance in the bank, jewelled baubles fools display. The things that really gratify are things that money cannot buy.

WEALTH is health, a cheerful heart, an ear that hears a robin's song, a mind content, some treasured friends, fragrant memories lingering long.

LIVING is an inward art, All lasting WEALTH is in the heart.

-- Alfred Walton

* * * * *

## What Counts

It isn't the money you're making, it isn't
the clothes you wear,
And it isn't the skill of your good right
hand which makes folks really care.
It's the smile on your face and the light of
your eye.
And the burdens that you bear.

Most any old man can tell you -- most any old
man at all
Who has lived through all sorts of weather,
winter and summer and fall,
That riches and fame are shadows that dance
on the garden wall.

It's how do you live and neighbor, how do you
work and play
It's how do you say good morning to the
people along the way
And it's how do you face your troubles
whenever your skies are gray.

It's you from the dawn to nightime; You
when the day is fair.
You when the storm is raging - how do
you face despair.
It is you that the world discovers,
whatever the clothes you wear.

You to the end of the journey, kindly
and brave and true,
The best and the worst of you gleaming
in all that you say and do,
And the thing that counts isn't money,
or glory or power but YOU!!

* * * * *

## Isn't It Funny

Isn't it funny. . .when the other fellow takes a long time to do something, he's slow. But when I take a long time to do something, I'm thorough. When the other fellow doesn't do it, he is too lazy; but when I don't do it, I'm too busy. When the other fellow goes ahead and does something without being told, he's overstepping his bounds. But, when I go ahead and do something without being told, that's initiative. When the other fellow states his side of a question strongly, he's bullheaded. But, when I state a side of a question strongly, I'm being firm. When the other fellow overlooks a few rules of etiquette, he's rude. But, when I skip a few rules, I'm original. When the other fellow does something that pleases the boss, he's polishing the brass; but when I do something that pleases the boss, that's cooperation. When the other fellow gets ahead, he sure had the lucky breaks. But, when I manage to get ahead, Man. . .hard work did it!!

Funny, isn't it -- OR IS IT?

* * * * *

## The Windows Of Gold

There is a legend that has often been told
Of the boy who searched for the Windows of Gold. . .

The beautiful windows he saw far away
When he looked in the valley at sunrise each day. . .

And he yearned to go down to the valley below
But he lived on a mountain that was covered with snow. . .

And he knew it would be a difficult trek,
But that was a journey he wanted to make. . .

So he planned by day and he dreamed by night
Of how he could reach The Great Shining Light. . .

And one golden morning when dawn broke through
And the valley sparkled with diamonds of dew. . .

He started to climb down the mountainside
With the Windows of Gold as his goal and his guide. . .

He traveled all day and, weary and worn,
With bleeding feet and clothes that were torn. . .

He entered the peaceful valley town
Just as the Golden Sun went down. . .

But he seemed to have lost his "Guiding Light" --
The windows were dark that had once been bright. . .

And hungry and tired and lonely and cold
He cried, "Won't You Show Me The Windows of Gold?". . .

And a kind hand touched him and said, "Behold!
High On the Mountain Are The Windows of Gold"

For the sun going down in a great golden ball
Had burnished the windows of his cabin so small. . .

And the Kingdom of God with its Great Shining Light,
Like the Golden Windows that shone so bright. . .

Is not a far distant place, somewhere,
It's as close to you as a silent prayer. . .

And your search for God will end and begin
When you look for Him and find Him WITHIN.

-- Helen Steiner Rice

* * * * *

When young men stop dreaming and old men aren't wise,
And the reason for failure is that man never tries,
Then the world will no longer have a reason for being
As mankind walks backward in a blindness called seeing.

When progression reverses and mankind is base
And morals have left the entire human race;
When "right" and "wrong" are words of the past
Then the right to exist will have left us at last.

When love has become just a word or an act,
With no lasting or spiritual emotion in fact,
When today is the day for which each man lives,
Tomorrow is the sad, empty, future he gives.

For a world without planning and a world without dreams
Is more hollow and empty than it ever seems
A mansion of cardboard in beauty may stand,
But the slightest of storms finds it buried in sand.

Our world has existed through strife and through tears
By the dreams of the young and the wisdom of years.
With energy provided by visions of youth,
Direction by wisdom has brought us to truth.

Today may seem filled with destruction and war
And sadness and doubt as to what man lives for;
But the saddest day ever for the sun to rise
Is when young men aren't dreaming and old men aren't wise.

-- John Milo Peterson

* * * * *

## The Mountain And The Vale

There's a mountain named "Stern Justice,"
Tall and towering, gloomy, grand.
Frowning over a vale called Mercy,
Loveliest in all the land.

Great and mighty is the mountain,
But its snowy crags are cold,
And in vain the sunlight lingers,
On the summit, proud and bold.

There is warmth within the valley,
And I love to wander there,
Mid the fountains and the flowers,
Breathing fragrance on the air.

Much I love the solemn mountain,
It doth meet my somber mood.
When amid the muttering thunders,
O'er my soul the storm clouds brood.

But when tears like rain have fallen,
From the fountain of my woe:
And my soul has lost its fierceness,
Straight unto the vale I go.

Where the landscape gently smiling
O'er my heart pours healing balm.
And as oil on troubled waters,
Brings from out its storm a calm.

Yes, I love both vale and mountain.
Ne'er from either would I part.
Each unto my life is needful,
Both are dear unto my heart.

For the smiling vale doth soften,
All the rugged steep makes sad,
And from icy rocks meander,
Rills that make the valley glad.

-- Orson F. Whitney

* * * * *

Watch The Switches In Your Life

The course of our lives is not determined by great, awesome decisions. Our direction is set by the little day-to-day choices which chart the track on which we run.

Many years ago I worked in the head office of one of our railroads. One day I received a telephone call from my counterpart in Newark, New Jersey, who said that a passenger train had arrived without its baggage car. The patrons were angry.

We discovered that the train had been properly made up in Oakland, California, and properly delivered to St. Louis, from which station it was to be carried to its destination on the east coast. But in the St. Louis yards, a thoughtless switchman had moved a piece of steel just three inches.

That piece of steel was a switch point, and the car that should have been in Newark, New Jersey, was in New Orleans, Louisiana, thirteen hundred miles away.

So it is with our lives -- a cigarette smoked, a can of beer drunk at a party, a shot of Speed taken on a dare, a careless giving in to an impulse on a date. Each has thrown a switch in the life of a boy that put him on a track that carried him far away from what might have been a great and foreordained calling. And as Nephi said ". . .thus the devil cheateth their souls and leadeth them away carefully down to hell." (2 Ne. 28:21)

--Gordon B. Hinckley

* * * * *

A kind philosopher went into the hills each day to study nature that he might be nearer unto God. Then each evening on his return, he gathered the people of the village about him to impart unto them the lesson he had learned. As in all good things, there arises skepticisms; for one morning, before he departed, one of his potential friends asked him to bring him back a hawthorn twig. Another asked him to bring back a rose, and a third asked him to bring him a lily. The kind philosopher assented to the requests of these three friends.

As the day wore on and the evening let down her curtain, the three stood by to receive their gifts from nature. As they took them in their hands, the first said; "Here is a dead leaf on my hawthorn twig." The second murmured: "Here is a thorn on my rose;" and the third cried out and said: "Yes, and here is some dirt on the root of my lily." The kind philosopher took them back, took the dead leaf from the hawthorn twig and placed it in the first friend's hand. Likewise the thorn and the dirt from the rose and lily. Then he said: "You have what attracted you first. I will keep the hawthorn twig, the rose and the lily for the beauty I see in them."

Those who grow most perfectly in life and in the service of the Lord are the men and women who find only that which is good in others.

* * * * *

## The Kite Is Held-Up By The String

While flying a kite, I once asked my father, "Dad, what holds the kite up?"

"The string," he replied.

"No, Dad, the string hold it down, not up."

"If you think so, let go of the string," he said, "and see what happens."

I let go and the kite began to fall! It seems odd that the very thing which seems to keep the kite down is actually what keeps it up. And this is true not only of kites but of life. Those strings that are tied to us, those rules and regulations that seem to hold us down, are actually holding us up.

And certainly in the realm of the spirit, in the field of faith, this same truth holds with even greater force. The word "religion" is said to come from a Latin root meaning "to hold back" or tie back. And this is what religion does. It provides the string to the soaring kite of our spirit; it keeps us from falling! It binds us to great values; it attaches us to great causes; it helps us fly high in the aid of God's truth and lifts us until our heads touch the stars and our lives take on the beauty of men and women who are bound closely to God.

-- Anonymous

* * * * *

## So You Can't Come To Church On Sunday

Actually there are very few valid reasons for not attending church. Off hand I can think of only one -- that being illness. Yet I'm sure we're all guilty of making up excuses, and magnifying them in such a way that we can justify our staying away.

Two Reverends were milling over some of the time worn excuses given for not attending church. And they decided to use these same excuses, only apply them to something that most people like to do, such as going to the movies. They came up with this list.

1. I don't go to the movies because the manager of the theater has never visited me.

2. I did go a few times, but no one spoke to me. Those who go there aren't very friendly.

3. Every time I go they ask me for money.

4. Not all folks who go to the movies live up to the high standards of the films.

5. I went to the movies so much as a child I've decided that I have had all the entertainment I need.

6. The performance lasts too long. I can't sit still for an hour and a half.

7. I don't always agree with what I hear and see there.

8. I don't think they have very good music.

9. The shows are held in the evenings and that's the only time I have to be home with the family.

You can easily see how ridiculous these excuses sound to us when they are used in this manner. The next time you feel like missing a meeting I hope you will give your excuse the movie test. See if it still sounds important enough to justify your staying away.

* * * * *

## The Stone Cutter

Long ago and far away there lived a stone cutter who, every morning took his mallet and chisel to hew slabs of rock from the mountainside, and polish them smooth for houses. He was very good at his work and so there was always plenty for him to do and he was happy. But one day, when he carried a finely polished block of stone to the house of a rich man, he saw all sorts of beautiful things such as he had never seen before.

"Oh!" he cried. "I wish I were rich. I wish I might sleep in a bed as soft as down."

Then he picked up his tools and started home, but the spirit of the mountain had heard his wish. Instead of the poor little hut he had left in the morning, there stood a wonderful palace, as full of beautiful furniture as the rich man's house. The stone cutter slept that night on a bed as soft as down. When he awoke he decided not to work anymore and looked out his window to see who was going by. As he watched, a fine carriage rolled along drawn by snow white horses. There were servants running in front and behind and a prince sat inside with a golden canopy over his head. At once the stone cutter began to be disappointed and discontented.

"Oh!" he said. "I wish I were a prince with such a carriage as that and a golden canopy."

And no sooner had he wished than it came to pass. He was a prince; he had servants dressed in purple and gold and he drove through the streets with his golden canopy. For awhile he was happy, but one day he noticed that the sun was drying his grass and flowers even though he had watered them.

"The sun is mightier than I am. I wish to be the sun."

The spirit heard him and the stone cutter was changed to the sun. He felt proud and mighty, so great and yellow in the sky. He burned the fields of rich and poor alike. But one day a cloud covered his face. Again he was filled with discontent.

"The cloud is mightier than I. I would be the cloud," he cried angrily.

So the mountain spirit changed him into a cloud and he lay content for awhile between the sun and the earth. He caught the sunbeams and would not let them go. He sent rain to earth and the flowers bloomed, but this was not enough for him. He began pouring down rain for days until the rivers overflowed and the crops were spoiled. He washed away whole towns, but one thing he could not move was the mountain.

"Is the mountain stronger than I?" he asked. "Then I will be the mountain."

At once the mountain spirit changed him into rock. For years he stood, proudly raising his head above the other cliffs and he did not feel the sun nor the rain. But one day he heard a sharp tap, tapping and he saw a stone cutter there working with his sharp tools, cutting into the mountainside. He felt a trembling inside him.

"Who is this that can cut into me? I would be that Man."

And a man he became once more, the same poor stone cutter he was before. Once again he lived in a hut and worked from morning to night. Yet he was happier than ever for he had learned it's the steady tap-tapping that moves mountains.

-- A Japanese legend found in a Cracker Jack box.

* * * * *

## An Open Letter to a Teenager

Always we hear the plaintive cry of the teenagers: What can we do. . . ? Where can we go. . . ? The answer is . . . Go Home!

Hang the storm windows, paint the woodwork. Rake the leaves. Mow the lawn. Shovel the walk. Wash the car. Learn to cook. Scrub some floors. Repair the sink. Build a boat. Get a job.

Help the Church. Visit the sick. Assist the poor. Study your lessons. And then when you are through--and not too tired--read a book.

Your parents do not owe you entertainment. Your town does not owe you recreation facilities. The world does NOT owe you a living. You owe the world something. You owe it your time and energy and your talents so that no one will be at war or in poverty, or sick, or lonely again.

In plain simple words: GROW UP; quit being a cry-baby; get out of your dream world; develop a backbone not a wishbone; and start acting like a man or a lady.

I'm a parent. I'm tired of nursing, protecting, helping, appealing, begging, excusing, tolerating, denying myself needed comforts for every whim and fancy, just because your selfish ego instead of common sense dominates your personality, and thinking, and requests.

--The Juvenile Court, Denver, Colo.

* * * * *

## Satisfaction

I wish it were wintertime. I am so tired of this heat. I'd be happy if it would just snow again.
Is this snow ever going to melt?
If I had a ten-speed, I'd be happy. That's all I want. . .a ten-speed bicycle.
Boy, I'll be happy when I get a car. No more begging for rides. . .
If I were just older. Old enough to date. . .then I'd be happy.
I'd be happy if I could stay out later at night. One hour later. Is that too much to ask?
I will never be happy until I am going steady.
Once I graduate from high school I will be happy.

I need a job. If I could just find a job, I'd never complain again.
I want to go to college.
I've got to get out of these dorms. The rules are starting to get me down. Once I get into an apartment, I'll be happy.
I need a place of my own.

I want to travel. How can I ever be satisfied with life if I never see the world?
I want to get married. . .settle down. I'm tired of roaming. I'll be happy once I'm married.

If we only had a little more money. . .
Children will make me happy. As soon as I have a baby, I will be satisfied.
If you could only talk. . .
I wish you were still a baby. . .

If I can get that job, I will never ask for another thing.
A house.
New furniture.
If the children could take care of themselves, I'd be so much happier.
If you buy me a second car, I promise. . .nothing else.
A dishwasher. How can I keep up with all these dishes? I need a dishwasher.
Boy, will I be happy when the kids go to school.
I wish the kids would come home.
I simply won't be satisfied until I get a housekeeper.
I've got it! A camper will make us happy. We could sneak off. . .enjoy one another. . .
Motorcycles. That's it!
Maybe a boat will make us all happy.
Once we get out of debt, we will be happy.
You know, we ought to take a long vacation. Not worry about the money. Really relax and enjoy ourselves. Maybe that would make us happy again.
I need a raise. Who can live on this salary? Everything would be better if I were making more money.
I need to get more involved in the community. . .
If I just had a church responsibility. . .
I wish I had more time to spend with my family. . .I'd be happier. . .they'd be happier.

We'll never be happy again unless we renew our courtship.
I want a divorce. Then I will be happy. I'd never ask for another thing if I could just be free again.
If I could just find a steady companion. . .someone to talk to. . .that's all I need.
A second chance at marriage. I'd make it this time. A second chance. Is that too much to ask?

We need a summer place. A place where we can be alone. We'd be happier if we were alone more often.
It is so lonely here. I wish the kids would spend some time here with us. What fun is a summer place without kids?
I'd be happy if the children were more independent. As soon as they go off to college. . .
Our kids never come to see us. Always off heaven knows where. After all we have given them, they ought to visit us at least on holidays.

Listen, if we had a few grandchildren, we would never ask for another thing.
Why can't they understand. . .we don't want to raise our grandkids. . .
When was the last time the grandchildren came to visit?

We won't be satisfied until we set aside some money for retirement.
I would rest easier knowing our cemetery plots are selected and paid for.
Once we retire and slow down, we'll be happier.
There is nothing to do. I need a hobby.
I wish I felt better. I'm always taking medicine. If I felt better I'd never complain again.
I'd be happy if we could catch up on these doctor bills.
We better sell this big house. Move into an apartment. Things will be easier in a smaller place.
Don't you miss the old house?
I wish the children would stop by to visit more often. I am so lonely. A few more visitors would make me so happy.
Can't people understand? I need my rest. . .
I'll be happy once I get into a good rest home.
No, I won't be happy until I move back home again.

I wish I weren't so sleepy all the time.
If my eyes. . .
If my legs didn't ache. . .
I'd be so happy if I were young again.
I'd be happy if it would warm up.
I can't stand the heat anymore.
I wish I had someone to talk to. I would be happy if I had a friend.
I want to sleep. Rest would make me happy.
If this would all just end. . .then I'd be happy.

As a rule,
Man's a fool.
When it's hot,
He wants it cool.
When it's cool,
He wants it hot.
Always wanting what it's not.
Never wanting what he's got.

--Peggy Ball Fugal
Reprinted with permission

* * * * *

# WOMAN

Be a real helpmeet. Never give a cross or unkind word to your husband, but let kindness, charity and love crown your works.

* * * * *

Treat him with mildness and affection. When a man is borne with trouble, when he is perplexed with care and difficulty, if he can meet with a smile instead of an argument or a murmur--if he can meet with mildness it will call down his soul and soothe his feelings; when the mind is going to despair it needs the solace of affection and kindness.

--Joseph Smith

* * * * *

Were I a woman. . .and had married a man and found myself deceived, he not answering my expectations, and I being sorry that I had made such a choice, let me show my wisdom by not complaining about it. A woman's wisdom and judgment has failed her once in the choice of a husband, and it may again, if she is not careful. By seeking to cast off her husband--by withdrawing her confidence and good-will from him, she casts a dark shade upon his path, when, by pursuing a proper course of love, obedience, and encouragement, he might attain to that perfection she had anticipated in him.

--Brigham Young

* * * * *

His (Pres. Harold B. Lee) counsel to the bride has been to stand by her husband's side, support him, be the mother of his children and one who gives him faith when he sometimes loses faith in himself. You are the one to make a happy home.

--Mrs. Harold B. Lee

* * * * *

It has been interesting to me that many couples who come for help--some of them with grown children--haven't the vaguest idea about some of the very basic considerations in the husband-wife relationship. Some women, long married, have no idea, it seems, about how a man is put together, and is to be lifted and inspired and encouraged. Now, first one suggestion with reference to him that you may want to think about. He needs to know that he is the leader in the family. He needs a wife and a sweetheart with whom he can share his love, with whom he can have its full, complete expressions. He needs to have a circle, a family circle with children.

This makes all that he must face in the world seem wothwhile. He needs to feel dominant. He needs to be the protector.

When he feels this he is a better man. He is a better husband. He is a better employee, a better employer. He is better adjusted and happier in life. He can do better work. He can even be more prosperous. But for the sake of all that is important, above all, he can be a better father, and a better holder of the Priesthood. Young sisters, if you take that role from him, the one he needs, you reduce his manhood. You take that which enriches not you and leaves him poor indeed.

--Boyd K. Packer

* * * * *

In the home the presiding authority is always vested in the father and in all home affairs and family matters there is no other authority paramount.

--Joseph F. Smith

* * * * *

The second role I would say in the responsibility of the mother is to put father at the head of the house. How does mother do it? Someone said that little children soon outgrow their need for affection, but fathers never do. Now that is the first way to put father at the head of the house. Even when he doesn't deserve it.

--Harold B. Lee

* * * * *

I know that you good women get annoyed and provoked and out of patience many times with your husbands, and at times justly so. They are not always as considerate of you as they ought to be; but if they provide for you and they are kind to you and otherwise treat you right, stay with them.

--Brigham Young

* * * * *

Children will not have the fear of losing their place in the eternal family circle if parents have done their part in building a wonderful hom life and if they are having their Family Home Evening.

--Harold B. Lee

* * * * *

A strong woman supports and reinforces her husband's position.

* * * * *

The woman is the neck that helps to make the head function properly.

* * * * *

## I am a Daughter of God

I am a daughter of God. God does care for me. He does tell me the way to reach eternity.

I am a daughter of God, I know what I must do. I know that my God lives, I know this Church is true.

In Satan's plan to destroy all, and capture us to his ways; he thought of several things to tell us to lead us all astray.

At first he said the Gospel wasn't true at all, and then he said, "I'll teach them it is <u>all</u> true but that they have lots of time.

Let's see how much time I have --
The days go awfully fast. It seems I never get the things done in a day that I've been asked.

Not much time for reading, the supper must be cooked,
Not much time for serving, the mending's been overlooked.
Not much time for children, the house is such a mess.
Not much time for anything I guess.

But when my house is leaking, I sure could use a hand,
And when my heart is heavy, will someone understand.
And when my money's gone, could I be blessed with more.
But my God's thoughts are elsewhere, like mine have been before.

Well, now my eyes are open and I can see much more,
What I'm really here for, not fantasy or lore.
I must really hurry, there's so much I have to do.
How can I teach my children if I don't know what's true?

Help me Lord I pray now, to remember who I am.
Each day that goes by, may I more fully understand.
May I strive to ever serve thee with my devotion and my care--
And do the things important to family and friends, everywhere.

I pray for help and wisdom to get me through each day;
To guide my thoughts to love, in every single way.
To be myself more fully; to freely give I pray,
In the name of Jesus Christ our Savior on this quiet lovely day.

--Sharon A. Tanner

* * * * *

# WORK

The Lord is no respecter of persons, and will give success to all who work for it. If I can only impress upon the minds of the youth of Zion the eloquence, the inexpressable eloquence of work, I shall be fully repaid.

-- Heber J. Grant

* * * * *

Our Heavenly Father loves us so completely that He has given us a commandment to work. This is one of the keys to eternal life. He knows that we will learn more, grow more, achieve more, serve more, and benefit more from a life of industry than from a life of ease.

-- Howard W. Hunter

* * * * *

Thomas Monson's "W" formula. . .

Work Will Win When Wishy Washy Wishing Won't

* * * * *

I am a great believer in luck - I find that
the harder I work, the more I have of it.

* * * * *

Bite off more than you can chew,
    Then chew it!
Tackle more than you can do,
    Then do it!
Hitch your wagon to a star,
Then keep your seat, and there you are!

* * * * *

The work will wait while you show the child the rainbow, but the rainbow won't wait while you do the work.

-- Patricia Clafford

* * * * *

Make your job important and it is very likely to return the favor.

* * * * *

The average person puts only 25% of his energy and ability into his work. The world takes off its hat to those few and far between souls who devote 100%.

-- Andrew Carnegie

* * * * *

Vision without work is daydreaming; and work without vision is drudgery.

-- Thomas S. Monson

* * * * *

He who complains loudest about the way the ball bounces is very often the one who dropped it.

* * * * *

The reward of a thing well done, is to have done it.

-- Emerson

* * * * *

O Lord, Thou givest us everything, at the price of an effort.

* * * * *

He who sits cross-legged with mouth open waiting for roast duck to fly in is going to have a long hunger.

-- Old Confucian Proverb

* * * * *

The story is told about a minister in Africa who called the natives to him one day and asked them to help him harvest his crop. He asked them to bring each a basket in which to carry the crop to market in the town. At the end of the day, the minister let each worker fill his basket for himself as a wage. Those who had brought big baskets had a great salary. But those who had purposely brought small baskets so that they would not have to work as hard were disappointed when their salary was small.

* * * * *

Thank God every morning when you get up that you have something to do that day which must be done, whether you like it or not. Being forced to work and forced to do your best will breed in you temperance and self-control, diligence, and strength of will, and a hundred virtues which the idle never know.

-- Kingsley

* * * * *

In shooing flies, or hauling freight
It's wiser to cooperate
For better things are sooner done
If two take hold, and work as one.

Now that's a truth all horses know,
They learned it centuries ago.
When days are hot and flies are thin,
Cooperation does the trick.

One tail on duty at the rear
Can't reach the fly behind the ear;
But two tails if arranged with craft
Give full protection fore and aft.

Let fools pursue the lonely course,
Let wisemen emulate the horse.
Two make a burden half as great
Use horse sense and cooperate!

* * * * *

The story is told of three stonecutters who were driving their chisels into a massive block of granite. A stranger who happened to be passing asked the first cutter what he was doing.

"I'm cutting stone," he growled, and it's a messy job."

"And you?", he asked the second.

"I'm working for two bucks an hour," he said.

When the question was put to the third, his face lit up with enthusiasm, "I'm helping to build yon cathedral," he said.

A worker can be an automaton, an opportunist, or an idealist. He can feel that he is serving time, or that he is serving himself, or that he is serving society. But unless he is capable of realizing the larger significance of his job, he does not realize its larger opportunities. . .If he does not have vision, he must have supervision.

* * * * *

WORK:
Thank God for the might of it,
The ardor, the urge, the delight of it,
Work that springs from the heart's desire,
Setting the brain and the soul on fire;
Ah, what is so good as the heat of it,
And what is so kind as the stern command,
Challenging brain and heart and hand?

WORK:
Thank God for the pride of it,
For the beautiful conquering tide of it,
Sweeping the life in its furious flood,
Thrilling the arteries, cleansing the blood,
Mastering stupor and dull despair,
Moving the dreamer to do and dare.
Oh, what is so good as the urge of it,
And what is so strong as the summons deep,
Rousing the torpid soul from sleep?

WORK:
Thank God for the pace of it,
For the terrible, swift, keen race of it,
Fiery steeds in full control,
Nostrils quiver to greet the goal.
Work, the power that drives behind,
Guiding the purposes, taming the mind,
Holding the runaway wishes back,
Reining the will to one steady track,
Speeding the engines faster, faster,
Triumphing over disaster.
Oh, what is so good as the pain of it,
And what is so great as the gain of it?
And what is so kind as the cruel goad
Forcing us on through the rugged road?

* * * * *

## White Rooster Story. . .A Sequel To The Little Red Hen

Said the Big White Rooster, "Gosh all hemlock. . . things are tough.
Seems like worms are getting scarcer, and I cannot find enough.
What's become of all those fat ones is a mystery to me;
There were thousands through the rosy spell, now where can they be?"

The Little Red Hen who heard him didn't grumble or complain,
She'd gone through lots of dry spells, she'd lived through floods or rain
So she flew upon the grindstone and she gave her claws a whet,
As she said, "I've never seen a time that there were no worms to get."

She found a new undug spot, the earth was hard and firm.
The Big White Rooster jeered, "New ground! That's no place to find a worm."
The Little Red Hen just spread her feet, she dug both fast and free.
"I must go to the worms," she said, "the worms won't come to me."

The Big White Rooster vainly spent his days and habits by the ways,
Where fat worms have passed in squads, in the rainy, rosy days.
When nightfall found him supperless, he growled in accents rough,
"I'm hungry as a fowl can be, conditions sure are tough!"

"It's worse with you,
For you must be not only tired, but you must be hungry too."
The Little Red Hen hopped to her perch and dropped her eyes to sleep,
And murmured in a drowsy tone, "Young man hear this and weep.
I'm full of worms and happy for I've dined both long and well.
The worms are there as always, but I had to dig like . . . heck"

O, here and there white roosters still are holding sales positions.
They cannot do much business now, because of poor conditions.
But soon as things get right again, they'll sell a hundred firms. . .
Meanwhile the Little Red Hens are out, a gobbling up the worms.

-- quoted by Vaughn Featherstone

* * * * *

There is a story told about a man who earnestly sought the Lord in prayer concerning the things he should do to get to heaven and to live with his Heavenly Father. The man humbled himself, and after 100 days of constant praying he opened his eyes and found he was in heaven. Two angels were with him and they asked him to follow them. He obliged.

After some distance the three of them came to a large valley with small rolling hills, and on the hills were strange - looking objects about three inches high and waving back and forth from where they stood. The objects looked like something he had seen before. He decided to stop and ask what they were.

"Pardon me angels, but could you tell me what those things are over there that are waving around?"

"Those are the tongues of the people who talked about Christ and the commandments but who didn't do anything."

"Oh, I see," said the man. "Do we stop here?"

"No," said the angels. "We go farther along this trail."

A short time later and some distance farther down the trail the man looked ahead and saw another strange sight. This time he noticed a large number of strange objects standing still but all in pairs. As he approached, these too looked familiar. Desiring to know about these, he again inquired.

"Excuse me, angels, but I can't help wondering just what those strange objects are there ahead of us."

"Those, dear sir, are the ears of those who heard the gospel, those who enjoyed the sermons, speeches, talks, those who said 'Amen' to all that they heard but did nothing more."

The man walked a short distance and then realized he was dreaming. His prayer had been answered and he knew what he should DO!

* * * * *